DEATH IN
BIG BEND

DEATH IN BIG BEND

STORIES OF

FATALITY AND RESCUE

IN THE PARK

BY

LAURENCE PARENT

IRON MOUNTAIN PRESS
Houston, Texas
2010

First Printing
June 2010

ISBN 978-0-9745048-7-2

Printed and bound in the United States of America

Cover photography and all photographs included in the text
by Laurence Parent

Cover design by Leisha Israel, Digital Tractor
Austin, Texas

IRON MOUNTAIN PRESS
Houston, Texas
www.ironmtnpress.com

This book is dedicated to the families and friends of those who lost their lives as chronicled in this book, and to those park rangers and others who have risked their lives to save people at Big Bend National Park.

ACKNOWLEDGMENTS

I wish to thank Superintendent Bill Wellman and former Chief Ranger Mark Spier for allowing this book to happen by giving me access to park files and assisting in many other ways.

Laura Van Inwagen, John Morlock, and Joel Yocum were hugely helpful in helping me find and sort through the relevant parts of the park files.

John and Adamina Morlock offered endless hospitality at their home during my park visits researching these incidents.

I also wish to thank the many people who patiently allowed me to interview them by phone and email, some many times. In particular, I appreciate those family members and friends who lost loved ones, but were still willing to talk to me. They are Tom Alex, Justin Baize, Doug Baxter, Cary Brown, Sally Butler, Victor Carrasco, Christa Coggins, Jon Cradit, Vidal Davila, Rob Dean, David Duncan, Bill Egger, Dave Evans, Lisa Evans, Andy Ferguson, Steve French, Glenda Green, Kathleen Hambly, George Howarth, Phil Koepp, Carol Kosarek, Mary Kay Manning, Steve McAllister, Roger Moder, Les Montgomery, Nova Montgomery, John Morlock, Jim Northup, Marcos Paredes, Marcy Reed, Reagan Reed, Clare Rhoades, Daryl Rhodes, Joe Roberts, Michael Ryan, Geary Schindel, John Sellers, Raymond Skiles, Mark Spier, Judith Springer, Melanie Springer-Tollett, Steve Springer, Michael Tiller, Kevin Tillman, April Trotter, Jim Unruh, Charles Van Driskill, David Van Inwagen, Laura Van Inwagen, Alyssa Van Schmus, Larry Voorhees, Sharilyn Voorhees, Judy Hooker Whittenton, Rick Womack, David Yim, and Mark Yuhas. Without all of you, this book would not have been possible.

TABLE OF CONTENTS

FOREWORD

It was my good fortune to work as a ranger at Big Bend National Park for almost ten years. Big Bend is a park unlike any other, with its isolated location along the Mexican border, its breathtaking 100-mile vistas from the top of the Chisos Mountains, its deep, narrow river canyons, and its vast, empty desert country.

Big Bend attracts some of the most dedicated visitors of any national park in the country. They drive for hours from all across Texas and beyond, sometimes for just a short weekend of wilderness. They bring everything needed for camping, boating, hiking, birding, and backpacking stuffed into or strapped to their vehicles. Most importantly, this loyal group of visitors brings a strong sense of caring and respect for the park.

However, as with any park, there are always a few visitors who fail to respect the park or use common sense in their visit, and so give the rangers job security. Early in every ranger's career, he or she will hear the basic job description that has been passed down from ranger to ranger for nearly a hundred years. "The job of the ranger is to protect the park from the people and the people from the park."

This has never been more true than it is today. Our national parks get millions of visitors every year, many of them coming from urban areas where people have little idea of the risks and hazards that can await them in the outdoors. In an age of extreme sports, wireless communications, global positioning systems, and 911 emergency service, people sometimes visit parks with unreasonable expectations about safety. They go for a short hike without proper gear or water, unaware of the limits of modern technology to save them from mistakes. What may seem to be minor, bad decisions can compound in the wilderness into a life-threatening situation. GPS batteries die, cell phones have no service, and the modern world is suddenly out of reach.

Big Bend National Park attempts to educate visitors about outdoor hazards that they might encounter at the park through brochures, books, signboards, and ranger talks. The vast majority of visitors have a safe and pleasant visit. However, every year at least a few people run into difficulty due to poor preparation, bad decisions, or sometimes just bad luck. Fortunately, when bad things do happen, the rangers at Big Bend are well prepared to help people in need.

The Big Bend rangers are highly trained professionals. Because of the isolated nature of the park, far removed from almost all outside help, rangers at Big Bend must maintain training and certification in law enforcement, emergency medical services, search and rescue, and structural and wildland firefighting. Any one of these functions is a full time career anywhere else. Complementing the formal ranger staff are many other equally dedicated, well-trained park personnel from other divisions who frequently set aside their maintenance work, interpretive visitor programs, or resource management projects to respond to an incident as a search and rescue team member or logistical support staffer.

During my tenure at Big Bend, the park responded to a number of incidents where a life was at stake. In every instance rangers worked tirelessly to do everything they could to help, sometimes even putting themselves at risk by doing so. Although the vast majority of incidents had a happy ending, sometimes the outcomes were tragic.

Few people realize the emotional consequences the types of incidents described in this book have on park staff. Every incident becomes personal at some level to the rangers involved. Major incidents often merit a critical incident stress debrief (CISD) where those who responded to an event involving serious injury or death can shed some of the emotional impacts those events cause. I clearly remember being with several rangers feverishly working to save the life of a two-year-old girl in the roadside debris of a drug and alcohol induced traffic accident, when I suddenly realized three of us at the scene had two-year-old daughters at home. The girl died. The CISD following that incident was difficult but very necessary for those rangers.

Rangers are sometimes assigned the role of family liaison to assist the family of a person who is lost or has died in the park. The ranger acts as the official link between what can be a large and confusing search or investigation and loved ones who are confused, frightened, angry, or grieving. This task is one of the most difficult performed during and after an incident. Not all rangers are good at it, and the ones who are probably get the job more often than is fair.

When a death is involved, family members often form a relationship forged in grief with the liaison ranger. The ranger is often hammered by difficult questions, some of which can never be answered. These relationships can last for years. It is not uncommon for a ranger to meet with family members on the anniversary of an incident for years afterwards. Some rangers have two or three such families for which they became "responsible." Sometimes when a ranger transfers to a new assignment at another park, another ranger who was involved in the incident inherits the role.

During my years at the park I saw cellular telephone coverage come to parts of Big Bend, life-flight helicopters stationed closer to the park, the common usage of GPS units for navigation, and the successful use of a PLB (personal locator beacon) to save a hiker's life. Emergency medical services in south Brewster County outside the park improved dramatically as well. Despite all this, the saying "if you're hurt bad in Big Bend, you might die in Big Bend" can still be true. Visitors need to be prepared and responsible. When they are not, Big Bend National Park has a group of professional rangers dedicated to doing everything possible to locate and help those in need.

Mark Spier
Superintendent, Palo Alto Battlefield National Historical Park,
formerly Chief Ranger, Big Bend National Park

INTRODUCTION

"Almost anywhere else is more dangerous than Big Bend National Park," says Ranger Marcos Paredes, who has the dubious distinction of having packed out more bodies than anyone else in the park. "We only fear what we don't know."

Paredes is probably right. Although this book chronicles a number of deaths and rescues that have occurred since the early 1980s, such events are actually quite rare, especially in proportion to the number of people who visit the park. Several hundred thousand people visit the park every year. For the vast majority, the worst thing that happens is a slight sunburn.

People don't judge risk well. People fear rattlesnakes, mountain lions, and bears, but no deaths have ever been caused in the park by those animals. The biggest cause of death at Big Bend? Motor vehicle accidents, just like anywhere else. The second largest cause? Natural causes, like heart attacks and strokes. Those heart attacks and strokes sometimes may have been brought on by exertion or heat at Big Bend for which the stricken people were not prepared, but the underlying physical conditions were there long before they visited the park. The most dangerous animal at the park? Probably deer, because of their tendency to cause car accidents.

Motor vehicle accidents at Big Bend have a sad history dating back even to the days before the park's creation. In the 1930s a major effort was begun between the United States and Mexico to not only create Big Bend National Park in Texas, but to create a sister park across the river in Mexico. On February 8, 1936, Secretary of State Cordell Hull appointed a high level commission to work with the Mexican government in creating international parks along the countries' common border. Among the appointees were George Wright, the most important early advocate of science and resource management programs in the National Park Service, and Roger Toll, the superintendent of Yellowstone National Park who was heavily involved in new park creation in the western United States.

On February 17, the American delegation arrived in Alpine where they met their Mexican counterparts for lengthy discussions and a tour of the proposed park lands in both countries. The men hatched the then radical idea of creating an international park involving both countries. After several days, the commission members departed with high hopes and a serious plan for creating the park. Tragically, less than 24 hours later, both Roger Toll and George Wright died in a car wreck east of Deming, New Mexico on their way to review potential park sites on the Arizona/Mexico border. Two prominent Chisos Mountains peaks were named for the men, but it did not make up for their deaths. Without their strong leadership, Park Service science programs declined for many years and the idea of an international park lost its momentum for 60 years. Efforts to create an international park did not resurrect themselves until the 1990s.

However, because motor vehicle accidents, strokes, and heart attacks occur everywhere, I have chosen not to include any of those events in this book. Instead, I concentrated on cases that are much more unique to the park and often required elaborate search and rescue operations. I chose incidents that have occurred since the early 1980s, because before that time it gets very hard to track down the rescuers, witnesses, and victims involved. Even within the relatively recent period that I chose, many people have retired, moved, married, or otherwise become difficult to track down. More than a few have died.

When I interviewed people for this book, accounts sometimes varied about a given incident. After enough time passes by, memories fade and change. Whenever there was a disagreement in fact between witnesses, I usually went by the Park Service reports written at the time of the incident. Sometimes the park reports didn't cover a given situation, so on occasion I had to pick what seemed the most likely version of a given incident when presented with more than one version. I apologize for any errors made.

The majority of the incidents covered by this book resulted in a fatality. I chose those incidents because they often were the most involved and interesting search and rescue stories, but they are far from the norm. In reality, there are many more successful rescues than not. Often those rescues are nothing more than a hiker getting overheated and dehydrated on a trail somewhere. A friend walks out and gets a ranger. The ranger hikes in with Gatorade, gets the person hydrated and cooled off in the shade, and hikes out with him.

I also often chose the fatalities because of the lessons to be learned. When someone dies from what seems a minor bad decision, it helps bring the lesson home. Some of the deaths in this book happened when someone wasn't properly prepared, underestimated conditions, or took unnecessary risks. Often the errors were very minor, such as going for a hike on a beautiful January day without extra clothes when a completely unpredicted snow storm rolled in suddenly, but ultimately caused a tragedy. In some cases, there was nothing that the victim did or didn't do that affected the outcome of the incident. It was purely bad luck.

To some degree, the causes of death have changed over the years. In the 1970s and 1980s, when the Rio Grande consistently had good flow, drownings were much more common. Today, with low water levels more the norm due to drought and Mexico's failure to release enough water into the Rio Grande, drownings have gotten rare.

Most people don't worry about violent crime at Big Bend National Park, and they shouldn't. Since 1980 five people have been murdered at the park, two of them in the same incident. I chronicle three incidents in this book. In only one of the four cases does it appear clear that the victim was not somehow related or known to the perpetrator. That kind of crime record would make any city green with envy.

Probably the most common thread in the stories in this book is heat and dehydration. People regularly underestimate the desert heat at the park. Take the park warnings seriously about carrying plenty of water, wearing proper clothes, and avoiding activity during hot times of the day and year. Respect the heat, use care near cliffs, wear a life jacket on the river, drive carefully, and your visit to Big Bend should be fun and safe.

CARL SPRINGER

"That one still haunts me," said Big National Park ranger and medic Michael Ryan, talking about the search and rescue effort made for Carl Springer.

He was one of the first to arrive on the scene when hiker Carl Springer was found by aerial searchers after an extensive hunt. Springer was severely dehydrated, but alert and oriented, when rangers reached him in the rugged southern foothills of the Chisos Mountains. Before Ryan arrived from park headquarters at Panther Junction by helicopter, Springer had been able to drink about a liter of water given to him by search and rescue team member Mark Yuhas. Upon his arrival, Ryan started an IV to help hydrate Springer. With the help of other rangers, Ryan then carried the lost hiker through rugged country to the helicopter landing site. Along the way, Springer began losing consciousness.

He was quickly flown to Panther Junction and transferred to the park ambulance where advanced life support was initiated by Dr. Hemant Vankawala, a park volunteer, and Ranger Marcos Paredes. Despite their efforts, soon after the trip commenced to meet a Midland-Odessa life flight helicopter at the Border Patrol checkpoint on U.S. 385, Carl Springer died.

"I still wonder if I should have done something differently when I arrived on the scene," said Ryan two years later. "Dr. Vankawala said that it was too late, that nothing would have saved him, but I still wonder sometimes."

Rangers at the park never like it, but they are familiar with arriving too late, after someone has already died. In this case they thought that they had saved someone, but it was not to be. Despite all their hard work and initial success, they ultimately lost a park visitor to the unforgiving desert of Big Bend National Park.

Carl Springer was the last person anyone expected to die on a hiking trip to Big Bend. The Conroe, Texas resident had traveled to the park for years and was very experienced. He'd hiked all over the park by himself and with others. He was 71, married for 45 years to Judith, and father of two grown children, Melanie and Stephen. He'd served in the Army and was a chemical engineer. For this trip he planned to do the Outer Mountain Loop, a strenuous 29-mile route that only serious Big Bend hikers in good shape attempt. It requires extensive climbing and steep descents on rugged trails as it goes up and over the Chisos Mountains high country twice. Although Springer had borderline diabetes that was controlled with oral medication and had recently suffered some mild short term memory lapses, he was otherwise in great physical shape. And it was a route he'd done many times before. The doctor who had tested his memory problems did not think that the trip was a good idea. However, the trip was already planned and his family did not want to discourage him from doing the thing he loved most.

Springer checked into the Big Bend Motor Inn on October 16, 2006, and reserved it until October 22. According to his daughter, Melanie Springer-Tollett, he was a meticulous man, not an uncommon trait in an engineer where the slightest design error can cost lives. Before he began his trek, he cached water ahead of time near the Homer Wilson ranch on Blue Creek. He obtained a backcountry camping permit from the park and filled out the solo hiker information sheet, so the park would know when to expect his return and could send out help if he didn't appear. He packed his gear, including detailed maps of his route. He planned to be on the trail for three days, ending on October 21.

Unlike the case in most rescues and fatalities at Big Bend National Park, the events were well documented by Springer himself in two small notepads that he carried with him. His journal left a record of his increasing travails and slow physical decline. He entitled one notepad "How I Got in Bad Trouble on Outer Mountain Loop." It was not an exaggeration.

On Wednesday, October 18, Springer left his room in Study Butte, leaving some items behind to be retrieved at the end of his trip. He drove up to the Basin, the big mountain valley hidden in the heart of the Chisos Mountains, and parked his car in the large lot by the lodge and trailhead. At about 9:30 A.M. he started up the Pinnacles Trail, the first leg of the Outer Mountain Loop, with three liters of water, food, and camping gear. Temperatures for hiking were pleasant, although plenty warm enough to make him sweat when carrying a heavy pack uphill; the high that day in the Basin was 79 degrees. The trail climbs 1,600 feet in 3.5 miles to reach the wooded high country of the Chisos Mountains, so Springer started sweating and breathing out large quantities of precious moisture immediately. He arrived at Boot Spring in a little over 3 hours. It lies in a narrow, rocky canyon shaded by pinyon and Arizona pines, junipers, Arizona cypresses, and bigtooth maples. The spring is not reliable and it's not clear from his journal whether he refilled his water bottles there. His journal simply states, "Left Boot Spring with 2 liters expecting to reach Upper Juniper Spring and water." Two liters were not an unreasonable amount of water to carry to Upper Juniper Spring. It's a short uphill climb, gaining about 200 feet of altitude, then a relatively steep descent of about 2.5 miles to reach the spring. If he didn't refill his water bottles at Boot Spring, it means that he only drank one liter in the long uphill climb to the spring, probably considerably less than what he lost through sweating and breathing.

Like Boot Spring, Upper Juniper Spring isn't always reliable. However, this time the spring was flowing well, but it didn't help Carl Springer. Somehow he missed the sign and short spur trail to the spring. In the subsequent search for Springer several days later, rangers John Morlock and Stephen McAllister reported, "There was abundant water flowing from this Upper Juniper Spring, with an obvious dipping pool for filling water bottles. This spring was in a campsite (approximately) 35 yards off the main trail. The campsite trail was signed 'Juniper Camp' at the junction of the main trail and the campsite trail. The campsite trail was easily seen leading into the trees within the Juniper Canyon drainage." There was no rainfall between Springer's journal entry of October 18 and the ranger's visit to the spring on October 23. How did Springer, an experienced hiker who had done the route many times before, miss the spring? His journal said, "Either Upper Juniper was dry or I did not find it." Obviously, he missed it. Was he tired? Even for a much younger person, it's a very strenuous hike from the Basin up and over the Chisos Mountains and then back down to Upper Juniper Spring. Did he suffer some sort of mental lapse as his doctor feared? Was he not thinking clearly because of exhaustion and dehydration? Regardless, Springer continued down the canyon, hoping to find water either at Lower Juniper Spring or with car campers at the campsite at the end of the Juniper Canyon Road.

The trail soon leaves the wooded upper slopes of the Chisos Mountains and enters high desert country with little shade. Lower Juniper Spring is more than two miles down Juniper Canyon, farther off the trail than Upper Juniper Spring, and much harder to find. It requires a bushwhack to reach. Unlike Upper Juniper Spring, there is no side trail to it. Did he find the lower spring? It's unclear. His journal said, "Did not find water at Lower Juniper Spring except for an unreachable stagnant pool." At this point he reported that he only had 1.5 liters of water left. Not only was it not enough considering his remote location, it also meant that he had not been drinking nearly enough that day unless he drank a large amount at Boot Spring. He was probably already quite dehydrated.

His journal reported that he reached the end of the Juniper Canyon Trail and the start of the Dodson Trail at the end of the Juniper Canyon

Road at 6:40 P.M. Undoubtedly he was very tired and becoming a bit desperate. He probably was not thinking clearly after hiking 11 difficult miles over the mountains with a heavy pack in a dehydrated state. The sun was setting, but he decided to head down the Dodson Trail, hoping to find water at Dodson Spring, rather than set up camp at the end of the road and wait for other hikers or a car to come by the next day.

The Dodson Trail continues the lengthy circuit of the Outer Mountain Loop. It is a strenuous route that crosses numerous ridges and drainages with substantial climbing and descending as it curves around to the west through the foothills of the Chisos Mountains. Dodson Spring lies 3.6 miles down the trail from the Juniper Canyon Road at the site of the historic Dodson Ranch. This section of the trail follows the route Harve Dodson used to get to his ranch headquarters long before Big Bend became a park. Then, as now, the only way into the rugged ranch was by foot or horse. When an early visitor asked Dodson how he got his family into such a remote spot, he replied, "Me and the old woman walked in, the kids was born there."

Springer arrived at or near Dodson Spring in the dark with only 0.5 liter of water remaining. The small spring is unreliable, hidden in thick brush, and difficult to find even in daylight. He was unable to find it that night or the next morning, October 19. From his journal, it's unclear whether he actually was at the spring or not. His writings describe his worsening situation. "Only hope is to get to Fresno Creek. I lost the cairns (trail markers) in dark somewhere. Backtracked and still could not find the trail. Thought I spotted a trail up on a hill. Spent my last energy and water to reach it. It led nowhere. I am stuck on hillside and cannot continue." Fresno Creek usually is reliable and has surface flow of water down a good length of canyon. It's fairly close to Dodson Spring and doesn't take long to reach by trail. However, Springer had lost the trail.

Alyssa Van Schmus, a ranger and EMT who was involved later in the rescue, said the trail was somewhat "overgrown." It was the end of the rainy season and during the search the "grass was up to our thighs even on the trail. It made it easier to lose the trail." Springer mentioned the tall grass in his journal. Van Schmus also said that there were lots of some sort of sharp needle and thread grass that constantly poked her through her pants and socks. Although Springer didn't mention it in his journal, she thought it was probably a distraction and added another layer of discomfort to his trek as darkness was falling.

Although lost and very dehydrated, Springer persevered as best he was able. He tried to get to the water at Fresno Creek, but was off the trail, lost, and weak. He set up camp on the hillside where he thought he saw the trail and continued to write notes in his journal over the following days. On Friday, October 20, he used his compass and topo map to try to locate himself on the map and find the Dodson Trail again. He was unsuccessful at locating himself accurately and remained on the hillside, continuing to weaken from lack of fluids and food. Although he had food with him, he couldn't eat it without liquid. The lack of food may have aggravated his borderline diabetes. He continued to take his blood pressure and diabetes medicines. His mood fluctuated from high to low and back. "The lack of expected water at both Upper and Lower Juniper Springs started this spiral of death," he wrote at one point that day. That afternoon he wrote, "Still on unknown hillside. Expect to die here. I am not due at Basin until noon 10/21/2006. Right now I think my survival odds are less than 25%. All mistakes were mine." Shortly after that he wrote, "I expect to die. I can't walk. I blame only me."

Springer wrote poignant individual notes to his two children, his son-in-law, and his grandchildren. His religious faith and love for his family came through strongly. To one grandchild he wrote, "I expect to die soon, lost on the Dodson Trail at BBNP. I made mistakes and did not have enough water. I had plans to take you on a train trip to Big Bend after Christmas. Sorry I messed that up. You are a fine boy with many talents. I love you."

Springer had a rough night with little sleep that Friday. At 5:30 A.M. on Saturday, October 21, he wrote, "My thinking is poor. Everything is a big effort. No water left, just a sip of Gatorade for meds. This may be my last note." But it wasn't, not by a long shot.

Later that morning he wrote, "My wedding ring is loose on dehydrated left ring finger. I choose to leave it there where Judy placed it 46 years ago." A bit later he added, "I must be content to lie here and hope for rescue which will not start until tomorrow at the earliest. Writing is difficult. This is probably my last note. I am ready. For rescue or to meet Jesus."

Near noon on that day he spread out his ground cloth to help make it easier for searchers to find him. "I waited almost too long," he wrote. "Cannot walk now. No strength in legs to stand on this hillside."

Springer's mood seemed to improve a bit late Saturday night. At 1:25 Sunday morning, October 22, he wrote, "I just produced 200 ml of urine. Normal looking in my pee bottle. I don't know where it is coming from. I'm shivering with all my clothes on. Temp is 45 degrees. That is air temp, not my body temp. Ha ha! This is the day a search for me should start."

At 7:30 A.M. on Sunday he wrote, "Another great pink-tinged sunrise. 40 degrees. I hope the people who will be searching for me just finished a good breakfast. When they find me they will say, 'how did that fool get so far off the trail?' I find writing difficult. This may be my last until after my rescue." A bit later he added, "I expect today searchers will find me." Unfortunately, he was wrong.

By 4:00 P.M. he was more realistic. He wrote, "This is too soon to expect searchers to find me, especially because I am way off the trail. I hope for an airplane search tomorrow. They can cover a wide area and spot the large ground cloth I finally got spread out."

Springer was suffering, but his sense of humor was still functioning. "My expectation for rescue soon is low. I can still say, 'all is well with my soul.' My soul is weller than my spelling." Later he continued writing in the same vein. "One poor choice is the one book I have in my pack: *Bitten, True Medical Stories of Bites and Stings.*"

Meanwhile, the park's search and rescue gears were beginning to turn. At about 3:00 P.M. on Sunday, the park communications center notified the ranger office that a solo hiker had not checked back in as scheduled on his permit. He was due in the day before, October 21. The park dispatch office called the pickup person listed on his permit, Barbara Edwards. She said that Springer had changed his mind about needing to be picked up and had brought his car to the park. She also said that Springer was a meticulous person and that it would not be normal for him to be late in getting back.

Ranger David Yim drove to the Basin parking lot and found Springer's car, a white Toyota Prius. He found that the car was unlocked. There was no backpack in the car or other sign that Springer had returned. He did find $200 in cash and a Discover card, which were removed from the car and placed in the park vault for safekeeping. Yim left a note in the car requesting that Springer call park dispatch upon his return.

Ranger Blake Trester drove to the Blue Creek parking area to look for Springer's water cache near the Homer Wilson ranch house. He also left a note on a trail sign requesting that Springer call the park office.

Park pilot Nick Herring was called out to fly the Outer Mountain Loop to look for Springer, and park volunteer Howard Benham was stationed at the Laguna Meadow Trailhead from 4:45 to 7:00 P.M. to question hikers as to whether any of them had seen Springer. The Laguna Meadow Trail is the last leg of the Outer Mountain Loop. No other hikers had seen him. West District Ranger Kevin Tillman assumed the Incident Commander position for the search.

Springer's friend, Barbara Edwards, called the Big Bend Motor Inn and was told that Springer had checked out. However, when Ranger David Yim called to verify that he had checked out, he was told that Springer was supposed to have checked out on October 22, but he had not been seen since he checked in on October 16. Yim asked if the motel staff could look and see if there was a large backpack in the room. Upon checking, the motel clerk reported that they had found only a small one.

At 4:35 P.M., Yim interviewed two hikers who had just returned from doing the Outer Mountain Loop and were at the Panther Junction Visitor Center. They had seen a single set of "big" hiking boot tracks ahead of them on the east side of the Dodson Trail when they began hiking that stretch of trail on the morning of October 21. Carl Springer was wearing size 13 Vasque hiking boots on his trip. The hikers lost sight of the tracks west of Fresno Creek where the trail begins climbing. The park rangers were concerned and organized a formal search.

At about 5:30 P.M., Nick Herring began an aerial search with the park plane of the Outer Mountain Loop. He searched the Dodson Trail area, along with the nearby Elephant Tusk and Smoky Creek trails. He also tried to search the Blue Creek drainage up to Laguna Meadows, but erratic winds prevented him from flying over that area. He recommended that Kevin Tillman contact the Texas Department of Public Safety or the Border Patrol for a helicopter search the next morning. Shadows were getting long by the time Herring was airborne, making it hard to see someone on the ground. He was unsuccessful at finding Springer and at about 7:00 P.M. he ended his search due to impending darkness.

At 6:00 that evening, Springer thought he heard people calling from way down the hill, although the park had not yet begun a ground search. "I hollered and blew my emergency whistle," he wrote in his journal. In his other notes, however, he stated that he couldn't talk well because his mouth and throat were so dry. He was able to whistle, however, and did so regularly. Unfortunately, he was either too far from the trail for anyone to hear it or no other hikers were in the area. He also wrote that evening, "I then thought I heard a plane circling. It came back but did not seem to spot me. I can still hear the plane in the distance. Sun has set in the West." Undoubtedly, he heard the park aircraft piloted by Nick Herring.

That night Incident Commander Tillman set up ground search teams for the next morning. Search and rescue team members Ron Sams and Mark Yuhas were assigned the route along the Laguna Meadows Trail and down the Blue Creek drainage to the Homer Wilson Ranch. The second team, Rangers Mark Cutler and Alyssa Van Schmus, was to search the Dodson Trail to Fresno Creek and onward to its east end at the Juniper Canyon Road. The last team, Rangers John Morlock and Stephen McAllister, was set up to cover the trail from the Chisos Basin to and down the Juniper Canyon Trail.

The next morning, Monday, October 23, at 5:30 Springer wrote, "Probably my last note," in worsening handwriting. "Love to all. Praise God from whom all blessings flow. Amen." But again it wasn't his last note. At 8:00 A.M. he wrote "Probably not my last note. That last liter of water lasted a long time. All gone now, but I did a verse of *Praise God* at the pink sunrise." His engineering background came through in a note written at 8:20 A.M. "I just urinated 450 ml into my pee bottle. Where does it come from with no input?"

The search and rescue operation accelerated first thing that morning. The rangers met with Kevin Tillman and headed out to their respective search areas. Ranger David Yim conducted a second search of Springer's vehicle, hoping to find something useful in the search. Nothing of value was found. Ranger Laura Van Inwagen then called Patricia Culp, the Big Bend Motor Inn manager, and received permission to search Springer's room. His belongings were still in the room, undisturbed. Van Inwagen took three items of worn clothing for use as scent items in case dogs were brought in to help with the search. She also took Springer's weekly planner, hiking trip plans, maps, a file labeled "2006 Oct. Trip," and a motel receipt.

A call to the Department of Public Safety found that their helicopters were down for maintenance, but a helicopter was secured through the Border Patrol station in Marfa. Park pilot Nick Herring was soon airborne again in the park's plane. As with the day before, he was unable to fly in the Blue Creek drainage or Juniper Canyon due to treacherous winds. Herring requested that the helicopter search those areas. Herring continued to circle the Dodson Trail area, looking for Springer.

At 1:30 that afternoon, Van Inwagen called Melanie Springer-Tollet, Springer's daughter. She and her husband had driven to Alpine the day before, wanting to be nearby to assist with the search. They stayed in Alpine because they thought her father would be brought to the Alpine hospital when he was found. Springer-Tollett told Van Inwagen that the Outer Mountain Loop was her father's favorite hike and that he had done it 12 to 15 times. She had done it with her father twice several years before.

"It was hard, it was harsh, you could get lost, and you had to be careful," she said when asked about the hike later. "Our nickname for it was the Outer Mountain Death Loop."

Springer-Tollett couldn't imagine that her father would be lost and thought that he must be hurt or dead to be two days overdue. He was very experienced and careful. Her father had never been lost before and he usually stayed on trails rather than hike cross-country. At about 2:00 P.M. Van Inwagen interviewed Springer's wife, Judy, and obtained more information, including hiking gear descriptions.

Two years later, son Stephen Springer repeated his sister's comments. He had also hiked the Outer Mountain Loop twice with his father.

"It's a difficult and remote area," he said.

He preferred other hikes in the park. He was the one who coined the family name for the hike, the "Outer Mountain Death Loop." He said that his father loved the hike simply because it was hard and a real physical and mental challenge.

By later that day, Springer had seen and heard the searching aircraft. He wrote, "I just heard and saw a plane or helicopter. I waved my red stuff sack on hiking stick. No response. I continue to blow three blasts on my emergency whistle every ten minutes."

Springer continued to contemplate his situation while awaiting rescue. "Why did I get so far off the trail? Once I realized I was on the wrong hill, I thought I spotted a trail above me that was trending in the correct direction. I put my last energy reserves in attempt to reach it, but failed." Later, he added, "I am so weak I can hardly stand on this rocky hillside. Too weak to think about going 50 feet. I do think about my loved ones." At 9:30 A.M. he wrote, "I hate to think about dying out here in this great wild place. It will cause much extra work for others and much extra worry and sorrow for family and friends. The good thing is that it is easy to have time to think about and talk to God. I have done that several times in the past two days."

At 10:30 A.M. he wrote, "I keep dozing off. I will not resist sleep. I am ready to go. I lived on 1.5 liters of water from October 18, 2:30 P.M., to now. Praise God from whom all blessings flow. I have fought a good fight. I still hope for an air search to find me. I think I will doze off now and hope to not awake. Now I lay me down to sleep. I pray the Lord my soul to take."

At 12:50 P.M. Springer was roused by the searching aircraft. He noted seeing and hearing planes several times over the next hour. His last note read, "2:06 P.M. Can hear plane."

At about 3:30 P.M. Springer was spotted by park pilot Nick Herring in the upper Fresno Creek drainage, between the South Rim and the Dodson Trail. Herring's eye was caught by the movement of Springer waving his walking stick with a red stuff sack tied on the end. Herring asked the helicopter to respond to evaluate Springer's condition. Within minutes Border Patrol pilot Milt Kennedy landed the helicopter, accompanied by search and rescue team member Mark Yuhas. Kennedy and Yuhas quickly made their way to Springer to check his condition and attend to his needs.

"He was conscious, looked okay, and was lucid," Yuhas said. "We gave him water."

At a little after 4:00 P.M., pilot Nick Herring, who was still circling above to help with radio communications, relayed to park headquarters that Springer was extremely dehydrated and that it would probably take 20 minutes to get him to the helicopter. Chief Ranger Mark Spier asked park medics Michael Ryan and Marcos Paredes to head for the helicopter landing site at Panther Junction with the park ambulance just in case. The park called Melanie Springer-Tollett, waiting anxiously in Alpine, with the good news that her father had been found alive.

At 4:54 P.M., Herring asked Van Schmus and Cutler to come to Springer's location to help get Springer to the helicopter. They were about two miles away when Springer was found. He asked Kennedy if he could fly to Van Schmus, who was also an EMT, in the helicopter to bring her to the site faster. However, the chopper was low on fuel and needed to fly to Panther Junction to refuel and pick up Michael Ryan. Despite having hiked all day, Van Schmus and Cutler made it across the rough intervening terrain in less than an hour to assist Springer.

At about 5:00 P.M., the helicopter made the short hop to Panther Junction to refuel and pick up Michael Ryan. Within about 15 minutes Kennedy was back at the landing site near Springer with Ryan. At about 5:35 P.M., Ryan successfully started an IV on Springer to aid in re-hydration. Rangers Cutler and Van Schmus arrived on the scene and all discussed whether to fly Springer out immediately. Ryan was concerned that the sun would soon be setting, preventing air operations. He thought that it was best to get Springer to medical care as soon as possible.

"I wanted him off that hill," said Ryan afterward. "We couldn't do much more for him there." Van Schmus was concerned that the move might have a negative effect on Springer, but who could really know? Ultimately, they decided to move Springer.

Although the helicopter was only 75-100 yards away, the route was steep and rough.

"We tried to help him up to the helicopter, but he couldn't walk," Yuhas said.

Finally, Ryan carried the 185-pound Springer piggyback up to the chopper, not a small feat even on flat, smooth ground.

At about 6:17 P.M., Ryan advised headquarters that Springer was losing consciousness en route to the chopper. At that point, Springer had taken about 0.5 liter of IV solution and had drunk about a liter of water before Ryan had arrived. Once Springer was loaded in the helicopter, Kennedy quickly flew to Panther Junction.

"I was in the back seat and Springer started nodding off," Yuhas said. "I was hoping he was just falling asleep, but he wasn't. He was unconscious by the time we got to Panther Junction."

Herring advised headquarters that Springer wasn't doing well and would need immediate medical intervention as soon as they arrived. Upon landing, Springer was quickly transferred to the park ambulance and care was transferred to Dr. Vankawala and ranger Marcos Paredes. The park called Springer's daughter to tell her that her father was going in and out of consciousness. Concerned, she and her husband hopped in their car and headed toward Odessa, location of the destination hospital.

Springer's condition continued to worsen. Advanced life support was initiated and within about 20 minutes the ambulance began the trip north to meet the Midland-Odessa life-flight helicopter. "We lost vital signs right as we were departing Panther Junction," said Paredes. Vankawala and Paredes tried to bring Springer back, but were unsuccessful. Despite the enormous effort made by many of the park staff to save his life, Springer slipped quietly away on the drive. Dr. Vankawala declared Carl Springer dead shortly after 7:00 P.M.

Melanie Springer-Tollett got the bad news as they drove toward Odessa. When she first got the news that he had been found alive, she thought, "That's it, he's going to make it. I was relieved." She was absolutely crushed to get the word only a short time later that her father had died.

"It was horrible," she said two years later. But she was "glad that they found him alive and that he had people with him when he died."

All rangers, vehicles, and aircraft were accounted for and returned to park headquarters by about 8:00 P.M. The operation was terminated and the dispirited rangers headed home.

Michael Ryan was still bothered about losing Springer two years later. "It's the worst rescue that I've dealt with. We did our job, we found him, he's okay. Springer was sitting up and even joking with Mark Yuhas. He was drinking water and eating a little. I was on standby at Panther Junction and didn't even think I'd be needed."

Then Mark Yuhas called in that Springer was very weak and needed a medic. So Ryan found himself on the helicopter flying to the site. Even after Ryan arrived on the scene he still thought that Springer was going to be okay. "He's tired, dehydrated, hungry. No one thought he was on the brink." When Ryan thinks about the incident today he says, "I wish I'd done something differently, but I'm not sure what."

"There was more going on physically with Springer than any of us realized," said medic Alyssa Van Schmus. "His talking and joking may have masked the severity of his condition. As you're trained, you give the best care possible, but you can't predict the outcome."

Marcos Paredes said, "Springer was too far gone from dehydration, exhaustion, and diabetes when we found him." He added that the family was very understanding and "didn't blame us. They said that Carl was probably happy going the way he did. He loved the park."

Two years later, his wife Judith repeated Paredes' words. She was really in shock at the time of his death, but "I'm at peace now," she said. "It's how he would have wanted to go. He used to tease us, saying that if he died at Big Bend, at least he'd die happy."

"He loved the park," Judith added. "After completing a trip he would book lodging for a trip for the next year before even leaving the park. Ironically, right before heading out alone on his last trip, he was showing some friends around the park and describing the hazards."

"I have nothing but praise for the Park Service," said Stephen Springer, now a Lutheran minister in Tucson, Arizona. "They did a great job."

John Morlock, one of the rangers who searched on foot from the Basin over the mountains and down to the Juniper Canyon road, said, "I think he (Springer) was already rationing water, already having trouble by the time he got to Upper Juniper Spring. Maybe already mentally impaired by dehydration and exhaustion. The side trail to the spring was clearly visible." He added, "It's a killer hike."

"By the time he got to Upper Juniper Spring, he was probably already dehydrated and exhausted, and maybe was not thinking clearly," said Laura Van Inwagen. "The combined distance (of the lengthy hike), dehydration, and warm weather made it more likely that he would miss the spring."

His daughter, Melanie Springer-Tollett, is a medical doctor in Houston and has some guesses about what killed him. "He was in excellent physical shape," she said. "He had had back surgery earlier in the year. He recovered well and was really looking forward to the hike. It was the best he'd felt in years. He would train and train for Big Bend trips. He would load up his backpack with 50 pounds of weight and walk around the golf course. People probably thought he was loony."

Her father was always a very careful man. "It just wasn't like him to head out on the Dodson Trail without enough water as night was coming on," said Springer-Tollet. "He must not have been thinking clearly."

"He knew the risk he was taking to hike it (the Outer Mountain Loop) alone," added Stephen Springer, "but he took all the precautions he could, such as registering with the park as a solo hiker and caching water." His actions on that trip "just weren't like him." He and his father had been going to Big Bend since he was a child in the 1970s. "I went out there with him almost annually after about 1981. When we hiked, my father would always say, 'your urine needs to be clear; if it's not you're not drinking enough.'"

And what finally killed him? "It was probably vascular collapse from dehydration and maybe acute renal failure," said Springer-Tollett. "He was so careful to take his drugs for treating his blood pressure and diabetes even without water, and they probably worsened his condition."

Not finding Upper Juniper Spring was obviously the first major cause of Springer's difficulties. His inability to locate water at Lower

Juniper Spring worsened the situation. If he had not pressed on to Dodson Spring that first evening and instead had spent the night at the end of the Juniper Canyon Road, someone might have found him in a day or two. However, it was likely that Springer was desperate and not thinking clearly by this point. His depleted state may have brought on some of the memory lapses that his doctor feared. In a sad, ironic twist, Rangers John Morlock and Stephen McAllister found two gallons of water in plastic jugs in the prominent metal bear storage box (to keep bears from accessing camper's food) at the campsite at the end of the road during the search. They were left there by another hiker who hadn't needed them. "Enjoy," said the note attached to them. Although there was no particular reason that Springer would have checked the box, the thought that he walked unknowingly within a few feet of two gallons of water is dismaying. The water would have saved his life.

JOHN GARY MONROE

On October 30, 1994, John Gary Monroe left his home in San Antonio for Big Bend National Park to hike and camp. That afternoon he obtained a backcountry permit for Pine Canyon Campsite #4 after arriving at the park . The campsite, like many others scattered across the park, is a primitive site with no facilities other than a parking area. The sites are kept primitive to allow a backcountry experience with few other nearby campers. His chosen site lay along Pine Canyon Road and was lined with large wooden beams to keep vehicles within the designated area. He reserved Pine Canyon #4 for two days, through November 1, but went to Panther Junction after only one day to switch to Pine Canyon #1. He also extended his stay to November 3. Pine Canyon

#1 and adjacent site Pine Canyon #2 lie 0.7 mile up the Pine Canyon Road from its start on the Glenn Spring Road. The Pine Canyon Road is 4.2 miles long, ending at the Pine Canyon trailhead. Pine Canyon #3 lies two miles up the road from the Glenn Spring Road; Pine Canyon #4 is 3.75 miles up, near the trailhead. The Pine Canyon Road climbs steadily up into the grassy foothills of the Chisos Mountains from the high desert.

Monroe had been coming to the park once per year for at least 15 years. He was the son of two school teachers in Houston and worked for AT&T in San Antonio. In a report Ranger Roger Moder wrote on January 12, 1995, "[Monroe] likes to come to the park to 'clear his head' and be close to God." When Monroe drove west that day from San Antonio, he left behind his wife, Christi. He had been married to her for about 12 years. Severe epilepsy had disabled her, but Monroe never resented her condition or the care that he had to provide for her. He was a dedicated husband and very religious person.

"He loved her and made her happier than we ever thought possible," his mother-in-law Carol Kosarek wrote. "He told me that we didn't ever have to worry about Christi being alone. That when we were gone, he would always take care of her, for as long as he lived. I have no doubt that was true."

Usually Monroe went with his wife or friends, but not this time. On the day that he left on this trip, his in-laws were uneasy when they learned that Monroe was going alone, and they tried to persuade him to go to their ranch instead. However, he was ready to go, mentally and physically.

"Carol, it's a national park. Nobody is going to bother me there," Monroe said right before he headed west.

On November 2, Charles Van Driskill, his wife Marilyn, and friends and family members Kent Hackett, Glenda Green, and Lydia Green drove up the rough, high-clearance Pine Canyon Road to the Pine Canyon trailhead at its end. From the trailhead, a popular path leads from the high desert grasslands in the eastern foothills of the Chisos Mountains into a dramatic canyon that cuts deep into the high country surrounding Lost Mine Peak. Heavy woods of Arizona pine, oak, juniper, pinyon pine, and the beautiful pink-barked madrone shade the narrow canyon. After two miles the trail ends at a 200-foot-high pour-off that becomes a small waterfall during wet weather. Yellow blooms of columbine dot the canyon floor and walls under the waterfall in spring. It was too beautiful a spot for the tragedy that was to occur nearby.

Van Driskill and his party reached the junction of the Pine Canyon Road and the Glenn Spring Road after lunchtime on their way to do their hike up the Pine Canyon Trail. As they drove past the Pine Canyon #1 campsite, Lydia Green noticed Monroe lying on the ground by his tent, but just thought that he was asleep. Her daughter Glenda Green explained later.

"My mother saw him lying there but wasn't too alarmed. The (Terlingua) chili cookoff was starting soon and sometimes people got drunk and slept on the ground," Green said.

At about 5:20 P.M., after doing their hike up Pine Canyon, they drove back down the road, again passing Pine Canyon #1.

"We were driving back by the campsite and my mother said, 'He's still there! Something must be wrong,'" Glenda Green said. "So we backed up and looked. It was pretty obvious he was dead. His face was very white."

Green's brother-in-law, Van Driskill got out and walked over to check on Monroe and immediately saw that he really was dead. He was lying on his back with his head against one of the logs that bordered the campsite. His feet lay against his tent. Blood covered the slightly distorted rear left side of his head. Small bits of gravel were stuck in his mouth and nose and his shirt was saturated with blood. Glasses and a blood-stained baseball cap lay on the ground next to his head. That Monroe was dead was not in doubt just from visual evidence. It didn't look like he had died peacefully.

"It looked like he was shot the moment he got out of the tent," Driskill said. "His pants weren't fastened and his boots weren't laced. My family was screaming, 'get away from there, get away from there!'"

Driskill immediately backed away. He recorded the license plate number of the maroon Toyota truck parked at the site and the group headed straight for Panther Junction to report what they had found.

"We were paranoid," Glenda Green said. "We didn't know what happened. We raced to Panther Junction. Van, Kent, and I went into the visitor center and reported it."

Except that the situation was so serious, their experience there was a little funny.

"There was a line at the desk," Driskill said. "Glenda went up to the desk and said that we needed to talk to a ranger. He told her that she had to wait her turn in line. She told him again that she really needed to talk to a ranger. He asked her again to please wait in line. Finally, she blurted out that we had found a dead man. It got really quiet and several rangers suddenly appeared. They took us in back and interviewed us."

The group had been tent camping on their trip. "It felt kind of creepy that night camping at Rio Grande Village," Green said.

"We didn't have a very good night," added Driskill.

The park's rangers leapt into action. Shortly after 6:00 P.M., rangers went to set up checkpoints at the three possible driving routes out of Pine Canyon—River Road East, River Road West, and Glenn Spring Road. The Border Patrol was notified of a possible homicide and were asked to record vehicle information on all vehicles leaving the park. Rangers Roger Moder, Marcos Paredes, and Gene Wesloh drove out to Pine Canyon #1, arriving at 7:49 P.M. The days are short that time of year, so it was dark when they arrived.

Moder cautiously approached the site and found that everything was as described by Van Driskill.

"It was pretty obvious Monroe was dead when we approached," Paredes said. "He maybe got shot right as he was stepping out of the tent."

"We were very careful to protect the scene," Chief Ranger Jim Northup said. "We cordoned off the area until the FBI's team arrived. We didn't want to disturb evidence."

Paredes and Wesloh checked the rest of Pine Canyon Road and found no other people. Paredes drove a number of miles over to Juniper Canyon Campsite #2 and questioned the people camping there, but the campers were unaware of the events in Pine Canyon and had no information. Paredes and Wesloh stood guard at the campsite until FBI agents arrived the next day. Because the crime had occurred on federal land, the FBI had jurisdiction.

At about 10:00 the next morning, agents Steve Morris, Mike Pearce, and Steve Malkiewicz arrived in the park from El Paso. Agent Tom Henrie came down from the FBI office in Midland to act as lead investigator. Agents Pierce and Morris arrived at the crime scene at about noon, accompanied by Ron Willard, a local justice of the peace and coroner, Chief Ranger Jim Northup, Roger Moder, and others. Ranger Paredes joined them in the preliminary survey of the campsite.

Willard examined Monroe and pronounced him dead, apparently of gunshot wounds. In addition to the tent, the investigators found a barbecue grill and cooking utensils, along with 12 or 13 crushed Coors beer cans and a number of cigarette butts. The area outside of the tent was orderly, with no apparent signs of a struggle. Many pieces of clothing and personal items were scattered around the interior of the tent, apparently coming from a suitcase and briefcase lying in the tent.

The agents examined the maroon Toyota truck parked at the campsite and found various, mostly camping related items in the truck's bed. The doors of the truck were unlocked. The glove box was open with its contents scattered across the passenger seat and floor. Several forms of identification were also spread across the front seat, including John Monroe's driver's license. Several bags of food, including fruit, bread, and nuts were also within the truck's interior.

The agents continued to explore the campsite, but failed to find any signs of a struggle. They also failed to find any useful footprints or vehicle tracks. The agents had a murder victim, but little to go on from their initial examination of the crime scene. The only things taken from Monroe were about $35 in cash, credit cards, his handgun, and a knife.

While the agents searched the campsite, park rangers overflew the crime scene looking for other vehicles in the backcountry area of Pine Canyon or anything else unusual.

The FBI agents and park rangers began to reconstruct events of Monroe's visit to the park leading up to his death. They talked to park employees and examined backcountry camping permits for that part of the park.

Two park employees, Betty Alex and Gene Foster, thought they remembered seeing Monroe's truck at the Glenn Spring pullout on November 1 at around noon. At about 10:00 on the morning of November 1, Dr. Ken Williams and his school class passed by Pine Canyon Campsite #1 on their way up the Pine Canyon Road to hike the trail. Monroe waved to the group as they went by. One member of the group thought that maybe someone was in Monroe's tent. After their hike, they drove back down the road at about 3:00 P.M., this time pulling slightly into Monroe's campsite to allow three vehicles that were driving toward the trailhead to pass on the narrow road. According to the supplemental criminal incident record written by Ranger Roger Moder on January 12, 1995, Williams' group reported, "Monroe was sitting in chair on north side of truck. Monroe did not wave or move."

The three vehicles driving up the canyon toward the trailhead were heading to Pine Canyon #4, their campsite for the night. The group, led by Nolan Lacy, did not notice Monroe or anything unusual in his camp as they passed Williams' group on the road by Monroe's campsite. At about 5:30 P.M., Jerry Needham drove by Monroe's campsite to camp at Pine Canyon #3 about 1.3 miles up the canyon from Monroe's site. Needham reported seeing a man standing on the side of the road that might have been Monroe about a half mile east of Pine Canyon #1, Monroe's campsite. The man did not wave. Needham didn't notice anyone in Monroe's campsite. Although Needham was only about 1.3 miles from Monroe's campsite, he did not hear any gunshots, vehicles, or anything else unusual during his stay there.

At about 10:00 A.M. the next day, Needham hiked up the Pine Canyon Trail, passing the six people of Nolan Lacy's group who were camping at Pine Canyon #4.

Interestingly, at 10:01 A.M. on November 2 someone used Monroe's credit card at a Texaco station in Alpine. Later interviews with the manager and the employee who took the credit card charge were not particularly fruitful. The signature used on the credit card slip did not match John Monroe's.

At about 11:00 A.M. on that day, Harvey Richard and some friends started to hike up the Pine Canyon Trail. They didn't notice anyone at Monroe's campsite while driving to the trailhead. They did see the vehicles of Needham and Lacy's party parked at the trailhead. At about noon, a member of Lacy's group did notice Monroe lying on the ground by his tent as they drove out, but didn't realize that he was dead. Needham left the trailhead at about 3:30 P.M., but didn't remember noticing Monroe's campsite on the way down the canyon.

On the evening of November 3, the park received confirmation that Monroe's wife Christi had been notified of her husband's death. Her brother called Roger Moder to confirm Monroe's identity and told Moder that Monroe had a .410 shotgun and a pistol for personal protection.

The next day, November 4, Christi Monroe and her father, Charles Kosarek, called Chief Ranger Jim Northup at about 9:00 A.M. to ask questions about the death of her husband. That afternoon an investigative team of rangers—Moder, Wesloh, and Bill Wright—was set up by Northup and Moder. Moder had a busy afternoon. He called Christi Monroe to let her know that the key to her house appeared to be on a key ring in the truck, as were personal checks of her and her husband. He called several people involved with the annual Terlingua chili cookoff that was in progress at the time to ask them to listen for anything interesting at the cookoff. He phoned the police department in Alpine to get information on a person wanted for murder who was supposed to be in the Terlingua area. He issued a BOLO (Be On the Look Out) for that person to all park rangers. He also tried to call Cathi West with the U.S. Attorney's office to setup counseling for Christi Monroe.

The next morning, November 5, Christi's brother, Steve Jones, and father, Charles Kosarek, called with questions and offered to send photos to the park. The investigative team called the Border Patrol and asked them to look for Monroe's stolen handgun. A ranger from Amistad National Recreation Area arrived to talk to people at the chili cookoff about the homicide. The team printed up "Can You Help" flyers to be posted in and around the park, hoping that someone would come forward with useful information.

On the morning of November 6, a checkpoint was set up at the chili cookoff to ask people if they knew anything helpful. At about 10:00 A.M. on November 7, Jerry Needham arrived at park headquarters to be interviewed by Moder and Wesloh. Needham wasn't sure that the man he had seen on the Pine Canyon Road on his way up to his campsite was Monroe, but he did remember that the man had a walking stick. Monroe's wife, Christi, had said that her husband had a number of walking sticks and liked hiking with them. Additionally, a walking stick was found lying underneath Monroe's body at the campsite, so it's very possible that Needham did see Monroe.

Needham reported that he had seen Nolan Lacy's group hiking down the Pine Canyon Trail as he hiked up. Earlier Lacy had told Ranger Wesloh that his group had seen Needham on the Pine Canyon Trail and then later at Langford Hot Springs. Lacy told Wesloh that he had asked Needham whether he had enjoyed the Pine Canyon Trail when he saw him again at Hot Springs. Lacy said Needham appeared to become nervous and denied that he had been on that trail. Lacy thought that Needham had been about to walk to the hot springs, but that he left the hot springs area right after Lacy's question.

Moder wrote in his report after the interview, "I asked Mr. Needham if he had been at the Hot Springs area after his hike on the Pine Canyon Trail. Mr. Needham appeared to me to become nervous, and he said that he had not been to the Hot Springs. I asked him if he went to the Hot Springs at any time while he was in the park on this current trip. Mr. Needham replied that he may have gone to the Hot Springs, but could not remember when. He said that he had travelled all over the park, and could not remember all the places he visited. Mr. Needham then said that perhaps he had gone to the Hot Springs two or three times during this visit."

Later that day Moder called U.S. Customs to learn more about a recent homicide that had happened at La Linda, outside of the park, to see if there were any similarities between the two cases. There did not appear to be any. Moder then connected with Cathi West of the U.S. Attorney's office. He explained the case to her so that West could get some help for Christi Monroe. Soon afterwards, photos of John Monroe arrived that were sent by Charles Kosark.

On the morning of November 28, Cynthia Cyne-York and Sam Hawkins appeared at Ranger Moder's office with information that they thought might relate to the murder of John Monroe. They had seen the "Can You Help" flyer on the Rio Grande Village bulletin board and had discussed the homicide with a friend of theirs, David Martin, who used to work for the concession in the park. He encouraged them to share their information with the park rangers.

On November 18, Hawkins and Cyne-York told Moder that while they were sitting in the restaurant of José Falcón in Boquillas, Mexico, across the river from Rio Grande Village, a stranger named Brian Keithley approached them and began a conversation. After visiting for awhile, Hawkins and Cyne-York left Keithley and returned to their campsite in Rio Grande Village. That afternoon they were surprised when Keithley appeared at their campsite. They had not told him where they were staying or what their plans were. They talked for some time and eventually invited Keithley to share the campsite with them for the night.

Moder wrote in his report of the interview, "During a subsequent conversation, Ms. Cyne-York brought up the fact that Mr. Monroe had been killed in the park. Mr. Keithley told Ms. Cyne-York that it would be easy to kill someone in the desert and get away with it. When Ms. Cyne-York asked him about this comment, Mr. Keithley changed the subject and refused to acknowledge a second question about it by Ms. Cyne-York. Ms. Cyne-York was alarmed by the comment and by Mr. Keithley ignoring her questions, and had the impression that Mr. Keithley was hiding something."

Cyne-York told Moder that from her conversations with Keithley that she thought that Keithley had been in the park when Monroe was murdered. Both Cyne-York and Hawkins thought Keithley was strange after talking to him for awhile. He contradicted himself and talked about things that weren't based in reality. They became frightened. During the night Hawkins heard Keithley talking loudly even though he was alone.

The next morning, November 19, Cyne-York and Hawkins went for a three-hour walk in the Rio Grande Village area, leaving their vehicle at their campsite. When they returned at about 10:30 A.M., Keithley was still there. They wanted to get away from him, so they packed up their gear. As they left, Keithley gave a quart of oil to Hawkins. Hawkins thought it odd, but took the oil.

On the way to Study Butte on the west side of the park, Hawkins' vehicle broke down by the Panther Junction gas station. It looked to Hawkins like someone had loosened the engine's valve cover causing the engine to lose most of its oil. Soon Keithley arrived and offered assistance. He gave Hawkins an oily adjustable wrench, already adjusted to the size of the valve cover bolts, to tighten down the bolts. Hawkins did the repairs and again headed toward Study Butte with Cyne-York. He broke down again, and again Keithley appeared on the scene.

Cyne-York said that Keithley made several attempts to separate her from Hawkins, including offering to put her up in a motel while the vehicle was repaired and offering money. She refused. Earlier Keithley had told Cyne-York and Hawkins that he had little money.

Ranger Moder wrote in his report, "Both Mr. Hawkins and Ms. Cyne-York were alarmed by the presence of Mr. Keithley, and thought that he might try to do them harm. They were trying to get away from him, but he kept following them. After the vehicle had been repaired at Study Butte, they no longer saw Mr. Keithley."

Hawkins told Moder that he might be able to identify Keithley from the camping fee envelope that Keithley had used to pay his camping fee. The self-serve envelopes at the campground entrance allow fees to be paid and ask for information such as name and vehicle license number. Ranger Dave Evans located Keithley's envelope. It had the license number for Keithley's vehicle, a 1984 Nissan pickup. A request was made to local law enforcement agencies to look for Keithley and his vehicle, but neither were found by January 12, 1995, the date of Moder's extensive report.

On January 4, 1995, Moder tried to call Cyne-York at the phone number that she had given him during the interview, but the woman who answered said that she did not know Cyne-York.

Later Moder tracked Cyne-York down for a follow-up interview on February 24, 1995. She provided an Oklahoma Native American driver's license as proof of identification. On it her name was shown as Cynthia Vela York. In the initial interview, her friend Eddie Dean Ramsey had falsely identified himself as Sam Hawkins. During the follow-up interview York said that she knew that Ramsey planned to use a false name. She said that Ramsey simply made up the name. However, the rangers challenged her with knowing a Sam Hawkins (the name of a former boyfriend). She then said that Ramsey must have looked through her personal phone book to get the name.

The March 2, 1995, report written by Ranger Steve Spanyer, said: "York said that Ramsey gave the false name because he did not want to get involved in a murder investigation. York stated that Ramsey told her people around here would kill you if you got someone else in trouble."

York said that Ramsey was from Odessa, Texas and had once owned a snow cone business with his stepfather. He had once been arrested for writing a check on his stepfather's account without permission. He had apparently made frequent trips to the park with his father when he was a child.

York and Ramsey had planned to return to San Antonio after their November visit to the park, but their van broke down. Their friend David Martin helped them get jobs at the Easter Egg Valley Motel in Terlingua. They planned to stay there until they earned enough money to replace the engine in their van.

The report also stated, "Near the end of the interview, York made the unprovoked comment that she and Ramsey were together the whole time they were in the park, that they weren't even in the park when the murder occurred and that Ramsey did not kill anyone."

None of these leads ever went anywhere. The FBI actively pursued the case with the support of the Park Service, but little turned up.

Two years after the murder in the fall of 1996, Daryl Rhodes, the park law enforcement specialist who replaced Roger Moder, was asked by Superintendent José Cisneros to review the case. Rhodes met with FBI agents Steve French and Tony Henrie and they read all the case files, interviewed additional witnesses, and even served a subpoena to get personnel records of a possible suspect.

"We didn't really find anything new," Rhodes said.

"The case just seemed to go cold after the gas purchase," Chief Ranger Northup said. "I don't think we ever determined where the assailant went after getting gas in Alpine."

John Monroe's mother-in-law, Carol Kosarek, has a hard time hiding her disappointment that the case was never solved, even though she can understand why.

"It's the perfect place to commit this sort of crime," Kosarek said. "The park has a very transient population of visitors. Here today, gone tomorrow. It makes it very difficult to investigate something like this. Jim Northup really tried. He wrote us several times afterward. He really seemed to care."

"The Oklahoma City bombing (of the Alfred Murrah Building) happened six months after the murder, which distracted the FBI from this case," Kosarek said. "We've never tried to revive it because our daughter had a really hard time and there didn't seem to be much point (in upsetting her again)."

Kosarek firmly believes that the assailant will eventually get justice one way or another.

Jim Northup would sure like that to happen. "It's a case that has haunted me for years," he said. "It bothers me that it's still unsolved."

"It's still an open investigation," FBI agent Steve French said. "We have not charged anyone in the case. It's my opinion that it was a random killing. Those types of cases are the hardest to solve. We would love to solve the case."

"It was a sad deal," Ranger Marcos Paredes said. "One minute he's out there enjoying his camping trip, the next he's been shot. I think he was just in the wrong place at the wrong time. An opportunistic asshole just happened by."

"A tragedy such as this changes the dynamics of an entire family," Kosarek wrote in an email. "Our lives have never been, nor will they ever be the same without him."

WILLIAM EGGER

At about 7:50 P.M. on December 30, 2006, the Search and Rescue Coordination Center at Langley Air Force Base in Virginia called the Big Bend National Park dispatch office to notify the park that a personal locator beacon (PLB) registered to William Egger, Jr. had been activated ten minutes earlier. The Federal Communications Commission approved PLBs for use in the United States in 2003, although they had been available for use in many other countries for years. The beacons are small, pocket-sized radio transmitters that are registered to their users. When activated in case of emergency, they send a 406 MHz signal to orbiting satellites that determine the beacon's location using the doppler shift in the radio frequency that occurs as the satellites speed by overhead. From there the signal is relayed to the U. S. Air Force and from there to state and local search and rescue agencies. More recent systems, such as the SPOT which debuted in 2008, use GPS satellites to locate the beacon. On the second to last day of 2006, Big Bend National Park got its first-ever call from a PLB of someone in distress.

San Antonio attorney Bill Egger got to the park on December 29, obtained his camping permit, and drove to the Elephant Tusk primitive roadside campsite in Big Bend National Park for the night. The next day he planned to climb Elephant Tusk. The campsite lies on the remote, rough Black Gap Road between Talley Mountain and the southeastern slopes of the Chisos Mountains. Elephant Tusk rises abruptly from the southeastern foothills, its steep, conical, symmetrical shape the most notable landmark in that part of the park. It lies about 4 miles northwest of its namesake campsite as the crow flies. Most people never get any closer than the campsite or the view of it from the South Rim of the Chisos Mountains. Egger's interest in climbing the peak had been piqued after seeing the peak from the South Rim and reading about it online. He had visited the park several times before, but had only hiked in the Chisos Mountains. An experience with a mountain lion pushed him into climbing Elephant Tusk.

"I was in Boot Canyon about a year before, lying in my tent just after dawn when I saw a mountain lion walk by," Egger said. "I yelled and it ran away. I went and took a picture of the paw print and then I turned around and saw that it had sneaked back to about 25 feet away, looking like it was going to pounce on me. I yelled loudly at it, using quite a bit of profanity this time, and it finally ran away. I thought I'd go try hiking in the desert next time."

So about a year later, Egger was in the desert. The morning after he arrived in the park, December 30, at about 8:30, Egger began hiking from his campsite toward the peak on the lightly used Elephant Tusk Trail. He was well equipped for a winter day hike, with a backpack, down vest, rain jacket and pants, pullover cap, three-liter CamelBak water bladder, two one-liter water bottles, space blanket, whistle, PLB, small LED light, a GPS unit, a pen flare gun, and food. After about four miles he left the trail and began climbing cross country toward the north side of the peak. As he ascended, the climbing got harder and harder, eventually narrowing into a steep, talus-choked ravine. As he got closer to the summit, he hiked up a steep ramp in the ravine to the base of a cliff with a climbable chimney in it.

"Unfortunately, I left my pack at the base of the chimney to make climbing easier," Egger said, "so I couldn't get to it later."

Very fortunately as it turned out, he did carry his space blanket, PLB, trail mix, LED light, whistle, and a little water with him in his pockets. He scrambled up the chimney without too much trouble, and reached a ledge. From there the climbing looked even harder, so he decided to retreat from the route, rather than continue to the summit. He tried to down-climb the chimney, but couldn't do it safely.

"I spent about four hours trying to self-rescue by down climbing, but was unsuccessful," Egger said.

Egger tried both the chimney and another spot, but was unable to get down either. Finally, with night coming on and realizing that he was not going to be able to down-climb, he activated his PLB.

"When the Air Force in Langley called my wife and sons to tell them that I'd activated my PLB," Egger said, "they freaked out. They told them that people usually only activated them if they were injured or had a serious emergency."

"I had done my due diligence in researching the climb before my trip," Egger said, "but it wasn't enough. I learned that it's a lot harder to down-climb than climb up. I later took some rock climbing lessons."

Temperatures fell below freezing that night, making it pretty miserable, although the view was spectacular.

"At about 10:00 P.M.," Egger said, "the wind started blowing at about 50 miles per hour down the chute I was in. I was really hypothermic from about 10:30 P.M. until 4:00 A.M. when the wind died."

He tied his PLB to a bush to keep it from blowing away. Egger was wearing only a cap, a long-sleeve shirt, pants, a t-shirt, and gloves. His pack with his warm outer layers was very close, at the bottom of the chimney, but unreachable.

"His pack was probably in sight," Ranger Michael Ryan said later. "It must have been frustrating."

"So near yet so far," Egger said. "I got down in a little hollow to try to get out of the wind and hunkered down. I was wrapped head to toe in my space blanket. If I hadn't had that space blanket I don't think I would have made it."

"Even with the emergency blanket, survival and death were rubbing against each other," Egger wrote shortly afterwards on a Big Bend online site. "My teeth chattered and my body shivered uncontrollably for hours. During the night I saw the white light at the end of the tunnel twice, but found the strength, somewhere in my soul, not to take that journey."

"But the thought of dying never entered my mind, surprisingly enough," Egger said later.

While Egger was trapped on his ledge, a rescue operation was in full swing. Upon getting the call from Langley Air Force Base that a PLB had been activated in the park, the dispatch office called Ranger Kevin Tillman who assumed Incident Command after arriving at park headquarters.

It takes a little while for the location information from a PLB to be processed. Between 8:00 and 8:30 P.M., Langley called with coordinates that indicated that Egger was somewhere between Elephant Tusk and Backbone Ridge which lies a little more than a mile to the south. During that time, Tillman found Egger's home phone number and talked to his wife. She told him more about her husband's hiking plans and what clothes and equipment he would have with him. She told him that he wouldn't have used his PLB if he was not injured or had some other form of emergency.

Tillman called Ranger Jeff Webb at Rio Grande Village and requested that he organize and begin a hasty search of the Elephant Tusk Trail and the area indicated by the PLB. He informed Chief Ranger Mark Spier of the situation and set up Ranger David Yim to help manage the search and rescue operation. Tillman faxed in a request to OnStar to locate Egger's Chevrolet Silverado. In cases of emergency, the General Motors service will provide vehicle locations to law enforcement personnel.

Webb and Ranger Joe Roberts left Rio Grande Village at about 9:15

P.M., long after dark that time of year. The drive to the Elephant Tusk trailhead and campsite is long and rough. At about 11:50 P.M., the men reported that Egger's vehicle was at the campsite and that they were hiking up the trail. The weather was cold and windy. They had headlamps plus some moonlight to light the way.

At about 12:20 A.M. on December 31, Langley called again to report that the estimated location of the PLB was about a mile north of the original location. The park radioed Webb and Roberts with the new information. The two continued hiking north on the Elephant Tusk Trail. Radio contact with the search team was lost at about 1:00 A.M., so finally at 2:40 A.M. Tillman asked Ranger Mark Cutler to go to the area to attempt to reestablish radio contact.

At about 3:15 A.M., Cutler reestablished radio contact with the team and reported that the men had been at Langley's estimated PLB position for about an hour, but had found no sign of Egger, other than a few unidentified tracks heading south toward a cottonwood grove.

"We had problems with the coordinates of the PLB," Tillman said. "Part of the problem was that we needed to convert the military coordinates into the type we were used to using. Mark Cutler, who had been in the Navy, knew how to convert the coordinates. The coordinates get you close, but not spot on."

"We arrived at a spring area," Roberts said, "supposedly only thirty feet from where the PLB was, but we couldn't find anything. We started to think the worst."

With the wind and darkness, the team was having little luck locating Egger. Webb asked for two more search teams and a helicopter to assist in the search beginning at first light. Tillman told the men to stay put and rest until dawn. Although they were better equipped than Egger, they too had a less than comfortable wait until dawn.

"We hunkered down for two to three hours until dawn," Roberts said. "We couldn't find any soft rocks or warm rocks to lie on. It was one of the coldest nights of my life. We didn't get much sleep."

At 4:00 A.M., Tillman called the Texas Department of Public Safety to request helicopter support at dawn while Yim began calling in other park personnel for the search teams. At about 6:15 A.M., Ranger Lance Mattson took over for Tillman. At about 6:30 A.M., the other rangers arrived and were briefed on the upcoming, expanded ground search. Gary Frable took over as the radio relay for Cutler, and the ground teams headed out to Elephant Tusk. Webb and Roberts resumed their search near Elephant Tusk at about 7:00 A.M. as light slowly appeared in the eastern sky.

"As soon as we got some daylight, we started hunting around again, at what were supposed to be the coordinates," Roberts said.

The men didn't have much luck, even with daylight.

Once the wind died after 4:00 A.M., Egger lit a small fire to try to warm himself up. Once a little daylight appeared he again tried unsuccessfully to down-climb the cliff where he was trapped.

At a little before 8:00 A.M., the DPS helicopter arrived at Panther Junction. After the pilots were briefed, they flew out to the Elephant Tusk area to begin their aerial search.

Egger heard the helicopter for quite awhile before it spotted him at about 10:00 A.M. Every time it was in sight, he would wave his space blanket to attract attention, but he was difficult to spot tucked as he was into a narrow, shaded notch on the northeast side of the mountain. In addition, the PLB location still wasn't very accurate and the search was concentrated some distance from him.

"The guy that spotted me must have had eagle eyes to see me because they were flying way down below me," Egger said. "I was just a flea on that mountain. Once the guy in the helicopter saw me and gave me a thumbs up, it was the most emotional moment in my life. They'd finally found me. I was bawling."

"I'm not sure that we would have found Egger if Don Sharlow (the observer in the helicopter) hadn't somehow spotted him," Mark Spier said.

Because fresh search teams were coming in, Roberts and Webb started hiking back toward the trailhead.

"We finally started down the mountain because replacements were coming in," Roberts said. "About the time we got down, the helicopter spotted him (Egger), so, since we were closest, we hiked back up."

Once Egger was located, the helicopter helped guide the search team to him. It then flew back to Panther Junction to fuel up and get some technical equipment needed by the teams to get Egger down off the mountain peak. Webb and Roberts were first on the scene.

"Jeff (Webb) scaled up to him (Egger)," Roberts said. "We got him his clothes and some food and water."

As the other search teams neared Egger, the helicopter brought the gear to the men, dropping it out while hovering just above the ground because there were no good landing spots.

"We met several guys that morning who were also planning to climb Elephant Tusk," Michael Ryan said. "We asked them if they wanted to help us. They ended up lending us some gear to help get Egger off. Radio communications were really bad out there and so the helicopter hadn't brought us quite the right gear. We used some of their equipment to get Egger down. They were excited to be involved in the rescue."

The search teams and hikers whom the men had met converged on the chimney in the cliff below Egger.

"It was pretty cold standing in the shade on the north side of the peak," Ryan said. "It was okay if you were climbing, but not standing around. Jeff (Webb) climbed up and got to him (Egger) first."

"The first ranger who arrived said to the other rangers below after seeing me to 'get out the ticket book, we've got an illegal fire here,'" Egger said.

In reality, the rangers were happy to find Egger alive and well, if not a little cold, fatigued, and hungry. Using ropes and technical climbing gear, the rangers lowered Egger down the cliff and the party began the long walk out to the trailhead, arriving late that afternoon at sunset. With a little food and water, Egger was able to hike out unassisted with the rangers.

"Late that afternoon I was sitting with the rangers eating an MRE and drinking hot tea," Egger said, "and I told them it was the best meal I'd ever had."

The operation wound down and the rangers all returned home. Egger followed them back to Panther Junction where he was interviewed that evening by Rangers Cutler and Yim.

Big Bend and other parks worried that when PLBs were first authorized by the FCC that they would get many unnecessary calls, but so far that has not been the case at Big Bend. Similar fears arose when cell phone service became available in some of the northern and western parts of the park.

"We thought cell phones would be a problem with too many people calling saying they needed help when they really didn't," Ryan said, "but they really haven't been a problem at Big Bend. I think Big Bend gets less idiots than some parks."

"I still remember when we got our first park cell phone call only a few years ago at Thanksgiving," Mark Spier said. "It was someone calling to report a motor vehicle accident on the road to Persimmon Gap. I was in the dispatch office and we all sort of stopped and looked at each other."

Spier sees benefits from the new communications technology, but also has serious concerns about PLBs, cell phones, and other similar devices.

"We're seeing new technology all over the world of search and rescue—satellite phones, GPS units, PLBs, cell phones," Spier said. "We have people assuming more risk because they feel that their technology will save them. It's like an insurance policy. But what happens when the GPS battery dies or the cell phone can't find a signal?"

"This incident marks the first time in Big Bend SAR (Search and Rescue) history a PLB was used by a hiker to initiate a rescue response," Spier wrote in a report two days after the Egger rescue. "Without the PLB and the assistance from the DPS helicopter the timely location and rescue of the individual would have been extremely difficult and it is probable the PLB saved the individual's life."

Tillman agrees with Spier.

"This is purely speculation, but I wonder if Egger may have gotten into that position in part because he had the PLB," Tillman said. "It may have given him some false confidence. However, overall I think they're a good thing."

Would the other climbers have run into Egger and saved him if he hadn't had the PLB? It's possible, but if they had taken a different route up Elephant Tusk, he might have stayed up there a lot longer in the cold without food, water, or shelter. It's very likely he wouldn't have made it through another night.

What did Bill Egger learn from his experience?

"First, I would sure have a PLB on any solo trek, and maybe even with a group," he said. "Second, know your limits."

Then he added jokingly, "Third, that Central Market Texas trail mix had too many endorphins in it, and it made me go farther than I should have."

"In a more philosophical vein," Egger said, "that trip changed my life. Compassion and forgiveness are the two things that I took away from Elephant Tusk—i.e., how much richer my life would be by bringing those into my life. This blossomed during the spring of 2007. Perhaps it was the near death experience that knocked something into place in my soul."

GEORGE GREGG

The Chihuahuan Desert in summer is not kind to unprepared visitors at Big Bend National Park. When George Gregg moved from the lush wet country of South Carolina to Del Rio, Texas in November 1993, he had no idea what the harsh Trans-Pecos country had in store for him.

George Gregg served as a Deputy United States Marshall in Del Rio. He was 41, tall at 6 feet 4 inches, and solidly built. He had two minor children. He met 45-year-old Judy Hooker at a neighbor's house about two months after arriving in Del Rio and began dating. She also had two kids. Neither had ever visited Big Bend National Park about 240 highway miles to the west. After making plans the week before, they drove to the park on September 3, 1994, in Gregg's 1981 Ford pick-up truck. He had bought the truck a short time before their trip.

On their first night in the park they camped at Cottonwood Campground along the Rio Grande on the park's west side. The next day they wanted showers, so they moved to a motel room at the lodge in the Chisos Basin. At around 4:00 P.M., they left the Basin to tour the park, taking along a cooler with ice and several sodas, but no food. They planned to return to the Basin for dinner that night.

Their first stop was Langford Hot Springs, where hot water bubbles to the surface in a stone foundation on the banks of the Rio Grande a few miles upstream from Rio Grande Village. Park visitors and locals frequent the spot to soak in the warm water that pools in the old foundation. Before the park was created, the springs were the centerpiece of a small resort established by J. O. Langford in 1909. The springs are popular year round, although mostly after sunset during the hot summer months.

After seeing the springs, Judy Hooker studied the map and suggested that they drive up the nearby Old Ore Road to the Telephone Canyon area, thinking it might be interesting. The 26-mile-long Old Ore Road traverses the east side of the park along the base of the rugged, nearly waterless Dead Horse Mountains. The road ends in the south on the Rio Grande Village highway near the Hot Springs turnoff. Until that highway was built, the Old Ore Road was the main access route to Rio Grande Village and the north end of the tramway that carried ore from mines in the Sierra Del Carmen of Mexico across the river into the United States. Wagons and trucks carried the ore from the tramway along the road north to the railroad in Marathon.

The road lies completely in almost shadeless desert country and is very hot from April through October. Few people travel the road in summer. The park maintains the road in a primitive state, so it's rough and rocky. The sign at the south end of the road warns that four-wheel drive is recommended.

"I said 'George, the road sign says four-wheel-drive and this truck isn't four-wheel-drive,' and he said 'I can drive it,'" Judy Hooker said years later. "George had only had the pick-up for a week so he wasn't really familiar with it."

Gregg and Hooker took the road despite having a two-wheel-drive truck. They reached the short spur road to the Telephone Canyon trail-head, about 14 miles up the Old Ore Road, near the midway point. They followed the spur and an old road a short distance. They soon turned around in an arroyo, although with some difficulty. The truck got stuck and Gregg burned rubber spinning the truck tires to get moving again. They returned to the Old Ore Road and drove back south on it less than a quarter mile before the truck overheated and broke down.

The unforgiving late afternoon sun beat down fiercely as they tried to restart the truck. Their only water was the melted ice in the cooler. It was a decent amount of water, about a bag and a half of ice. However, rather than save it for drinking, Gregg used it to fill the radiator in his vain efforts to restart the truck. They had no food, but they did have the Pepsi sodas. Gregg fired the handgun he was carrying three times as a distress signal, but in summer that road is little used and no one heard the shots.

They finally spread out their sleeping bags, Hooker in front and Gregg in the bed of the truck, and settled in for the night. Gregg had a bottle of vodka in the truck which he mixed with the Pepsi that he drank. Unfortunately, alcohol dehydrates the body.

"I told George to wake me up after I got a couple of hours of sleep," Hooker said, "but he didn't wake me up until it was already getting hot. We should have walked at night."

So, rather than get an early start the next morning, September 5, to beat the heat, they slept until about 8:00. They attempted to start the truck again with no success. The back wheels got stuck when they tried to push-start it. They decided to walk north to the park's north entrance highway, even though it was close to 15 miles away and farther away than the highway at the south end from which they had driven the day before. Initially, temperatures were bearable, but it didn't take long for the sun to change that. Neither was dressed appropriately for the desert, particularly Gregg. He had on a t-shirt, shorts, ball cap, and tennis shoes without socks and was very exposed to the sun. Hooker had only beach flip-flops rather than good walking or hiking shoes. On the other hand, she was wearing a long-sleeved shirt, and a good hat, according to Ranger Marcos Paredes.

"Those items made all the difference," Paredes said.

"We had half a can of Pepsi left," Hooker said. "George wouldn't drink any. He made me drink it as we walked. He probably saved my life. We didn't think we were going to die when we started out, we just thought we'd have a hot walk."

Initially they walked together, Gregg carrying Hooker's purse with his handgun in it because it was heavy. Hooker couldn't keep up with Gregg, so he sometimes walked ahead and waited for her in small bits of shade to catch up. The temperatures increased steadily as the sun climbed higher and higher. The road lies completely exposed to the sun. With only shorts and a t-shirt, Gregg began to sunburn. Breathing and sweating slowly drained their bodies of fluid.

Although Gregg had better shoes and started out faster than Hooker, he eventually started lagging. Hooker walked, bicycled, and swam daily to stay fit. Gregg apparently didn't exercise much, smoked, and had high blood pressure.

Heat exhaustion was probably settling in with both walkers, bringing headaches, cramps, weakness, and nausea. With heat exhaustion, the body is stressed but still able to make some effort to cool the body by sweating. Eventually they reached the top of the draw that contains McKinney Spring more than 5 miles north of the truck. Hooker returned to the scene more than two weeks after the ordeal with Park Ranger Roger Moder. Moder wrote in his report that Hooker commented to him that when she reached that point above the spring, "she had wanted to lay down and die."

"She said that she had wanted to take a picture of the area for others to know where she had died, but that Mr. Gregg would not allow her to stop or die," Moder wrote in his report of the trip with Hooker. "Mr. Gregg forced Ms. Hooker to walk on."

A sign in the bottom of the draw marks McKinney Spring and a primitive car campsite. They saw the sign, but continued on, even though the lush green cottonwoods that mark the spring are visible from the road only a few hundred yards up the arroyo. The cottonwoods offer thick shade and a generally reliable spring. Salvation was at hand, but Hooker and Gregg were not thinking clearly and passed it by.

From McKinney Springs, Hooker wanted to cut across country straight west to the highway visible about 2 to 3 miles away, much shorter than the 9 miles remaining to pavement on the Old Ore and Dagger Flat roads. Gregg, however, wanted to stay on the road in hopes someone would come along. But it was not a busy day on the Old Ore Road. Considering their inexperience in desert travel and the related risk of getting lost, the road might have been the better choice even though it was much longer.

In his report Moder also wrote, "on the slope going up and out of the (McKinney Spring) drainage, Ms. Hooker again wanted to lay down and die. Mr. Gregg continued to force her to go on. Ms. Hooker now thinks that she owes her life to Mr. Gregg's insistence that she continue walking out."

They trudged on, northward on the Old Ore Road, the heat worsening steadily. Heat waves shimmered across the desert in the blinding sunlight. Temperatures that afternoon would reach 108 degrees Fahrenheit at Rio Grande Village in the shade. And there was no shade on the Old Ore Road.

Sometime after McKinney Spring, Hooker's better physical condition began to pay off, and she found herself walking alone ahead of Gregg. She looked back and didn't see him, so she turned around and went back. She found him, probably suffering from the ravages of heat stroke.

With heat stroke, the body is so overheated and dehydrated that its temperature regulation mechanism breaks down. It's often the next and much more serious condition after heat exhaustion. Sweating, the primary method of cooling, stops and body temperature soars. In addition to the symptoms of heat exhaustion, flushed dry skin, breathing difficulty, and a rapid pulse are common. As body temperature rises, disorientation, confusion, strange behavior, and even hallucinations can result. Without treatment, unconsciousness, coma, and death will follow. Heat stroke is a medical emergency. A person afflicted with it can suffer permanent injury or death in a short period of time if the body temperature is not brought down.

Hooker found Gregg lying on the side of the road, sitting up, and lying down again. He was very delirious and was yelling what sounded like "Parsons, I'm coming" to her. She assumed that he was referring to an old friend who had died some time ago. His speech was slurred and he didn't understand her words. He was shaking and she later described his eyes as appearing "weird." He was even trying to take off his clothes in his unstable mental state, probably because he was literally burning up.

Earlier Gregg had told Hooker to fire the handgun in case of an emergency. This definitely qualified, so she fired the gun several times. Gregg was in such bad shape that he didn't even seem to be aware of her firing. As with the night before, there was no one within miles, so no one responded to the gunshots. She thought he might be dying, so she walked on to try to find help for him.

"George had said before that he wanted to die alone, so I left him," Hooker said. "I didn't know he was going to die, but he didn't look good."

She later thought that she left him at about 1:30 P.M. She took the gun with her. She later tried shooting again, but to no avail. The gun was now out of ammunition.

"I carried the gun for a long time," Hooker said, "thinking that George was going to want it back. It got too heavy so I finally hid it along the road."

By now the sun was high overhead, beating down on her unmercifully. The temperature in the shade was probably pushing over 100 degrees. Finally, in desperation, she crawled under a bush to take advantage of its meager shade and rest.

"The ants kept bothering me," Hooker said, "but they might have kept me alive by keeping me from going to sleep."

Wisely she stayed under the bush until the sun was slanting down to the west. At sunset, about 7:50, she resumed walking north on the rocky road. Her feet tortured her in her flip-flops. Thirst ravaged her. Darkness slowly fell across the desert after the sun sank below the horizon. While it got harder to see, the slight break in the heat was welcome.

"Even after dark I was hot," Hooker said, "so I took off my blouse and bra and tied them around my waist."

"After George collapsed, Hooker started making some pretty good decisions, like resting in the shade during the afternoon heat," Chief Ranger Jim Northup said later. He wondered if Hooker was actually a little more experienced outdoors and whether some of the decisions that led them into their predicament were pushed through by Gregg.

"At one point I laid down on the road after dark and thought that 'I can't go anymore,'" Hooker said. "I started to have hallucinations. A star seemed to be moving toward me and I wondered if it was my death star or my salvation star. I finally thought, 'I have to get up, I have two kids to raise.'" She got up and kept walking.

Hooker had the park brochure map with her and had studied it while she still had light to see. When she finally reached the end of the Old Ore Road, she knew to turn left toward the highway on the Dagger Flat Road. She could see the lights of distant cars passing on the highway across the open desert country.

"I kept seeing headlights on the highway," Hooker said, "and thought I was almost there, but I wasn't."

After two long, exhausting miles she finally neared the highway. Seeing headlights coming again, she quickly put her blouse and bra back on and hurried to the road as fast as her battered feet and body would let her. The driver, Craig Carter, saw her waving and stopped. He quickly took her to Panther Junction to get water and help. Hooker was obviously pretty tough. She had just walked 15 miles in flip-flops through the worst conditions the Chihuahuan Desert could throw at her in summer and survived.

Chief Ranger Northup got a phone call at about 10:30 P.M. at his home at Panther Junction from Lyn Carter, the manager of the Chisos Remuda in the Basin. His son, Craig, was at Panther Junction with a woman he had found walking along the highway near the Dagger Flat Road. She was exhausted, dehydrated, and very concerned about her friend who was still somewhere out in the desert along the Old Ore Road. Northup met Carter and the woman, Judy Hooker, within ten minutes at park headquarters. The woman was in bad shape, dehydrated and exhausted. "She had trouble sitting up and conversing with me," he wrote in his report later.

"My feet were so bruised, they were black," Hooker said.

Hooker managed to relay her story to Northup in spite of her condition. At 10:45 P.M. Northup called rangers Roger Moder and Jim

Unruh and asked them to report posthaste to headquarters for a search and rescue operation. Ranger Gene Wesloh was also summoned to give medical assistance to Judy Hooker. At 11:00 P.M. Northup briefed Moder and Unruh. They quickly set off for the north end of the Old Ore Road.

Northup took Hooker to the District Ranger Office where he examined her. She was weak, agitated, restless, and breathing rapidly. Wesloh arrived within a few minutes and assisted with treatment. She slowly began to improve with rest and re-hydration.

At Hooker's request, Northup called Paul Evans of the U.S. Marshall's Service in Del Rio to report the situation. Jim Brown, the Chief Deputy with the U.S. Marshall's Service soon called back to learn more about the search for Gregg.

"I was a teacher," Hooker said. "At the ranger station I told the ranger that I needed to call the principal to tell him I was going to miss work. The ranger told me that, all things considered, my boss would probably be okay with me missing a day of work."

Hooker ended up missing a week of work.

Meanwhile, rangers Moder and Unruh were moving slowly south along the Old Ore Road looking for Gregg. Even though it was dark, it didn't take them long to find him. He was lying in the road where Judy Hooker had had to leave him 3.1 miles south of the junction with the Dagger Flat Road. The desert had claimed an unwary, unprepared victim. He was lying next to the gravel berm on the east side of the road with his arms straight and parallel to his body. The sun had burned his exposed skin from dark red to almost black. His clothes were partly torn off. A number of 9 mm cartridge shells lay near and under his body from Hooker's vain attempts to attract help with gunshots. At 12:15 A.M. on September 6, Moder radioed in that they had found Gregg's body. He then summoned the coroner, Ron Willard. Willard arrived at 2:40 A.M. with ranger Marcos Paredes. After his examination, Willard released Gregg's body to Paredes who transported it to a funeral home to await an autopsy.

When Paredes first saw the body on the road he was surprised. "When I came up on him," he said, "he looked like a black man. He was so severely burned."

"(He) was lying in the middle of the road with spent cartridges all around," Moder said. "I wondered at first if it was a murder."

Rangers Unruh and Moder continued south on the Old Ore Road and found Gregg's pick-up where they expected, about 0.2 mile south of the Telephone Canyon spur road junction. Later that morning Hooker took Moder and others out to recover the handgun in daylight. At the same time, Gregg's truck was towed to Panther Junction and impounded.

When Moder saw the small, inadequate bush that Hooker had sheltered under, he was surprised.

"The ranger said, 'That was the bush you were under!'" Hooker said.

An autopsy was requested by the park because of the circumstances of the death.

"An intriguing part of the case was that the woman was carrying a handgun," Chief Ranger Northup said. "Because of the gun involved and the woman surviving, part of the reason we did the autopsy was to make sure that there was no foul play involved."

Several days later the autopsy confirmed that Gregg had died of heat stroke.

On October 12, a Board of Inquiry was convened at park headquarters at Panther Junction. The National Park Service requires that such hearings be held "to examine all available information regarding the circumstances surrounding the fatality, identify the proximate causes of the fatality, and provide recommendations to park management on possible actions to be taken to prevent similar incidents in the future."

Jim Northup chaired the inquiry into George Gregg's death. The conclusions were very clear. Gregg had died of heat stroke after a long walk in summer under the hot desert sun with inadequate clothing and no food. Neither Gregg nor Hooker had had much experience with desert travel or survival. Both they and their vehicle were poorly equipped for desert travel. Upon entering the park and paying the entrance fee, they had received the official park map and brochure, along with the *Paisano*, the park newspaper. The paper had a section of safety tips entitled "Reading This Could Save Your Life."

Under the heading "Heat," the paper reads, "Desert heat can kill you. Carry plenty of water and wear a hat, long pants, long-sleeved shirt, and sun screen when hiking the sun-drenched trails. At least one gallon of water per day is necessary for a safe journey." It continues with, "Avoid hiking during mid-day in summer. Travel as wild animals do, in early morning or late evening hours rather than during the heat of the day. Drink water frequently whether hiking, camping, floating, relaxing, or seeing the park by car."

Despite these warnings, Gregg and Hooker decided to attempt to hike out from their disabled vehicle with no water or protective clothing in the heat of a summer day.

The park map and brochure labels the Old Ore Road as a "Primitive Road (Four-wheel drive, high clearance vehicles only)." The brochure also states, "Check on road conditions before driving unpaved routes" in the section "Regulations and Safety, Driving." Another section of the brochure reiterates the need for large amounts of water when hiking.

Like the warning in the park brochure, the warning to use a four-wheel drive vehicle posted on the sign at the start of the Old Ore Road was ignored by Gregg and Hooker.

The board determined several other factors that may have contributed to Gregg's death. An interview with his mother indicated that he may have been particularly susceptible to heat, having had a heat-related illness while in the military. His heavy smoking, high blood pressure, and the consumption of alcohol the night before the walk may have added to the stress his body was forced to endure. A park mechanic inspected the pick-up truck after it was towed into Panther Junction and found that a loose fan belt may have contributed to the vehicle problems experienced by Gregg and Hooker.

The board found that the safety wording in park publications was adequate and did not need changing. The board also recommended that the park continue to pursue funding to build entrance stations to ensure that more park visitors would receive the safety information contained in the publications. Although it was not a factor in Gregg's death, because he and Hooker stopped at Panther Junction and received the publications when they paid their entrance fee, the board felt it could have been a contributing factor if they had not stopped and received the material. The board also recommended that park aircraft continue to be used to patrol remote areas of the park. Since the time of this incident, entrance stations have been built at park entrances.

There really were no substantive changes that the board could recommend to lessen the risk of the desert claiming more victims in the future. Park visitors need to follow safety advice and be careful when entering harsh terrain very different from that encountered in everyday life. The desert is not forgiving of mistakes, especially in summer.

"This story (of the tragedy) can really have some benefit to park visitors. They'll learn what not to do in the desert," Ranger Paredes said."

"We made mistake after mistake after mistake," Hooker said.

Jim Northup summed up the incident. "It was a collection of errors with tragic results."

"I cried every day for two years afterward," Hooker said. "George was such a nice guy and good to my kids. I think that's why I fell in love with him."

ELLWOOD VOORHEES

Many times when a crisis develops at Big Bend National Park, the people involved are at least partially responsible for the events that occur. Bad decisions and small errors can compound into life-threatening situations. That was emphatically not the case with Ellwood Voorhees of Menomonie, Wisconsin in February 2003. Sometimes, nothing but bad luck is all than can be blamed for a bad turn of events.

Fifty-four-year-old Ellwood Voorhees was a successful surgeon at a Menomonie, Wisconsin hospital. He stood about six feet tall and had a medium build. His wife Sharilyn was a nurse. They wedded young and had been married for more than 33 years when they arrived at Big Bend that winter. Ellwood was very fit and loved the outdoors. Hiking, backpacking, and biking were favorite physical activities. Forestry was a hobby of his.

"He had lots of forestry equipment, even a portable sawmill," Sharilyn said. "He cut the lumber for the house that we built ourselves. He loved being out in the woods."

Ellwood and Sharilyn Voorhees came to Big Bend National Park toward the end of a two week driving vacation. They had driven down from Wisconsin in their new truck with attached camper. It was their first trip to Texas. They drove all over the state, hitting highlights like San Antonio and the coast. Their visit to Big Bend was going to be "the grand finale of the trip," Sharilyn Voorhees said. "We had a great time. I liked San Antonio and would like to visit the city again."

They arrived at the park on the evening of Tuesday, February 18, and found a campsite in the Chisos Basin Campground for the night. The next morning they explored the Basin area together. Ellwood Voorhees wanted to do a short backpack into the high country of the Chisos Mountains before they headed back to Wisconsin to return to work. Sharilyn Voorhees couldn't go, but he didn't mind going by himself.

"I would have gone," Sharilyn Voorhees said, "except that I had just had rotator cuff surgery and was getting over a case of pneumonia."

So on the afternoon of February 19, Voorhees donned his backpack and headed up alone into the high country of the Chisos Mountains for an overnight trip. After getting his backcountry camping permit, he hiked up the Pinnacles Trail to the Emory Peak 1 primitive campsite. It lies on a short side spur about a quarter mile up the side trail that leads to the summit of Emory Peak. The Emory Peak Trail forks off the Pinnacles Trail just below its highest point at a saddle between Emory Peak and Toll Mountain. The Pinnacles Trail climbs about 1,600 vertical feet in 3.5 miles from its trailhead in the Basin to the junction with the Emory Peak Trail. The campsite rests at an elevation of a little more than 7,100 feet in a thick, scrubby forest of pinyon pine, juniper, and oak. The rocky summit of Emory Peak, the highest point in the park at 7,835 feet, towers into the sky about 0.75 mile to the southwest. Tremendous views lie within a very short walking distance of the campsite. Normally it's an idyllic spot.

Voorhees' wife stayed the night in their camper at the Chisos Basin Campground. That night it got cold in the mountains. Their truck and camper were new, but the heater didn't work as she soon discovered. She remembers being a little aggravated at the time.

"It was really cold," she said.

Ellwood Voorhees was a seasoned backpacker and was well-equipped for the trek. He was planning to be gone for one night only, returning no later than the evening of February 20.

"The next day I just hiked around the Basin while waiting for my husband to return," Sharilyn Voorhees said. "It started raining at about noon, about the time that he should have been coming back down. I didn't realize that it was snowing up high. We had a break in the weather, but then it started raining again. I thought that maybe he didn't come down because of the rain."

Ellwood Voorhees was experienced in the outdoors and, as a resident of Wisconsin, no stranger to cold weather. Sharilyn had no real reason to worry until her husband didn't show up as planned that evening.

"I spent another cold night in our camper," she said. "I started to get worried that night."

Because of her shoulder injury, she wasn't able to drive their truck, so early the next morning she asked another camper to give her a ride up to a phone so that she could report that her husband was missing. At that time there was no cell phone service in the park. Even today, in 2010, cell service only covers very limited areas in the northern and western parts of the park.

At 7:45 A.M. Sharilyn Voorhees called the park dispatch office and relayed her worries. The call was transferred to Ranger Marcos Paredes. He obtained a description of her husband. She told Paredes that Ellwood was in excellent physical condition and described his appearance and clothing. The weather was still cold and wet. Paredes put together a search plan. He asked her to wait a little while in case her husband was on his way down that morning.

Before leaving park headquarters at Panther Junction, Ranger Paredes sent two people out to the trails that come down off the mountains at Blue Creek and Juniper Canyon to make sure that Voorhees wasn't hurt or lost out there and coming down from the high country a differ-ent way. The other two trails that lead up into the high country are the Laguna Meadow Trail and Pinnacles Trail. Both of those feed down to the lodge, ranger station, and other facilities in the Basin.

Paredes then drove up the winding road to the Basin, the big valley tucked into the heart of the Chisos Mountains in the middle of the park. He met Sharilyn Voorhees at the Basin Campground and got more information from her about her husband and his plans. He then sent out searchers into the high country to locate Voorhees. The park's trail maintenance crew was already in the high country and began hunt-ing for him first. The search didn't last long. Trail crew member Aaron Robinson found Voorhees at his Emory Peak campsite at 10:40 A.M. and radioed Paredes. The news was bad. Voorhees was "Code Red," deceased. Paredes asked if Robinson was sure. "One hundred percent," Robinson replied.

Paredes closed the Emory Peak Trail to hikers and asked Robinson to secure the scene until investigators arrived. Rangers David Yim and Kyle Green donned packs and hiked up the Pinnacles Trail to the campsite, reaching it about an hour after Robinson located Voorhees. They found Voorhees lying on his back near the entrance to the cleared camping area, his eyes wide open staring blindly into the sky. Snow had drifted partially over him.

Meanwhile, Sharilyn Voorhees had been waiting anxiously at her campsite in the Basin Campground.

"About two hours later (after talking to Ranger Paredes), two park vehicles drove up to our truck with two people in each," she said. "I had a bad feeling. Sure enough, they told me that 'he had passed on.' I was in denial at first. I couldn't believe it."

The rangers tried to comfort her, but it was difficult for her.

"They initially told me that they thought that it was a heart attack," she said. "I told them no way."

She turned out to be right. Rangers Yim and Green were busy exam-ining the scene. Closer inspection revealed clues to Voorhees' fate. Two inches of snow had initially obscured much of Voorhees' body and rel-evant evidence.

"When Aaron (Robinson) got there he almost tripped over the body because it was mostly snow-covered," Yim said. "He (Voorhees) was wearing a watch cap that had burn marks on it. A tree had a big limb split off about 20 feet from him."

Further examination revealed that Voorhees' pants were ripped down the legs and a shoe was blown off.

"The change was blown out of a pocket," Paredes said. "One of the coins looked a bit melted."

The cause of death was apparent—lightning had abruptly ended the life of Ellwood Voorhees. He never knew what was coming.

"He was probably hit on the head and a shoe was blown apart where the bolt left his body and grounded itself, " Paredes added.

From the investigation, it appeared that Voorhees had camped there the night before, eaten breakfast on the morning of February 20, had packed his gear, and was set to head down the mountain when he was struck by lightning.

"It looked like he was all ready to go," Yim said. "His pack was leaning on a tree."

The trails were icy, complicating the retrieval of Voorhees' body. The Pinnacles Trail is steep and gets little sun in winter.

"I brought a horse up to carry the body down," Paredes said. "I went up the Pinnacles Trail and decided to come down the Laguna Meadow Trail because it (the Pinnacles Trail) was treacherous."

"We loaded his body on a horse," Yim said. "We took the body down by the Laguna Meadow Trail because it was less steep with the ice."

The park rangers didn't want to show Voorhees' body to his wife, but she insisted on seeing it.

"I'm a nurse," she told them. "I've seen dead bodies before."

The rangers relented, but it was worse than she expected. Any remaining doubts she had died immediately. Her husband was gone.

"It was hard," she said. "The park said that an autopsy had to be done, but it couldn't be done until the next Tuesday (five days later). I said I couldn't wait. I don't know anyone here and have no heat in the truck."

"It was difficult for her," Paredes said. "We tried to do what we could to help."

She needed to be with family. Park staff drove her to the Midland airport the next day and took her truck to Midland, too. She flew straight home.

Two of Ellwood Voorhees' brothers, Larry and David, flew down to Texas immediately after the incident.

"My brother David and I went to the park right after it happened, even before the funeral," Larry Voorhees said. We literally ran much of the way up the trail to the site where my brother died. We just wanted to see it."

The two brothers drove the camper truck all the way home to Wisconsin after visiting the Emory Peak campsite. It was a long, stressful drive. They got home before their brother's body arrived for the funeral.

His family all miss him to this day. He was survived by his wife, four children, multiple grandchildren, his father, three brothers, and two sisters. The medical profession lost a respected doctor.

"His patients loved him," Sharilyn Voorhees said. "That's not common for doctors," she added with a laugh. "I should know."

"All of us, his brothers and sisters, looked to him for help with problems," Larry Voorhees said. "He (Ellwood) used to say that you have a better chance of getting struck by lightning than winning the lottery. As it turned out it was almost like an omen."

"The rangers told me that he was the only known lightning death in the park," his wife said.

Ranger David Yim confirmed that it was the only one that he knew of at Big Bend. "I take lightning more seriously now," he said. "I pay a lot more attention to the sky."

Sharilyn Voorhees has never returned to Big Bend. "It's a beautiful area," she said, "but I don't think I'll ever go back."

Snow storms are rare at Big Bend National Park, even in the high country of the Chisos Mountains. Usually no more than three or four per year occur, and sometimes none at all. Additionally, lightning is not common in snowstorms. What could Ellwood Voorhees have done differently to avoid his fate? Nothing, really. He was just in the wrong place at the wrong time.

JOSEPH GOTTSCHALK

When Reagan and Marcy Reed of Terlingua, Texas hiked up to the South Rim in Big Bend National Park on June 21, 2003, they expected to have a relaxing overnight backpack to one of the most spectacular places in Texas. Their trip didn't turn out as they planned.

The South Rim of the Chisos Mountains is a prominent escarpment that towers more than 5,000 feet above the stark desert along the Rio Grande, reaching an elevation of about 7,400 feet. It marks the abrupt southern edge of the Chisos Mountains, where the pinyon pine and juniper forest of the high country falls away in a series of high cliffs and steep slopes to the drier country below. Despite the strenuous hike of about 6 miles and 2,000 feet of elevation gain from the Basin required to get there, it is one of the most popular spots in the park. The dramatic views across much of the park and far into Mexico combined with the shady woodland attract many day hikers and backpackers. Because the Rim's high elevation moderates summer temperatures, the hike is one of the few in Texas that gets at least a few hikers even in summer. Because of the popularity of the South Rim and the rest of the Chisos Mountains' high country, the park has set up designated primitive backpacking campsites and limits the number of overnight campers to prevent environmental damage to the area.

The Reeds hiked up the Pinnacles Trail to the South Rim. It's the steeper and harder of the two routes to the South Rim, but the most scenic. At about 7:00 P.M., they reached their campsite, designated SW4 for Southwest Rim Site #4. The site lies in the woods a short distance from the towering cliffs of the South Rim. They set up their camp, ate dinner, and relaxed after the long hike up to the Rim with heavy packs. That time of year the sun sets at about 9:00, so they had plenty of daylight for eating and camp chores.

"Around 8:15 P.M. Reagan decided to go watch the sunset, while I stayed in the tent reading," Marcy Reed later wrote in her statement.

He watched the sunset for about a half hour. When he returned to the tent, he noticed some shoes and a water jug sitting on the rim a short distance away.

"My husband came back to the tent and said 'get your shoes on, come out with me,'" Marcy Reed said. "'There's a mystery I want to show you.'"

She put on her shoes and walked with her husband back to the area of the rim where her husband had seen the shoes and water bottle.

"When we got up closer Reagan yelled 'Hello' twice," Marcy Reed wrote. "What I noticed was a pair of black, military-like boots upright, one right next to the other. Left of that, black jeans, black shirt, both items sitting on top of a white t-shirt maybe. I looked to see if there was a wallet in one of the back pockets but did not see one—I did not touch anything."

"They were folded up nice and neat," she said. "I had a weird feeling about it."

"The whole thing seemed kind of odd to me," Reagan Reed said. "I had called around and had not gotten any answer."

"Reagan walked over to the edge a little away from me and kneeled down to look over the edge," Marcy said. "He said, 'Oh my God!' and rocked back on his heels."

"I peered over the edge and saw a body," Reagan Reed wrote in his statement. "It looked like a white male about 50-60 feet below."

They were both shaken up by their discovery and unsure how they should proceed. There was no cell service on the Rim and no other way to call 911 or a park ranger. No one else was anywhere around.

"He was asking me, 'what do you want to do?'" Marcy said, "and I said I'm not staying up here with a dead man."

"We also wanted to get down to notify the park so they could start planning a search and rescue," Reagan said.

"We immediately went back to camp, packed up, and left around 9:00 P.M.," Marcy Reed wrote.

It was getting dark as they started down the six miles of trail to the Basin. Both were upset over their discovery and nervous about hiking down in the dark, but they kept moving rapidly.

"We were worried about losing the trail and about rattlesnakes," she said. "We saw two red eyes glowing in our light once. I asked my husband if he saw them and he said, 'just keep going.'"

"We got down the trail on adrenaline," he said.

"The body was found at 8:50 P.M.—I looked at my watch," Marcy wrote. "We arrived at the Basin at 10:45 P.M. My husband called 911 in Alpine."

The Reeds' idyllic camping trip was over.

At about 11:00 that night, Ranger David Yim received a 911 call from the Alpine Police Department relaying the call made by Reagan Reed. He immediately drove to the Basin Visitor Center and met the Reeds. They told Yim about their discovery.

"Marcy Reed had not wanted to spend the night up there after they found the body," Yim said.

After taking their statements, Yim called Chief Ranger Mark Spier with his report.

Spier placed Yim in charge of investigating the incident and then began to assemble a search and rescue team that had the technical climbing skills necessary to reach and retrieve the body.

At about 6:00 the next morning, June 22, Yim started hiking up the Pinnacles Trail to the South Rim after a short night's sleep. Ranger Michael Ryan followed him soon afterward. Not only did they want to get to the body as soon as possible, they also wanted to make sure that no evidence was disturbed by other hikers.

Yim reached the South Rim at 9:05 A.M. He found the clothing about four feet back from the edge of the rim as described by the Reeds.

"I looked over the edge but was unable to locate the body," Yim wrote in his report.

At 10:17 A.M. Michael Ryan arrived at the scene. After a few minutes of hunting for the body by the two rangers, Ryan spotted it about 150 to 200 feet below the rim, farther down than what the Reeds had estimated. It was a naked white male lying in the prone position.

After some scouting, Ryan found a route down to the body through a break in the cliffs about 200 yards east. It could be down-climbed reasonably safely without much exposure. Ryan remembered it from a previous incident.

"In maybe 2000 or 2001 another man, David Kelly, either fell or jumped off at the same spot. That one looked like a suicide, but it was hard to be absolutely certain," Ryan said years later. "At that time we found the non-technical route down the big cliff."

Ryan and Yim scrambled down to the body, which had numerous cuts, scratches, and abrasions. Substantial patches of blood covered the chest, abdomen, and face. Later examination of the body found broken bones and internal injuries, all consistent with a major fall.

The rangers measured a distance of 28 feet between the body and the base of the cliffs. About eight feet up the steep slope from the body was a patch of disturbed soil and broken branches, probably created by the impact of the man when he fell from above. From there the body appeared to have tumbled a short distance farther down the slope. They found a black bandanna near the point of impact.

Ryan reported their findings via satellite phone to the park dispatch office and requested the gear necessary to retrieve the body. At about 11:30 A.M. the search and rescue party began their hike up to the South Rim via the Laguna Meadows Trail, arriving at about 3:00 P.M. The team rigged ropes and began the body recovery.

"With Kelly, he had fallen farther down the slope, so we got him out with a helicopter and long line," Ryan said. "For this victim we used ropes and hauled him up the cliff."

"We put him in a body bag," Yim said, "wrapped it in a tarp, and put it in a litter. We raised him up to the rim with a winch with maybe a ten-to-one mechanical advantage. The litter hung up on ledges several times, but we pulled it free and got it up to the top. We put him on a mule to carry him down to the Basin."

Meanwhile, back at park headquarters, Chief Ranger Mark Spier and Ranger Kathleen Hambly were attempting to identify the victim. Rangers on the scene had not found a wallet or any kind of identification with the clothing left on the Rim. Initially the rangers considered a man who had inquired about obtaining a backcountry permit for the Outer Mountain Loop at the Panther Junction visitor center. They found a vehicle with Minnesota license plates by using the permit information, but the focus soon shifted to another individual.

Kym Beckwith, an interpreter at the Panther Junction visitor center, reported a conversation on June 20 with an individual who came to the park by himself on a motorcycle. He asked about hiking to the South Rim.

"He did not look like the hiking type so I recommended the Lost Mine Trail and he was intent on the South Rim," Kym Beckwith and Anita Johnson, another interpreter stationed at the visitor center, wrote in their report later. "He was surprised to hear how long it was and how long it would take to get there. He was very interested in the cliffs. I was under the impression he was worried about being too close to the edge, so I reassured him our trails were far from the cliffs (as he kept calling them). When he saw the picture on our map of the High Chisos trails, he was very interested in the picture of a person standing on a ledge out on the South Rim and wanted to know exactly where that was. I pointed out the area of (the) Southwest 4 (campsite) and reminded him to be careful."

Their report mentioned dark-colored clothing and crooked teeth.

"Man struck me as unusual," they wrote. "Talked fast. Antsy type. Never asked about entrance fees, I assumed he had paid at an entrance station but they were closed that day. He spoke of no other part of the park, only about the South Rim."

Mark Spier realized that the clothing found at the South Rim was mostly black, so he checked with the volunteers stationed at the Basin visitor center. The parking lot in front of the visitor center is used as the main trailhead for the High Chisos Mountains trails. The volunteers checked outside and confirmed the presence of a covered motorcycle that had been there for two days.

Kathleen Hambly drove up to the parking lot and located a black BMW motorcycle with Texas plates. A check run on the plates indicated that it was owned by Joseph Gottschalk of San Antonio. Hambly took the cover off the bike and found the motorcycle's key tucked between the seat and the right rear pannier. Using the key she opened the pannier and found a wallet with Gottschalk's driver's license, credit cards, cash, and other items. She also found a cell phone, watch, and house keys. Spier and Hambly thought it unusual that such items would be left with the motorcycle with no real effort to secure them or the bike itself. The motorcycle was taken down to the impound yard at Panther Junction.

Once Hambly returned to Panther Junction, she and Spier spent the first half of the afternoon trying to reach a friend or family member of Joseph Gottschalk to check on his welfare. Calls to the dozen or so Gottschalks listed in San Antonio all ended with no answer, busy signals, or disconnected lines. Spier left a message on Joseph Gottschalk's answering machine asking him to call the park.

At 2:47 P.M. the park dispatch office received a call on their emergency line. It was answered by Park Dispatcher Jessica Erickson.

Dispatch: "Big Bend emergency line, please state your emergency."

Caller: "(garbled) uh, my brother (garbled)."

Dispatch: "Hello?"

Caller: "Yes, hello? Can you hear me?"

Dispatch: "Yes."

Caller: "O.K. (garbled) the past few days has been talking about committing suicide. Over the couple of days has made reference to jumping off the South Rim there at your park. Do you all have a South Rim there?"

Dispatch: "We do have a South Rim, yeah. Let me transfer you to our Chief Ranger."

Caller: "Thank you."

The call was transferred to Mark Spier. The caller identified himself as Paul Gottschalk, the brother of Joseph Gottschalk. He told Spier that his brother had been talking about suicide recently and seemed fixated on the South Rim of the Chisos Mountains, a place that he used to visit years before with his wife. He said that his brother was unemployed and depressed.

Paul Gottschalk went on to describe his brother. He said that his brother's prominent crooked teeth were "the first thing you notice." He also added that his brother would be tanned all over because he frequently went out nude or near nude. He didn't have any tattoos, but had a scar on his back from a bicycle accident. He added that his brother dressed in dark clothing and wore a black bandanna on his head.

Spier didn't have good news for Paul Gottschalk. They had found his brother's motorcycle in the park and a body at the South Rim.

"I explained that while I could not provide a positive identification of the body, based upon the information he had provided it was very possible the body was that of Joseph Gottschalk," Spier wrote afterwards in his report.

Spier then explained that the body recovery was under way and the Brewster County Justice of the Peace would examine the body and that an autopsy would be done to determine the cause of death.

Paul Gottschalk asked Spier if his brother was naked when found, and Spier affirmed that he was. Gottschalk explained that his brother had achieved a certain level of fame in San Antonio by riding his bicycle around town in a thong. His actions had led to some problems with the local authorities that were covered by the media. He added that his brother never used drugs or alcohol.

"My memory is that it was just a coincidence that Paul called about his brother," Spier said later. "I don't think our unsuccessful calls spurred his call."

At about 5:30 P.M., the mules carrying the body and rescue equipment started down to the Basin via the Laguna Meadow Trail. David Yim accompanied the mule train down, arriving late that evening.

At about 9:45 P.M., Spier and Yim met with Justice of the Peace Williams to examine the body. Williams noted the damage to the body, including obvious broken bones. Because of poor light and the body's lividity, she was unable to find the scar on the back, but the crooked teeth mentioned by both Kym Beckwith and Paul Gottschalk were apparent. Positive identification of the body as that of Joseph Gottschalk was made when the driver's license photo found in his wallet from his motorcycle pannier was compared with his face.

Joseph Gottschalk was an unconventional man. He rode his bike around San Antonio wearing only a thong, leading to his moniker, "Thong Man." He seemed to enjoy pushing society to the limit on civil liberties and eventually got arrested for his near-naked rides.

He worked many jobs over the years, doing everything from attending Catholic seminary to become a priest to driving a gravel truck. During the Vietnam War he was drafted into the Army and spent much of his time behind bars because he was a pacifist and wouldn't perform his duties.

He was married for almost 25 years and fathered four sons. Even after he and his wife divorced in 2000, he would still do favors for his ex-wife.

"He was an interesting character," Spier said. "The indications were certainly there that he committed suicide, but it's hard to know for sure. Unfortunately, the national parks seem to attract a good number of suicides."

While a few questions may always linger over the cause of Gottschalk's death, it is certain, however, that he left behind friends and family that miss him. Even people like the Reeds who found his body, were impacted by his death.

"I go back regularly (to the South Rim)," Reagan Reed said, "but Marcy's not too keen about going back up there to camp."

GUADALUPE ROMERO-HERNÁNDEZ
JUAN LUIS CARDONA
JUAN ENRIQUE ROMERO

On June 5, 2008, Michael Tiller drove to Big Bend National Park to spend his days off from work. He had long wanted to drive the Old Ore Road and he had his four-wheel-drive truck, so this was his chance. He planned to take some photos and enjoy a quiet trip through a part of the park that he hadn't seen before. June brings some of the worst heat of the year to the park, so Tiller wouldn't have to contend with crowds in the desert country of the Old Ore Road. He drove east on the Dagger Flat Road and then turned south onto the Old Ore Road. His trip would turn out far differently than he planned.

The Old Ore Road follows the base of the Dead Horse Mountains from near Rio Grande Village to the Dagger Flat Road on the north end of the park. The mountains are a northern extension of the much higher Sierra del Carmen of Mexico. They are separated from each other by the Rio Grande and its path carved through the mountains, Boquillas Canyon. The rough, 26-mile-long road requires a four-wheel-drive vehicle to drive it. It passes through rugged desert terrain sparsely vegetated with cacti, yucca, lechuguilla, creosote, and other hardy Chihuahuan Desert plants. Michael Tiller began his drive expecting a pleasant day of sightseeing and photography.

"Up ahead I saw a giant dagger yucca that looked interesting to photograph," Tiller said.

Because it was morning, he was facing into the sun, making shooting the photograph difficult. He decided to drive past it to get the sun more at his back for his shot.

"As I drove up to get a better angle for a photo, I saw what looked like some clothes lying by it," Tiller said. "I then thought that it was a mannequin that someone had placed there as some sort of bad joke." After close inspection, he realized that it wasn't a joke. It looked like an actual human being. He put a long telephoto lens on his camera and zoomed in for a closer view. He saw that the person was not breathing and called 911. Unlike much of the park, this section now has cell service in some areas, so he was able to make contact.

"They told me to wait there, even though it was really hot. So I just sat there with my truck running for about 45 minutes until the rangers came. I got out and walked over to about ten feet from the body just to make sure he wasn't alive, then got back in my truck. I didn't want to disturb anything. I was a little unnerved, so I locked my doors."

Tiller's quiet photo trip down the Old Ore Road was over. After being interviewed by the rangers he continued his drive south on the road. However, the rest of the day he was upset and nervous.

"He (the victim) had gotten within three miles of the highway after walking all the way across the park," Tiller said. "It shattered my naivety about people coming across that desert."

Ranger Joseph Roberts and Border Patrol agent Sam Acosta were the first to respond to Tiller's call. Their initial impression was that the victim, a young Hispanic man, died of heat stroke. The later autopsy confirmed their guess.

The victim had an empty water container with him, but no pack. His other possessions were meager: two cigarette lighters, a knife, an aluminum foil package of 6 Naproxeno tablets with two missing sections, and a bandana. He wore a tan t-shirt, Wrangler jeans, a tan belt, and brown boots. The ground was disturbed all around the large yucca, indicating that he had moved as the sun changed position to stay in its shade. Roberts photographed the scene, then he and Acosta searched the immediate area in about a 1/8-mile radius around the body. Acosta found only one set of tracks coming from the south. They matched the victim's boots. The body was removed and transported to El Paso for autopsy. The victim had no identification, so the challenge now was to identify him.

Because of the dead man's clothes and his tracks coming up from the south, it appeared that the dead man may have been a Mexican citizen illegally entering the United States. That evening, Roberts showed photos of the victim to the Diablo firefighters who were temporarily stationed in the park because of the current high fire danger. The Diablos are a crew of men from the villages of Boquillas and Las Norias across the border from Rio Grande Village. The park has trained them as firefighters to help with wildland fires at Big Bend and other western parks and forests. Roberts thought that there was a possibility that one of them might recognize the dead individual, however, they all said that they did not. The next day the Diablos returned home to Mexico.

On June 9, the park received a call from Chris Mendoza concerning the unidentified fatality in the park. She explained that she was calling on behalf of the Romero-Hernández family. She said that she believed that the victim was Guadalupe Romero-Hernández, a relative of her husband. She said that her brother-in-law, Diablo firefighter Juan Romero of Las Norias, had recognized the boots on the victim as belonging to his son, even though he didn't say anything to park rangers when the firefighters were questioned several days before. When Romero asked his son about the boots, his son said that he had given them to Guadalupe Romero-Hernández. Juan Romero, when interviewed, said that he had visited Guadalupe Romero-Hernández's mother in Las Norias and described the clothing that her son was wearing when he was found. She said that it matched what he was wearing when he left home. She told the park rangers that Romero-Hernández was traveling with two other men. After receiving the information, the park began a search in an attempt to find the other two individuals. Because that area has several springs, it was possible that the other two men were still alive.

Coincidentally, earlier on June 9, Ranger Marcos Paredes had volunteered to go out to the site where the man had been found dead by the Old Ore Road. He wanted to try to backtrack along the man's path to see if anyone else had been traveling with him. By searching carefully, he was able to find the man's tracks on the Old Ore Road about 100 yards south of where he died. He followed them south until he came to a drainage that crossed the road. He found another set of tracks there that came out of the arroyo and then went back down it. Only the original set of footprints continued north on the road. He found a water jug that still had a few ounces of liquid in it wrapped in blue cloth on the south side of the dry wash. He then followed the new tracks down the arroyo and found a t-shirt, cap, socks, and pair of shoes about 30 or 40 yards down the wash under a persimmon tree. He continued down the wash for about 15 minutes and discovered a second body at about 1:30 P.M.

"I got a whiff of him before I found him," Paredes said.

The body was that of a thin Hispanic man not much more than five feet tall who was lying face down. He was wearing only his underwear, although a pair Wrangler jeans lay close to his feet. From the amount of decomposition that had occurred, it appeared that the man had been dead for at least several days. He was about 1.1 miles southeast of the first fatality.

Heat stroke was a likely cause of death. It occurs when the body's cooling system breaks down. It's not uncommon for people in the late, delusional stages of heat stroke to tear off their clothes in an effort to cool themselves.

At this point, Paredes received a radio call telling him of the interview with Chris Mendoza and that the first victim might be traveling with two other men. He told them that he had just found a second dead individual and requested assistance, including a couple of horses to help pack out the body.

While he waited for help to arrive, Paredes hiked farther down the wash to its confluence with Javelina Draw looking for others, but found no sign that anyone had walked that far down the drainage. The park aircraft was returning to the park at that time, so he radioed it and asked the pilot to search the area around him from the air. The plane looked for about a half hour with no success as Paredes walked back up the arroyo to the second body.

"At this point I was getting overheated myself with temperatures exceeding 110 degrees," Paredes wrote in his report later. "The glue on the soles of my boots melted from the heat on the rocks and I lost the sole to one of my boots. I shaded up in an overhang and waited for assistance to arrive."

Two of the park fire crew arrived first, gave Paredes water, and searched the area more thoroughly, but without success. Justice of the Peace Jim Burr then arrived at the scene. Paredes had cooled off and re-hydrated some by then, so he continued to walk south down the Old Ore Road. He found another water bottle, but never saw more than the two sets of tracks of the victims who had already been found. At the point where Javelina Draw crossed the road, he turned around and walked back, getting there just as the horses arrived. The park personnel, Border Patrol agent Sam Acosta, and Jim Burr helped secure the victim in a body bag and load it on top of a mule. The body was packed out to the Old Ore Road and loaded on a funeral home truck and taken to Alpine. From there it was transported to El Paso for autopsy.

Like the first victim when he was first found, the identity of the second man was also unknown. It would be determined, but not for a few days.

Now that the park knew that there was probably a third man lost out in the desert, the search resumed with a passion early the next morning, June 10. Initially, rangers Paredes and Roberts did another search of the arroyo where the second man died, but found nothing new. They then moved south along the Old Ore Road to where Paredes had found the water jug the day before. All they found was the same two sets of tracks. They also saw a bicycle track, but didn't think it was connected to the two men.

At the spot where Javelina Draw crossed the road, the footprints and the bicycle track went down the dry arroyo. The bicycle track stopped in a short distance but the footprints went a ways longer. Paredes tied off his horse and continued down the drainage on foot while Roberts rode along on the rim above. When they reached Muskhog Spring, they turned around.

"The spring had plenty of water and shelter and had any of our subjects made it down there," Paredes wrote in his report, "it is quite probable that they would have survived there for several days. But it was apparent that no one had made it that far down the arroyo in quite a while."

As Paredes was climbing up the rock ledges of the canyon bottom above the spring, he had an unnerving experience.

"I was going up these rock steps from Muskhog Spring when I felt something hit my leg," Paredes said. "I looked down and I saw a rattler hung up on my jeans with its fangs. I freaked out and jumped around wildly to shake it off. My cowboy boots saved me. I was wearing them because my hiking boots got damaged the day before. Losing my boot sole the day before ended up saving me from getting snake-bit because my cowboy boots go farther up my calf."

As Paredes hiked back up to the road he found an overhang where it appeared that at least two people had holed up in the shade. Because he found a piece of green cord that matched that tied to the other two water jugs that he had found, he was sure that the two victims had been there.

Four Border Patrol agents, including Sam Acosta, joined the two rangers and continued the search. They walked down the road to McKinney Spring, but never saw more than two sets of tracks. After awhile the tracks faded out, probably due to a light rain that some of the area received two days before. The lush green cottonwood trees of the spring lie near the road and are easily seen. A reliable trickle of water flows under the cottonwoods, but there was no sign in the damp sand lining the tiny creek that the two men had gotten water there.

Paredes was surprised not to find any traces of the men at McKinney Spring. He thought that the only way that the two men could have missed it is if they had taken a route sometimes called the Old Old Ore Road. It was once an old road that ran east of the current road between the Telephone Canyon Trailhead and primitive campsite to the south and a spot north of McKinney Spring where the Old Ore Road turns southwest from its general southeast track. It bypasses the McKinney Ranch site and McKinney Spring, cutting off a little mileage. It was abandoned years ago, but because the desert heals so slowly can still be easily followed. Another abandoned section runs from near Willow Tank on the Old Ore Road to the site of the ore terminal ruins at the north end of the old tramway which carried ore from mines in the Sierra del Carmen of Mexico across the river. Some of that section is used as a hiking trail today in Ernst Basin.

At this point they had no tracks to follow, so when Paredes, Roberts, and the Border Patrol agents received word that a Border Patrol helicopter was coming to help with the search, they returned to the area where the bodies had been found. The ship searched the area for an hour and a half at which time they ended the day's searching. The afternoon heat had become unbearable, and no one wanted any more casualties in the desert.

The next day, June 11, Ranger David Van Inwagen and pilot Jim Traub searched the area from the north end of the Old Ore Road all the way south to the Rio Grande at the Marufo Vega Trailhead using the park plane. After more than three hours in the air, they only found some footprints and what looked like travois drag marks on the Old Old Ore Road about a mile southeast of the Ernst Basin primitive campsite located on the Old Ore Road.

On June 12, Van Inwagen hiked four miles from the Marufo Vega Trailhead on the park road near Boquillas Canyon all the way to the ore terminal in the brutal summer heat. The trail gains about 800 feet and is not a recommended hike that time of year. Shade is almost nonexistent along the route. Because of the hard soil and rocks, he was unable to find any footprints. On his return, he was only able to find three of his own tracks that he had just made.

The next day, Ranger Roberts hiked 2.5 miles into the Ernst Basin area on the Old Old Ore Road south of the Ernst Basin primitive campsite to check out the tracks that Van Inwagen and Traub had seen from the air two days earlier. He discovered that the travois marks were bicycle tracks unrelated to the illegal aliens. He did find some old footprints and an aluminum sleeve from drug packaging.

On June 14, Paredes and Roberts interviewed Teresa Hernández, the mother of first victim Guadalupe Romero-Hernández, at the Boquillas crossing of the Rio Grande. Several other members of the victim's family attended, but most of the discussion was with his mother. Hernández said that her son left on May 30. She had packed some food for him and wrapped two water bottles in blue cloth to keep them cool.

Hernández told the rangers that two other men from Múzquiz, a larger town quite a few miles south of Las Norias and Boquillas, had accompanied her son. She knew little about the two men, other than their names: Juan Enrique Romero and Juan Luis Cardona. One of the first victim's brothers added that Cardona was short and thin, matching the stature of the second victim. The third man, Juan Enrique Romero, was taller and the heaviest of all three men. He also said that Romero had several tattoos. Another family member added that Romero is *"mala gente,"* or bad people, and that he charged to smuggle people into the United States. Whether that was actually true is unknown.

Teresa Hernández said that the two men came to Las Norias from Múzquiz looking for her son. They told her that her son, Guadalupe, needed to go back to Grand Prairie, Texas, where he had been living until recently because his baby was sick and his wife Maxima needed his help. He had been deported two weeks earlier for illegal entry into the United States. She said that her son wasn't prepared to go, but was talked into it by the men. She said that the men had been drinking, but were not arguing with each other. The men were all on good terms when they left. The two men from Múzquiz weren't as well prepared as her son. Her son had a backpack, three days of food, some cash, and the two water jugs that she had prepared. Cardona had a pack and a one-gallon water jug. Romero had a pack but no water jug. It wasn't much for a multi-day hike across the Chihuahuan Desert in the peak of summer heat.

Hernández then asked Paredes if the body of her son had been identified yet. He told her yes, but only by physical description. He told her that he had photos of the body if she was prepared to look at them. She was willing and gave Paredes and Roberts a positive identification.

"The last thing she told us was that she would be willing to help raise her grandson," Paredes wrote at the end of the report, "and asked me if I would please relay that message to Maxima which I did, later that day."

After Paredes and Roberts talked to Teresa Hernández, searchers checked the area around the Boquillas river crossing, along the Boquillas Canyon road, and along the trail that connects the north side of Rio Grande Village to the Ore Terminal Trail. All they found was some clothing at the Boquillas Crossing.

On June 15, Paredes and Roberts used horses to search the area starting from where Roberts had ended his search in Ernst Basin two days earlier. They hunted all the way down to the Boquillas Canyon road via the Ore Terminal Trail. They found only one water bottle and some footprints. That night they met with Ranger Alyssa Van Schmus and discussed possible routes where the third man could be.

"We narrowed the possibilities down to the most likely route—the Old Old Ore Road north of the Telephone Canyon campsite," Van Schmus said. "I've long been interested in the routes that smugglers and immigrants use in the park. It helps us determine how to intercept them. I had just done that route earlier that year."

"Marcos (Paredes) and Joe (Roberts) were pretty tired from all the searching in the days before," Van Schmus said, "so I volunteered. I was fresh, having just come back from vacation. As they were leaving after the meeting, they both said 'I think you'll find him.'"

The next morning at about 10:00, Van Schmus and Ranger Steve McAllister hiked north from the Telephone Canyon primitive campsite carefully looking for signs of the three men. They followed the route of the Old Old Ore Road that Paredes had suspected might have been the men's travel route after finding no evidence of their having obtained water at McKinney Spring. Van Schmus also thought it was the most likely route, given the evidence that they had found thus far. Just north of the Telephone Canyon campsite, they found a two-foot-deep, 1.5-foot-diameter hole dug into a dry wash that appeared to them to be from someone digging for water.   Most of the likely routes north used by smugglers and illegal immigrants in the Old Ore Road area don't hold tracks well because the ground is too rocky. However, some of the route taken by Van Schmus and McAllister north of the campsite is very sandy and holds tracks well.

"We're seeing lots of footprints, but I couldn't tell if it was two or three people," Van Schmus said. "Then I got a whiff and walked right up to him."

After walking about a mile, they found food cans and the body of what appeared to be a Hispanic man lying face down under some bushes in a wash. Van Schmus had no doubt that the man was dead because the skin was decomposing and discolored, and the smell was terrible. About 100 feet north of the body she found marks in the sand of the wash where it appeared two other people had slept. Numerous opened food cans were scattered around the area.

"They were only drinking the liquid," Van Schmus said. "They were desperate."

"He might have been alive when the other two left him," Van Schmus said. "For shade there was a blanket over him, but it looked like he'd pulled it down in his mindless state at the end. They'd left their packs with him and made a flag to mark him with toilet paper and a sotol stalk. The body was in the shade when we found him in the morning, but in the afternoon the place cooks."

Van Schmus called Chief Ranger Mark Spier via satellite phone to report their discovery and then set up the body recovery with Roberts and Paredes. They decided not to start the recovery until 5:00 P.M. to avoid the worst of the day's extreme heat. She and McAllister then hiked about five miles north on the Old Old Ore Road to its junction with the Old Ore Road without seeing any other evidence of the men other than a footprint or two. They also wanted to make sure there wasn't anyone else out there.

"It was hot," Van Schmus said. "We got overheated and finally shaded up at a lone yucca that was the only shade around."

To prepare for the hike, McAllister froze his water bottles to keep them cold until all the ice melted, but it wasn't enough to keep him cool.

"It was pretty brutal," McAllister said. "There's hardly any shade out there. I was going through my water so fast that I drank all the liquid faster than the ice could melt. We had water and those guys didn't. I can't imagine what they went through."

They arrived at the junction with the Old Ore Road at about 4:00 P.M., where they found another hole dug in a dry wash, probably where the first two victims had tried to find water.

It was too hot to do anything but wait in the shade for a ranger to pick them up. They crawled under some bushes to get out of the sun, McAllister scaring a deer out of its spot in the process.

"I felt like I was getting a little heat exhaustion," Van Schmus said, "and, unlike the immigrants, we had plenty of water that still had ice in it."

Ranger Roberts picked them up and they returned to the Telephone Canyon campsite to help with the investigation and body recovery.

At about 5:00 P.M., Border Patrol Agent Jeff Johnson met Roberts, Van Schmus, and McAllister at the campsite and they began hiking north back to the body. Roberts observed the food cans that had been found earlier. He and the other people also found an empty medicine bottle, a tan blanket, and four packs in the area near the body. At about 6:50 P.M., Paredes arrived with Justice of the Peace Jim Burr and a mule. They lifted the body out of the brush and placed it in a body bag. They then rolled it over to take a face photo for identification purposes. The bag was closed and secured, and then five people lifted it up onto the mule and strapped it down. The mule packed the body out to the dirt road.

"I was surprised that the mule didn't run off at the smell from the body," Roberts said.

They carried it out the Old Ore Road in Border Patrol agent Johnson's vehicle to the park highway. From there it was transported to Alpine and then to El Paso for an autopsy. The third body was later positively identified as that of Juan Enrique Romero.

"We probably should have looked sooner to see if there were any other guys," Paredes said. "They usually don't travel alone. However, I'm sure that they were all dead by the time we found the first guy."

"I was a little surprised that they (the dead men) had problems," Roberts said, "because I believe that at least one had done the same trip before. Maybe it was a cooler time of year. They'd still be alive today if they'd found one of the springs. Maybe hungry, but alive."

The autopsies of the three Mexican men indicated that all had died of heat stroke, with no evidence of foul play. The desert at Big Bend National Park can be cruel to the unprepared, especially in summer. Three young, healthy men slipped illegally into the United States the night of May 30 near Rio Grande Village. Guadalupe Romero-Hernández was going to see his wife and baby in Grand Prairie, Texas. The other two men, who it turned out were relatives of his wife, went along to accompany him. They had too little water and didn't know the terrain ahead and the locations of springs and other water sources.

"I didn't finish dealing with the case until near Christmas," Paredes said. "I returned all the personal items then—money, packs, cell phones, and other things —to their families. They were really shaken up. It hit the whole community pretty hard. I sure hope no one down there tries it again."

On the first full day of the three men's trek, the temperature in the shade reached 107 degrees Fahrenheit at Rio Grande Village. On the succeeding days, the high temperature ranged from 110 to 114 degrees. It was not weather to be hiking in the desert, especially with inadequate water. Juan Romero, by far the heaviest of the three, made it about 17 miles before succumbing to the heat. Juan Cardona walked another 8 miles before collapsing. Guadalupe Romero-Hernández's body failed only about one mile farther north. A paved highway and possible assistance was only about three miles away when he died under the scorching West Texas sun. The three young men paid a high price for their illegal entry into the United States.

JEFF WINTERROWD

Jeff Porucznik, a seasonal park ranger at Big Bend National Park, and his friend, park volunteer Jeff Winterrowd, met each other in September 1995 during training at the park. They hit it off and became friends while working together at the Persimmon Gap Ranger Station/ Entrance Station at the north end of the park. It's a very isolated part of the park with only a few people assigned there; for more social opportunities they had to drive to Panther Junction, Marathon, or Terlingua. They socialized and went on hikes together, including several overnight backpacks. They had talked about doing a backpacking trip to remote Mesa de Anguila on the west side of the park, but it didn't come to fruition until December of that year.

Mesa de Anguila, a large, high desert mesa, rises abruptly from the lower desert at its base. It's most notable as the huge sheer-walled mountain on the U.S. side of the Rio Grande at Santa Elena Canyon. The mesa continues on both sides of the river, but is know as the Sierra Ponce on the Mexican side. No easy, non-technical routes lead to its top on the eastern side in and near Santa Elena Canyon. Several faint, little used trails lead up onto it on the western side from near Lajitas and the river upstream of Santa Elena Canyon. Although the top appears flat from below, in reality, cliffs, canyons, and rolling hills break up the terrain. Chihuahuan Desert plants such as lechuguilla, sotol, prickly pear, creosote, and desert grasses cover the dry mesa. No springs lie hidden in its heights. After good rains, water pools temporarily in a few natural rock basins called *tinajas* hidden in the bottoms of the canyons that cut across the mesa. The views are spectacular from atop the high cliffs lining the edges of the mesa, but few hikers see them. The faint, easily lost trails, high temperatures much of the year, and lack of reliable water discourage all but the most hardy desert hikers from visiting.

On December 11, Porucznik and Winterrowd began their hike up onto the mesa. By then, they had had plenty of experience on other park trails and were ready to visit the remote place. The two spent the night before at Porucznik's house and headed out that morning, stopping for a backcountry camping permit at Panther Junction. They paused briefly in Study Butte to buy a pint each of light and dark rum for the trip and then started their hike at about 11:00 A.M. from the Lajitas trailhead.

Along the way, the two stopped for lunch on the trail. They had no particular destination in mind for a campsite that night, but found what Porucznik called a "neat place overlooking the Tinaja Rana" at about 2:30 or 3:00 P.M. It was a flat site that lay on the rim of the deep canyon containing Tinaja Rana and the southwestern edge of the mesa. It offered dramatic views to the south and west. They left their packs there and did a day hike to Tinaja Blanca.

After the two young men returned, they relaxed at their campsite talking and enjoying the sunset. In his statement given to Chief Ranger Jim Northup and Ranger Bill Wright three days later on December 14, Porucznik said that Winterrowd and he "broke open the rum and limes" before preparing dinner. He said that their drinking was casual and that they each drank about an equal amount of rum from their first bottle. It was dark by the time they ate dinner. They continued to drink the rum while eating dinner.

After dinner the two men continued to relax at their campsite, drinking rum and visiting. They finished the first bottle of the light rum and opened the second. Porucznik didn't like the flavor of the dark rum as much and didn't drink as much of it as he had of the first bottle.

By about 8:30 P.M., Porucznik was getting tired and was ready for bed. He walked over to the cliff edge to brush his teeth, while Winterrowd remained sitting in camp. He returned to camp and arranged his sleeping pad and bag for comfort. He and Winterrowd were no longer conversing and he was only vaguely aware of Winterrowd's movements. In his statement he said that he was "getting into sleeping mode...thinking about drifting off to sleep." Porucznik couldn't remember whether he was already in his sleeping bag or just getting into it when he vaguely noticed Winterrowd getting up from his camp chair.

Porucznik's statement details the subsequent events.

"Porucznik stated that approximately one to one-and-a-half minutes after Winterrowd walked towards the cliff edge," Northup wrote in his report on the statement, "while he (Porucznik) lay in his sleeping bag, on his side, facing away from the cliff face, he heard Winterrowd call out a vague, descending 'Whoa.' Porucznik said that he had never heard a voice 'descend' in this way. Porucznik said that he sat up quickly in his sleeping bag, called 'Jeff' in an alarmed state, and then heard what he believed to be Jeff's body hitting or landing on the ground below. Porucznik said that he immediately grabbed his headlamp, went to the cliff edge and spent 'three to five minutes' shining his light and calling Jeff's name with no response. Porucznik said that after the fall, he first recalled looking at his watch at 8:50 P.M."

Panicked, Porucznik quickly packed up his gear to hike out for help, leaving the campsite at about 8:55 P.M. He hustled back down the approximately 6 miles of trail to Lajitas in the dark.

"He got freaked out and hiked back in the dark to the first house he could find with lights on," Ranger Mary Kay Manning said.

At 10:45 P.M. Porucznik made a 911 call from Jim and Katricia Cochran's home in Lajitas. The call information was relayed from the

Alpine Police Department to Ranger Kathleen Hambly at about 11:00 P.M. The police department gave her the number of the Cochran residence in Lajitas. She notified Ranger Bill Wright of the incident and then called Porucznik to get more details. Porucznik told her that he believed that his hiking partner, Jeff Winterrowd, had fallen from a 200-300 foot cliff on Mesa de Anguila. Wright reported the incident to Chief Ranger Jim Northup and assumed incident command.

Wright and Northup quickly assembled a response team consisting of Rangers Wright, Manning, and Marcos Paredes to hike to the scene of the accident as soon as possible. Their goal was to find the victim and render medical attention if he was still alive. Paredes was also a park medic.

Hambly and Wright left Castolon in the park at about 12:15 A.M. for Lajitas. Because he would be hiking out onto the mesa, Wright turned over incident command to Jim Northup. The two arrived at the Cochran home in Lajitas at about 1:30 A.M. Hambly conducted the initial interview with Porucznik. According to Wright's report written later, Porucznik "appeared very upset and shaken."

"He was sick about it," Hambly said.

Porucznik identified the victim as Jeff Winterrowd, a park volunteer, and showed the two rangers the location of the accident on the U.S.G.S. topgraphic map of the mesa. He told them that he and Winterrowd had set up camp about 50 feet from the cliff edge and that the two men had drunk about one and a half pints of rum before the fall. He was unable to see the bottom of the cliff through the darkness with his light and came to Lajitas for help.

The rest of the initial response team arrived and drove to the Lajitas trailhead. Wright, Manning, and Paredes geared up and headed out soon afterward.

"We started hiking at about 2:30 A.M.," Manning said. "We had a full moon which really helped. We didn't need headlamps much."

"I remember turning my headlamp off and I could see better," Paredes said. "Considering the remoteness of the area, I thought we got out there pretty fast."

The team arrived at the spot identified on the map by Porucznik at 5:23 A.M. and found the campsite after about 15 minutes of hunting in the dark. It lay only about five to eight feet from the cliff edge and the Tinaja Rana canyon rim.

"It was perched right on the edge of the cliff," Manning said.

Park recommendations for backcountry camping call for a minimum of 100 yards between camp and a cliff edge.

"It's not an offense (for which people can be fined)," Manning said, "but it's sure safer."

"We got out to the point and started calling around," Manning said, "but we couldn't do much until we got some daylight. We tried to bivouac and stay warm. It was cold."

"We called out a bunch," Paredes said, "but never heard anything. I remember a white sock gleaming in the moonlight about one to two feet below the rim. I thought that wasn't a good sign. It was pretty apparent that he'd gone to the edge of the cliff, maybe to urinate. It was just black down below in the canyon."

By about 6:30 A.M. enough light had seeped into the sky from the east that the rangers were able to resume their search for Winterrowd. Wright discovered what he believed to be a body at the bottom of Tinaja Raja Canyon about 200 feet below the canyon rim at about 7:05 A.M. By 7:15 the light had grown bright enough to confirm that they had indeed found a body that they believed to be Winterrowd's. Access to the body was slow and difficult in the rough, vertical terrain. Wright and Paredes finally reached the body at 8:35 A.M. by climbing and rappelling down the canyon walls. They quickly confirmed that it was Winterrowd and that he was dead. Before disturbing the body, they photographed it.

His torso had some obvious deformity and there were multiple injuries to his head. He was wearing jeans, a t-shirt, a thermal underwear shirt, a cap, and one sock. Three other socks, one of which was extremely tattered, lay at various points down the cliff face. The jeans were also ripped and tattered. Blood was found on the rock around and above his body. The blood evidence and torn clothing indicated that Weatherrowd had hit the cliff several times as he fell. It did not appear that he had moved from his final resting point, indicating either that he received a fatal blow as he fell or that he never regained consciousness after falling. Wright smelled what he thought to be alcohol about five feet down canyon from the body.

The rangers photographed the campsite as enough daylight appeared. It appeared as described by Porucznik, except that it was much closer to the cliff edge than the 50 feet that he had described. Relatively smooth rock surfaced the immediate campsite area, but it was surrounded by jagged, sharp rock. Lechuguilla plants grew scattered across the site, as is typical for the Chihuahuan Desert. Careful observation indicated that the spot from which Winterrowd fell was only a few steps from his sleeping bag.

Wright and Paredes climbed back up to the canyon rim to prepare for recovery of the body and to finish the investigation. A Border Patrol helicopter had flown in that morning to help with the rescue effort. While Wright, Manning, and Paredes did the initial search, a team of rangers was forming up to help extricate the body.

"It was a difficult recovery from a remote location," Ranger Hambly said. "The helicopter was critical for ferrying people in and out and for getting the body out. It would have taken days without it."

By 9:30 A.M., the helicopter had begun ferrying other rangers to the scene of the accident on Mesa de Anguila. By 1:00 P.M., all 14 additional personnel were on site. One of the first to arrive was Ranger Jim Unruh at about 10:15 A.M. He climbed back down to the body with Wright and Paredes for additional photos and a more thorough examination of the body. When they first moved the body at about 12:05 P.M., the smell of alcohol was still present. The injuries were severe, and included severe lacerations and contusions on the head, a crushed jaw, deformity of the right scapula, back, and chest, multiple broken and crushed ribs, deformity of the pelvis and spine, deformity of both knees and ankles, and multiple lacerations, contusions, and abrasions on many parts of his body. The injuries were consistent with a fall from great height. The rangers placed Winterrowd's body in a body bag.

Wright climbed back up to the rim to prepare the newly arrived rangers for retrieval of the body. Hambly finished photographing the campsite, and collected and inventoried all the items. At about 1:00 P.M. the recovery effort began.

The body was strapped into a litter, and using a rope belay system for safety, the rangers slowly worked the body up the rugged canyon bottom.

"Moving a body in difficult terrain just requires a lot of manpower," Manning said. "We found a way around most of the cliff because it was safer for the rescuers."

The team was forced to set up a rope haul system to get the recovery téam and the victim up an unavoidable, thirty-foot vertical pitch.

"We had trouble at a notched pour-off (on the thirty-foot pitch) that kept hanging up the litter," Manning said.

Finally, at about 3:35 P.M. the victim's body and the entire team were out of the canyon. The helicopter soon departed with the body and Wright and carried it to the nearby Lajitas airstrip. At about 4:00 P.M. Justice of the Peace Ron Willard arrived and pronounced Winterrowd dead.

The helicopter resumed ferrying people and equipment off the mesa and back to the Lajitas airstrip, racing against oncoming darkness. Ranger Hambly was the last one out as the sun settled on the horizon, approaching the limit on safe flying time. The multiple trips in and out had drained the chopper's fuel reserves.

"The pilot said we were running on fumes on the way out," Hambly said.

At 6:00 P.M. all the rangers and equipment were on the ground in Lajitas and the operation wound down.

In the case of a death, the park follows up with an investigation. Three days after Winterrowd's fall, Chief Ranger Jim Northup and Bill Wright quizzed Porucznik about that day's events. He said that their camp was "50 feet" from the cliff edge, "perhaps 25-30 feet," when in fact it was five to eight feet. He said that he and Winterrowd never discussed that camping so close to a cliff edge violated park safety rules. He also admitted that he was "probably" legally drunk at the time of the accident based on the amount of alcohol that he had consumed. Obviously, he was not very drunk because he was able to hike six miles out for help in the dark with a heavy pack. However, if Winterrowd had drunk a similar amount of alcohol, it might have been enough to slightly affect balance when standing on a cliff edge in the dark.

Northup's lesson from the accident was very simple. "Don't camp that close to the edge when it's so easy to stumble or trip in the dark."

Although there were absolutely no suspicions of foul play in Winterrowd's fall, the park must always check for it in situations like these. In the interview, Porucznik denied that there were any rivalries, jealousies, or disagreements between the two. Nor had they engaged in any form of horseplay that might have contributed to the accident. Follow up interviews with rangers that knew both men found that the two were best of friends and that they did not engage in horseplay or practical jokes with each other. The death of 25-year-old Jeffrey Winterrowd was a tragic accident, nothing more.

"We held a little ceremony, kind of a memorial service, for him afterwards," Hambly said. "Quite a few park people knew him."

"We all felt so bad for his family," Paredes said. "We (the park staff) named an unnamed spring for him at Mesa de Anguila. We really value our volunteers."

SHANNON ROBERTS

On March 31, 2000, District Ranger Cary Brown stopped an extended cab truck with two men in it for a traffic violation on the main park highway north of Big Bend National Park headquarters at Panther Junction. Brown walked up to the vehicle to check licenses, registration, and insurance. Two Hispanic men occupied the vehicle.

"I don't recall exactly now, but I saw or smelled what I thought to be marijuana stacked behind the seat under a tarp," Brown said years later. "I went back to my car and called dispatch for backup and to run the plates. I walked back up to the pickup and asked the driver and passenger to get out of the truck. The driver started to get out, but at the same time the passenger started to reach under the seat for something. I got very nervous. However, the passenger just grabbed a water bottle and ran off into the desert. I couldn't leave the driver and truck, so I called dispatch again and requested assistance and explained the situation."

The dispatch office called out more rangers and the Border Patrol to the scene.

"Pretty soon all kinds of people were pursuing this guy," said Brown, "rangers on horses, a Border Patrol helicopter, people on foot."

Brown returned to Panther Junction to deal with what turned out to be 400 pounds of marijuana and the driver who was still in custody.

"I was in Chief Ranger Bill Wright's office when a call came in that the searchers had found a skeleton," Brown said. "We first thought it was probably some historical skeleton, but that opinion soon changed. Bill and I went out there and met several people at the scene."

Border Patrol agents Mark Bartlett and Andy Graham had responded to the scene to help find the suspect who had run. A simple traffic stop had escalated into a major drug bust, but the situation was about to turn even more serious.

Agents Bartlett and Graham had headed east of the park highway in pursuit of the suspect. After some time following the suspect's tracks, they reached an old, unused earthen stock tank that dated back to the area's ranching days before it became a park. The tank lay about three or four miles east of the highway, about two miles south of the Dagger Flat road, and a little less than a mile west of the Old Ore Road. Creosote, cacti, and sparse desert grasses vegetate the open desert area surrounding the tank. Bartlett and Graham were distracted from their pursuit of the suspect when they saw part of a partially decomposed body, the skull and upper torso, protruding from disturbed ground on the north edge of the tank. A multi-colored blanket lay just north of the body that looked like it might have been covering the upper part of it. Chicken wire that was also partly buried covered the torso. Several bones lay about 20 feet south of the body, along with a piece of gray duct tape and some other items. Some tent stakes were driven into the ground near the body.

The pursuit of the truck's passenger suddenly received a lower priority.

"Once the body was found," Brown said, "everyone forgot about the drug suspect. We never found that guy."

The searchers had a probable crime scene on their hands. Wright and Brown got everyone away from the site to prevent the evidence from being contaminated. Texas Ranger David Duncan came out to the scene to look it over and help plan a course of action. Ranger Lance Mattson was left overnight to guard the crime scene.

"He didn't have a very fun night out in the middle of nowhere with a dead body," Brown said.

The next day, April 1, Ranger Brown brought FBI agent Steve French, Texas Ranger David Duncan, Park Ranger Matt Stoffolano, and Brewster County Justice of the Peace Cliff Heslip to the scene. The officers were careful not to disturb the site or damage evidence. FBI agent French decided to call out the El Paso FBI Evidence Response Team to investigate the site and exhume the body. The officers left for the evening, leaving Stoffolano to protect the scene from disturbance until the evidence team could get there the next morning.

Duncan arrived at the scene at about 7:45 the next morning, April 2, followed by Heslip. Soon after, Brown, French, and the Evidence Response Team arrived, followed by Chief Ranger Bill Wright. The evidence team proceeded to photograph the scene, collect evidence, and remove the body. They carefully dug around the body so that it could be removed in one piece. It became apparent that the blanket had covered the upper portion of the body and that chicken wire had been laid over the body prior to burial. A pair of size 13 Nike shoes were found in the bottom of the grave and collected, along with the bones, and other items.

As a required formality, Justice of the Peace Heslip declared the subject dead and ordered that an autopsy be performed by the Lubbock County Medical Examiner's Office. The body was placed in a bag and carried to the Old Ore Road from where it was transported to Lubbock.

The next day, April 3, Brown, Duncan, and French drove to Lubbock for the autopsy. The victim was male, about 5 feet, 9 inches tall, and weighed an estimated 150 to 165 pounds. He had had a lot of dental work and probably wore braces. His wisdom teeth and maxillary premolars had been removed. X-rays revealed a two-inch screw in his left ankle due to the repair of multiple fractures. The screw would prove important in identifying the victim.

Because of the body's deteriorated state, discovering a cause and time of death was difficult. A cause was not able to be determined from the remains. The medical examiner estimated that the person had died about a year prior to the autopsy. However, a forensic entomologist from Texas Tech University studied the remains and bugs found at the scene and estimated a time of death of three to five months earlier. His estimate later proved to be more accurate although still too lengthy.

Texas Ranger Duncan called the Missing Persons section of the Department of Public Safety in Austin on April 4 and asked for a list of missing persons that matched the description of the victim. Duncan received a list of people later that day. One missing person from San Antonio, Shannon Roberts, had a metal pin in one of his ankles according to the police department's entry. The next day, San Antonio detective Wise called Cary Brown at Big Bend. After discussing the find at the park, they concluded that the remains were probably those of 43-year-old Shannon Roberts. In addition to similar height, weight, and hair color, the ankle pin and size 13 shoes made the match likely.

Brown and Duncan learned that Roberts was a medical student at the University of Texas Health Science Center in San Antonio. One of Robert's classmates, Jason Schillerstrom, had called the San Antonio Police Department several times inquiring about the missing Roberts. A search of camping permits at Big Bend found a backcountry permit for January 18, 2000, for Roberts. It listed Dagger Mountain as the campsite and showed Roberts as a "Sol. Hiker," probably meaning solitary or solo hiker. The vehicle listed on the permit matched that of Roberts'.

Roberts' dental charts were faxed to the Lubbock medical examiner. They appeared to match the teeth of the victim, but Shannon's actual X-rays were needed for absolute confirmation. Brown arranged for the X-rays to be sent to the medical examiner.

On April 10, Brown, French, and Duncan traveled to San Antonio to meet with San Antonio Police Department detectives. They learned that Roberts had originally been reported missing to the police by his father, George Roberts. The father had become concerned after receiving a call from Dr. Leonard Lawrence, the Associate Dean of Student Affairs at the University of Texas Health Science Center. Dr. Lawrence had become concerned when Roberts stopped attending courses after August 3, 1999, even though he had paid his tuition in advance for that fall and the spring of 2000. When Roberts' father was unable to reach his son, he filed a missing persons report with the police department on March 9, 2000. The next day the police sent a detective to check Roberts' apartment, but he wasn't there.

When Dr. Lawrence told George Roberts that his son had not been in class since August, he was surprised. He told Roberts that he had been communicating with his son during the fall of 1999 and in January 2000. His son had told him that he was going to school.

After Brown, French, and Duncan interviewed Dr. Lawrence, they visited Shannon Roberts' apartment and talked to the manager. She told them of receiving a concerned phone call from his father. Roberts had paid his rent in advance through March. The March rent had been paid in late January. She had only been working there for six months and didn't know Roberts very well.

The next day, April 11, the officers met with Roberts' classmate Jason Schillerstrom at the Health Science Center. He told them that he had met Roberts at the University of Texas at Austin which Roberts was attending to complete his pre-med classes. Both had then enrolled at the Health Science Center and were in the same third year group of 25 students. Schillerstrom said that Roberts had not been attending school that spring or the prior fall of 1999. He said that Roberts was depressed about academic problems. Although he wasn't in school, Schillerstrom had seen him at the library using the internet. He told them that Roberts was a big email user and should have extensive email files. He also added that Roberts was homosexual and had a boyfriend whom he called "Sweet Thing." He didn't know the name of the boyfriend. Schillerstrom gave officers the name of some of Roberts' other friends, however.

Later that same day, the officers talked to Patti McDaniel, the former manager at Roberts' apartment. She told them that Roberts had several young male friends who used to hang out at his apartment. One of them was a young man known only to her as Jonathon.

The next day Duncan headed back to Alpine. Brown and French conducted more interviews over the next two days. Through their investigation, Brown and French identified "Sweet Thing" as John Michael Baker.

On April 18, Tiffany Anthony, a friend and fellow student of Roberts, called Duncan to tell him that the press had been interviewing medical students at the Health Science Center about Roberts' death. She said that she had been quoted in one newspaper story and had then received a call from Ray McQueen, a longtime friend of Roberts'. She also told Duncan that she knew that Roberts had a boyfriend who was either married or had a girlfriend.

Duncan proceeded to call McQueen. McQueen told him that he had been a friend of Roberts during his tenure as a geophysicist at Atlantic Richfield. After getting laid off after working there for 11 years, Roberts decided to go to medical school. McQueen thought that Roberts left Dallas in 1995 to begin pre-med courses at the University of Texas at Austin.

McQueen told Duncan that Roberts had sent him an email on January 29, 2000, telling him that he was going to the border to work in a family service clinic. A few days later, Roberts called McQueen to tell him the same thing about going to a clinic in Laredo. However, Jason Schillerstrom later told McQueen that Roberts had already completed his required work at the clinic. McQueen also told Duncan that Roberts was having a homosexual relationship with a "young man" in San Antonio. Roberts and the "young man" were stopped by the police and then arrested because the "young man" had cocaine in his backpack. Later investigation made it appear that the backpack belonged to Roberts. McQueen remembered that Roberts told him that he had been having a sexual relationship with the "young man" for some time and that the "young man" had a girlfriend or was married. The family of the "young man" would be upset if they learned of the relationship.

On April 19, 2000, the medical examiner in Lubbock called to confirm the identification of the victim as Shannon Roberts. The dental X-rays matched perfectly the teeth of the victim. However, the medical examiner also could not determine what caused Roberts' death or more than a rough estimate of the date or time of death.

"He (Shannon) was pretty well gone," Brown said. "It was impossible to determine the cause of death. There wasn't enough soft tissue left."

Meanwhile, Cary Brown had obtained Shannon Roberts' bank and debit card records. The records showed a debit at a Hilton Hotel in New Orleans on March 7, 2000. There was also a debit purchase labeled "Phillips," probably a gas station, on February 2, 2000, in Sanderson, Texas. Sanderson is a small town that lies along the main route between San Antonio and Big Bend National Park.

The investigators learned that John Baker was Roberts' lover before Roberts' disappearance, his "Sweet Thing." Additionally, they found that Baker and two friends went to Mardi Gras in New Orleans in March of 2000 at the time that the victim's debit card was used there. They were able to identify Baker as the user of the card in part because he had used it online under his real name to track down old girlfriends with a people search website. That really pushed the investigators toward Baker. He was now considered a suspect in the case, but they didn't have much of a case for anything other than fraud related to use of Roberts' debit card.

The case moved slowly for the next two years. They learned that Roberts had many personal and financial problems. His student loan debt was huge, and he thought that he might fail medical school even though later discussions with faculty at the Health Science Center indicated that Roberts was doing okay. The evidence collected at the crime scene was analyzed but didn't reveal much in the way of fingerprints or usable DNA. The parents of Shannon Roberts gave blood to the investigators to help with the DNA work.

During that time the investigators learned that Roberts had talked about suicide for a long time. He had approached people about assisting him in committing suicide. He had even gone to the extreme of placing an ad in an underground newspaper requesting such assistance. When an individual responded to the ad, the individual was asked by Roberts to help him commit suicide. The individual refused and called the police after hearing about Roberts' death at Big Bend. Ranger Cary Brown interviewed the individual about his experience with Roberts.

"Baker's name came up early on," Duncan said, "it just took a long time to build a case. "All of us (the investigators) being so far from San Antonio slowed the case down some."

On April 22, 2002, Brown, French, Duncan, and Chief Ranger Mark Spier consulted with the FBI's Behavioral Sciences Unit on an approach to use for questioning John Baker. The unit recommended telling Baker that they knew that Roberts had been soliciting assistance in committing suicide. Maybe Baker would admit to assisting Roberts in committing suicide. The investigators met with Assistant United States Attorney Jim Blankenship in Alpine and all agreed to take that approach with Baker.

On May 6, the investigators questioned Kathryn Fazio at her home in San Antonio. She confirmed that she and her boyfriend had gone to New Orleans with Baker in March 2000. She also told officers that Baker was attending college at Southwest Texas State University (now Texas State University) in San Marcos.

With the assistance of Texas Ranger Tommy Ratliff, the investigators located Baker and approached the university police. Ratliff accompanied them to San Marcos. They went to Baker's dorm room and found him there. Baker agreed to let them interview him at the police department offices.

When asked by Brown, Baker said that he remembered Brown from two years before. The investigators told Baker that he wasn't under arrest and could leave at any time. Brown, Duncan, and French proceeded with the interview. They told Baker that they knew of Roberts' many personal and financial problems. Apparently Roberts was concerned about failing medical school, being unable to repay college loans, his sexuality, and with becoming older and unattractive. They strongly believed that Roberts intended to commit suicide. They had talked to individuals in California and San Antonio whom Roberts had approached about helping him commit suicide. Brown explained that there was no federal statute prohibiting assisted suicide, but the state did have one. Duncan explained that the state statute was a Class C misdemeanor. Based upon interviews and evidence, they told Baker that they firmly believed that Roberts' death was an assisted suicide. He was told that they wanted to close the case and give closure to Roberts' family.

When Baker was asked about his relationship to Roberts, he said he had met Roberts when he was in high school. His girlfriend lived at Roberts' apartment complex with her brother and introduced Baker to Roberts. He told the investigators that Roberts let him and his girlfriend hang out at his apartment, and bought alcohol and cigarettes for them and some other teenagers. Baker and his girlfriend even had a key to Roberts' place. Baker said that Roberts associated with teenagers while he was attending medical school. He was "weird," but very entertaining. He was intelligent and helped them with their calculus homework. He said that Roberts was a reliable friend who would do a lot for you. Baker knew that Roberts was gay and was sometimes embarrassed by it. In contradiction to what Roberts had told his friends prior to his death, Baker told the officers that he was heterosexual and that Roberts had never made a pass at him. When Baker was asked what his relationship was with Roberts, he paused and then said that Roberts was a "friend."

Baker said that Roberts became obsessed with suicide and that he wanted his death recorded as a snuff film. He said that Roberts frequently talked about it when he was with Baker and others. Roberts was even talking about suicide the first time Baker met him. Baker, however, denied knowing that Roberts had tried to get help in committing suicide.

"I first met Doc (Shannon Roberts) in '97 or so and was introduced to him by my girlfriend at the time," Baker wrote in a statement made about nine months later, "From the first day I met him, he started with questions like, 'Have you ever wanted to kill someone for money?' At the time I took it as him being strange, that and the fact that he was very openly gay. After I'd known him for awhile, it hit me that he wasn't even remotely joking. The questions about killing him were almost a daily thing, that and the sexual advances. During this time he pretty much gave me whatever I wanted, booze, cigs, weed, mushrooms, and cash when I was broke. Figured it gave him someone to talk to."

"Probably around '99," Baker wrote in his statement, "he started getting a little more edgy/pushy about the killing issue. Several times he called to say 'goodbye,' a couple times he stopped by my mother's house, and dropped off crap. Some of the times he told me things like, 'I found someone that would do it for free, and they are coming in from out of town,' and 'I put an ad in the S&M personals, and found someone to do it.' But all those fell through for whatever reason."

When Duncan asked Baker if Roberts had ever given him gifts, Baker said that he had, but nothing of value. Brown followed up by asking if Roberts had given him anything the last time that he had seen him. Baker said that he couldn't remember receiving anything. Brown then asked when Baker had last seen Roberts. He said that he had last seen Roberts at Roberts' apartment after meeting him at Jason's Deli on January 31, 2000. When Brown asked Baker if he had ever been to Big Bend National Park, Baker said that he had been there with his parents as a child, even though his parents didn't recall ever going there in an earlier interview. Brown then bored in more deeply and specifically asked if he'd ever been to Big Bend with Roberts. Baker said that he had not.

Brown, French, and Baker then told Baker some details about finding Roberts' body and some of what they had learned in their investigation of the death. Brown told Baker that Roberts' wallet and car keys were never found and that Roberts' car was parked at his apartment complex instead of out in the desert at Big Bend. Baker said that he had seen Roberts with a small purse that he used for a wallet, but that he hadn't seen it since the death.

Duncan told Baker that information that they possessed indicated that Baker knew more about Roberts' death than he was disclosing. He told Baker that they had enough information to present a criminal case against Baker to the district attorney's office, even aside from any involvement in the death of Roberts. Those charges involved Roberts, but weren't related to charges in Roberts' death. Baker denied committing any crimes related to Roberts. Duncan wrote "Debit Card Abuse" on a sheet of paper and placed it face down on the table so that Baker couldn't read it and again told Baker that they were only interested in closing the case. Baker responded by saying that the officers were trying to trick him by not reading him his rights. Brown said that if Baker meant a Miranda warning, that they weren't required to do that because he wasn't under arrest, could leave at any time, and didn't need

to answer their questions. Brown and Duncan explained custodial inter-
rogation to Baker and again told him that he could leave at any time.
Baker said that it would be "stupid" for him to leave. French again said
that Baker could leave at any time, but Baker made no attempt to do so.

Baker told the investigators that he had applied to join the National
Guard so that he would get some help in paying for his college expenses.
They told him that they would recommend to prosecutors that no
charges be brought against Baker if he would cooperate in helping solve
the case of Roberts' death. Baker seemed perplexed by the possibility
of additional charges and said that he would have to talk to someone
before commenting on any information he had. At this point, the officers and Baker took a short break.

Upon resuming the questioning, Baker told the investigators that
telling them about what had happened was like jumping into cold
water. He was unsure of the exact date, but said that he had gone to
Big Bend National Park with Roberts, because Roberts had paid him
$1,000 before the trip and that he wanted Baker to kill him. They
had driven at night and gotten there early in the morning before the
park's entrance station had opened. He said that Roberts took him to a
remote, large, clear, sandy area where Roberts had already dug a grave
on a previous trip. The earlier trip was consistent with what the investigators had found in their investigation. He told the investigators that
rather than pay Baker $1,000 up front that Roberts originally planned
to put the money in his apartment mailbox and swallow the key. Baker
said that Roberts wanted to be staked out and have his bowels cut open.
If he swallowed the key he thought that whoever killed him would have
to cut him open to get the key and money. Baker said he was unable to
disembowel Roberts. He told them that Roberts was really "stoned" on
"Ambiens." Baker finally hit Roberts on the head several times with a
shovel, but it didn't seem to affect Roberts much. According to Baker,
he told Roberts that he couldn't kill him, so they both drove back to
San Antonio. The date of their return trip matched the date on an ATM
transaction made in Sanderson. Even though he hadn't killed Roberts,
Baker kept the $1,000 that Roberts had given to him. Baker told them
that at a gathering that they attended on January 31, 2000, after returning that Roberts made a "lame excuse" for his bloody head. The officers'

investigation revealed that Roberts had told others that the injuries were from hitting his head on a curb in a bicycle accident. Baker said that that was the last time that he had seen Roberts, although he had talked to him on the phone after that. He reiterated what he told the officers in a statement he wrote nine months later.

"Early the next morning," Baker wrote, "we headed out to Big Bend, the booth wasn't even open when we got there. He drove to a very specific spot that he had picked out, and had already dug part of a grave. After we got to the spot, he started to dig, when it was to his liking, he said it was time to get started. At this point the thought of tying him down and cutting him open was turning my stomach, so I hit him over the head with a shovel, several times. That really did nothing. After that lame effort, we left, he was kinda depressed and said things like, 'I really hadn't planned on coming back to town.'"

Baker then told the investigators that he didn't know anything else about the death of Roberts, but he seemed to be disturbed and thoughtful. Duncan told him that they still thought that he knew more than he had revealed so far. Baker told them that the other charges that could be brought against him must be related to the use of Roberts' debit card. Duncan turned over the piece of paper that he had written on earlier and showed it to him. It said "Debit Card Abuse." Baker told them he should have known better than to use the card.

Baker then proceeded to tell the investigators that about one or two weeks after their first trip to the park that he and Roberts drove to the park again in Baker's car.

He wrote in his statement nine months later, after the first failed attempt to kill Roberts, "For the next week or so (I think) he kept giving me shit about it, until I finally broke down and said okay."

Baker's dates were consistent with what the investigation had shown. The last that anyone had heard from Roberts was an email received on February 10, 2000. Baker said they left at night in his Volvo. He wasn't sure what time that they had left San Antonio, and that he had slept in back while Roberts drove. Baker woke up at about daylight as they were driving into the park. Roberts took Baker back to the same spot where the grave had been dug. Baker said that Roberts was drinking tequila or vodka. After some conversation that Baker said was "really weird," Roberts again wanted Baker to stake him out and kill him by cutting him open. According to Baker, he told Roberts that he couldn't do it. At this point while he related the story to the officers, Baker was visibly shaken.

Finally, Roberts sat in the grave and Baker used a rope to strangle him from behind. Baker filled in the grave on top of Roberts and covered him with wire. He told the officers that Roberts had brought the wire "so that dogs wouldn't dig him up." When Brown asked about the blanket that had been placed over Roberts body, Baker said that it must have come from his car. Duncan then asked Baker about the tent stakes that they had found next to Roberts' grave. Baker said that Roberts had placed them there so that he could be staked out and disemboweled. Baker's statements about what happened were consistent with the physical evidence that the investigators had discovered at the crime scene. Baker then drove back to San Antonio. Because he had been sleeping while Roberts drove to the park, he had some minor problems finding the way.

Brown asked Baker if Roberts had paid him any money to come to the park with him to assist in the suicide. He said that Roberts paid him $2,000 to $2,500. He added that Roberts gave Baker his debit card and said to use it until the account was empty. He said that Roberts had even made the reservations in New Orleans so that Baker could go to Mardi Gras.

In the statement that Baker wrote nine months later, he wrote about the killing of Roberts.

"He went through the same spiel about wanting to be tied down and cut open," Baker wrote. "After repeated refusals from me, he started getting irritated, from the hole, he started grabbing at me with the pick axe he had. I honestly don't remember everything that took place, but eventually I ended up with some rope that he had brought to be tied down with, and choked him with it. After that I started filling in the hole, and stopped before it was full. On the way back to the car I left all the 'tools' on the ground (all over). Left Big Bend, came home, got the money, and figured that would be the end of it."

The interview ended. Baker was told that they would discuss the case with the United States Attorney's office in Alpine and get back to him about the case. They drove Baker back to his dorm. "Thanks for the interesting afternoon," he told them.

The investigators were tired after the five-hour interview and needed a break.

"We went to eat after the interview," Brown said, "and said, 'this isn't assisted suicide, it's murder.'"

The investigators presented their case to the new Assistant U.S. Attorney in Alpine, Gary Trombley, hoping that charges would be brought against Baker after all their work on the case. However, the attorney thought that he needed a stronger case and wanted them to try to get a written confession. So Brown, Duncan, and French re-interviewed Baker about Roberts' death at a hotel in San Antonio where they were staying on February 9, 2003.

When Baker arrived at the hotel that evening, the group gathered in a conference room by the lobby. Baker asked what they needed to know that he hadn't already told him. Brown told him that their job was to gather as much information as possible to give to the U.S. Attorney. He also told Baker that there was no interest in pursuing any other charges against Baker except concerning Roberts' death. The decision about whether any criminal charges would be brought against Baker would be made by the U.S. Attorney's office. Baker said that he understood.

Brown then tried to get answers to some remaining questions that they still had about the case. When Brown asked if anyone else had gone to Big Bend on Baker's two trips with Roberts, Baker said no. Baker said that the tools, sleeping bag, blanket, and other items found at the scene were Roberts' and that he had not brought anything with him. Baker was asked who had driven the metal stakes into the ground at the site. He couldn't remember who drove the stakes into the ground by the grave, but said that those were the stakes by which Roberts wanted to be tied down and cut open.

Brown asked Baker if he threw Roberts' tennis shoes in the grave with the body. He said that he couldn't recall exactly, but thought that he probably had. The shoes had not been on Roberts' feet. Baker did say that Roberts had his shoes on when he walked to the site from the car.

Brown then asked about the duct tape found at the scene. He told Baker that they had not run the hair found on the tape through DNA testing because of the expense and wondered if Baker knew whose hair it was. Baker said that the hair was Roberts' and that the tape was used to bind either his hands or ankles, but he couldn't recall which.

After more questioning, Baker again denied that he had had any sexual relationship with Roberts, even though Roberts had made sexual advances over the years.

They ran through some of the events of the first trip to Big Bend. Baker said again that Roberts wanted to be staked out and cut open while still alive, but that he couldn't do it. He told them again about hitting Roberts in the head with a shovel. Brown paraphrased Baker's comment in his report. "It's not like in the movies. I hit him as hard as I could and it hardly phased [sic] him." This time Baker said that Roberts paid him about $500 for trying to assist him in his suicide.

On the second trip to the park Baker said that he thought he would be paid about $4,000 for killing Roberts, but he retrieved only about $2,000 from Roberts' mailbox after his death. Baker said that he must have had the mailbox key to get the money from the box.

When the officers asked more questions about the chicken wire that covered Roberts' body, Baker said that it was Roberts' idea to keep the "coyotes" from digging up the body. He didn't know where the shovel was that he used to cover the body and was surprised that it wasn't at the scene. He added that Roberts dug most of the grave on an earlier trip to the park before their first visit and that Roberts finished it during their first visit to the park.

Baker said that Roberts was acting "weird" on their second trip to Big Bend, getting in and out of the grave several times. While in the grave, Roberts tried to pull Baker closer to him with the pick-axe. At this time, Baker said that he got behind Roberts with a cord and choked him to death. Brown asked Baker how he knew that Roberts was dead before burying him. Baker did not have a specific answer, but knew that Roberts was dead before he covered him with dirt.

Brown asked Baker if he was willing to write down a summary of his statement for the investigators. Brown agreed, so they left him alone to write it. After he finished it, Brown and French witnessed it. Baker left the hotel after the officers told him that they would notify him after the Assistant U.S. Attorney reviewed the case and made a determination about its disposition.

"After we got the written confession, we gave it to the attorney in Alpine," Brown said. "It went to the Attorney General's office in Washington for a decision on the charges. They decided on second-degree murder."

The charges were brought against Baker and he was arrested. Before the trial, he was housed at the Reeves County Jail in Pecos, Texas. In an interesting twist, Baker managed to escape from the jail on August 13, 2003. He turned himself in near Abilene only two days later. On August 25 he pled guilty to second degree murder in the death of Shannon Roberts before United States District Judge Robert Junell in Midland, Texas.

It took more than three years, but the dogged efforts of Park Ranger Cary Brown, FBI agent Steve French, and Texas Ranger David Duncan brought justice in the death of Shannon Roberts.

"It was the first conviction for homicide at Big Bend National Park," Brown said later. "Shannon Roberts was a remarkable guy in many ways, but very troubled."

"It was one of the strangest murders that I've ever been involved in," Duncan said.

Brown, French, and Duncan attended the sentencing hearing on November 12, 2003. John Baker was sentenced to 210 months in prison by the judge, the maximum under federal sentencing guidelines for second degree murder. The jail escape added to the sentence. He is scheduled for release on August 3, 2018.

As Baker was being led out of the Midland courtroom afterward, he paused to talk to the investigators.

"I've got to congratulate you guys," Baker said. He directed his last comment to Brown. "I'll never think of a park ranger the same way again."

BRYAN BROCK

When John Sellers picked up his friend, Bryan Brock, late on the stormy winter night of December 13, 1984, at the Midland/Odessa airport for their trip to Big Bend National Park, he expected to have a fun adventure over the next few days. He was right about the adventure part. He was horribly wrong about the fun part.

On earlier trips Sellers had attempted to descend Cattail Canyon from its headwaters high in the Chisos Mountains down to its abrupt exit from the mountains in the Chihuahuan Desert. His first attempt was in 1977 with two friends. They failed when they hit high pour-offs in the canyon bottom. The most rugged, difficult terrain in Big Bend National Park lies in and around Cattail Canyon. The canyon is many hundreds of feet deep, narrow, and mostly sheer-walled. In December 1983, Sellers attempted to descend the canyon once again, this time with five partners, a 300-foot rope, 165-foot rope, and technical climbing gear. The trip was arduous, with numerous rappels down sheer drops of up to 100 feet in the canyon bottom. Some of the coldest winter weather in park history blew in, freezing the scattered pools of water into treacherous sheets of ice. Temperatures well below freezing made hiking, camping, and particularly fumbling with ropes difficult and painful. Where water had dripped down the pour-offs, the climbers had to rappel down slick sheets of ice. Some of the rappels dropped into ice-covered, frigid pools of water. One member of the party, Mark Mosier, had brought a wet suit, so he was often the first to descend, breaking the ice and swimming across the pool to the far side. He would anchor the rope so that the others could lower gear and descend without getting wet. Little of the slanting winter sun found its way down into the bitterly cold, dim canyon.

"I think it got down below zero in the mountains," Sellers said years later. "It was challenging, but beautiful with ice everywhere."

After many treacherous rappels, the group reached a pour-off that floored them. Although they had 465 feet of rope with them, the drop was so high that they were unsure that the rope would reach the bottom. There was no way to see the bottom from their perch in the narrow section of canyon suspended above the drop. In addition, without being able to double the rope for the rappel, there would be no way to retrieve the rope when they were done even if it was long enough to reach the bottom. Doubling the rope would only give them a working length of about 200 to 230 feet, depending on the anchor. However big the drop was, they knew it was far more than 230 feet. Not only did they not want to abandon expensive ropes, they might need them for more drop-offs farther down the canyon. Reluctantly, they went back upstream until they could climb out of the canyon and find a detour around the huge pour-off. The detour was difficult, but they eventually got around the massive pour-off and continued down canyon, over more drops and through more ice and pools of dark water. It took them two full days to traverse a mere three miles of canyon. Ranger and experienced rock climber George Howarth later said that Cattail Canyon is "probably the most complicated and dangerous area in the park as far as technical climbing."

Even with the miserable weather and incredibly difficult travel, the trip inspired John Sellers. He was determined to return and complete the entire descent of Cattail Canyon from top to bottom, including the massive pour-off that had turned his party away in December, 1983. Now he was here a year later with his friend, Bryan Brock, the older brother of one member of the 1983 trip. After hearing about the previous year's trip from his younger brother, Bruce, and John Sellers, Bryan Brock wanted to go on this attempt. Brock was very fit and athletic and had had a moderate amount of climbing experience. His wife Sasha was pregnant with their first child, an event of great importance in his life.

After Brock arrived late at the icy Midland/Odessa airport, he and Sellers drove to the park, arriving very late and camping in the Basin. The next morning they packed their gear, including a massive 765 feet of rope and lots of other technical climbing equipment, and got back-country camping permits. They also needed to get a climbing permit, but did not, possibly because of some confusion on the ranger's part as to whether rappelling constituted climbing. However, a later hearing concluded that Sellers and Brock had good equipment and were experienced, so they would have been issued a permit.

Brock and Sellers set out up the trail to Laguna Meadow at about noon, burdened by enormous 80-pound packs. Climbing ropes and related gear are not light.

In addition to all the camping and climbing gear, Sellers said, "I had a ridiculous amount of camera gear."

They ate lunch and rested at Laguna Meadow before leaving the established trail. They hiked up over the low saddle that separates the meadow from the headwaters of Cattail Canyon and began their descent. Initially, the canyon drops fairly gradually, and is broad and nicely wooded with oaks, pinyon pines, and alligator junipers. Sun shone on their shoulders as they walked down the gently sloping draw.

After passing a small masonry dam that dates to the park's ranching days, the canyon begins to curve north. Vegetation becomes sparse and more bare rock lies exposed by erosion. The sun reaches less and less of the canyon floor. Soon they hit the first of many pour-offs that ended in a pool of water at the bottom. They were tired after a short night's sleep and the long hike up into the canyon with very heavy packs. With rain spitting down, they fixed dinner and, with some difficulty, found a flat enough spot for their tent.

The next morning, the two continued their descent. They climbed around the first pour-off without using ropes and continued down the steepening, narrowing gorge. With heavy packs, they had to delicately traverse around the edges of deep pools of standing water by clinging to the canyon walls. The next drop they had to rappel, a tricky maneuver with an 80-pound pack strapped on one's back on a wet, slick nearly vertical wall. A metal rappelling device is clipped with a carabiner to a seat harness worn by the climber. The rope is solidly anchored to a large tree, boulder, or climbing chock wedged in a crack. The rope is then threaded through the metal rappelling device. The device adds lots of friction to the rope as it slides through, making it possible to descend a cliff at a very controlled rate of speed.

The second cliff was short enough that they were able to use their shorter 165-foot rope as a double-rope rappel. To do a double-rope rappel, the rope is looped through or around the anchor at the top of the drop and its ends are tied together. The doubled rope is fed over the cliff with the knot at the bottom. The climber then rappels down with the doubled rope feeding through his or her rappel device. Brock was less experienced with technical climbing, so Sellers made sure that Brock was rigged correctly. Brock descended first with no problem. After Sellers descended, they unrigged the rope by untying the knot and pulling one end of the rope out of the anchor above and down to them. The anchor is left behind. Once the rope was down, they were committed. They could not return back up the cliff. Without serious climbing to get out of the canyon, they had to continue their descent.

They soon came to the second pitch needing a rope. This time they had to use the 600 foot rope. A rope that long tends to get tangled and becomes a nuisance to coil and uncoil every time it's used. From the bottom of that drop, they continued downwards, deeper into the canyon.

"The canyon seemed endless," Sellers later wrote in a lengthy account of their trek posted on the BigBendChat.com website. "The weight of our packs wore upon us. We came to the third pour-off, and a fourth."

They got through those pitches with the slow, tedious effort of uncoiling the rope, preparing an anchor, hanging the rope, rappelling down with their packs, coiling the rope, repacking gear, and continuing onward.

They soon hit a fifth pour-off. Sellers began to wonder if he'd remembered the number of pour-offs correctly. By lowering their packs down, they managed to down-climb it without rigging ropes and rappelling. By the next drop, they had tired of endlessly coiling and uncoiling the 600-foot rope. They laid it out and cut it exactly in half, making two 300-foot segments. It would be no problem at the huge drop ahead to knot the rope back together. Although cutting the rope was a sensible move, the decision would later change not only the outcome of the entire trip but their very lives.

Very quickly they hit yet another drop. This one they were able to carefully down-climb without ropes. Sellers moved ahead a short distance and yelled excitedly back at Brock. They had reached the enormous pour-off that had foiled Sellers and his party the year before. The narrow slot that they were in opened up into an enormous chasm, the bottom of which, as they later discovered, lay by their measure 435 sheer, vertigo-inducing feet below. The incredible magnitude of the drop awed them. The canyon below was much deeper than it was wide, forming a tremendous gorge. Scattered trees in the bottom appeared as little dots.

With a mixture of excitement and dread, the two began setting the anchor and rigging the rope. They tied the two 300-foot lengths together for the main rope. Sellers was unsure of the length of the drop. Even with 765 feet of rope he was nervous about having enough to reach the bottom. Using a complicated system at the top, he set up the ropes to allow a rappel of the first 300 feet of rope. If that wasn't enough, a braking system that they rigged at the top would allow Brock to gently lower Sellers the second 300 feet. Sellers looped the 165-foot rope over his shoulder to tie to the bottom of the combined 600 feet if necessary. Additionally, he tied a knot at the end of the bottom 300-foot rope to ensure that he wouldn't accidentally rappel off the end of the rope if it didn't reach the bottom. He also carried two prusik knots with him in the event the entire 765-foot length didn't reach the bottom. Although it would require great effort, the prusik knots would allow him to climb back up the rope to the top.

Sellers and Brock agreed that if Sellers could reach the bottom with only 300 feet of rope that Brock would lower their packs and then follow Sellers down the cliff. Otherwise, Brock would lower the packs and then descend the detour route that Sellers' group had found the year before, taking one of the 300-foot ropes with him for the shorter rappels along that route.

They checked the rope rigging system one more time. Sellers clipped his rappel device to the rope, looked at Brock, and said "I'm scared out of my wits." With great trepidation, he stepped over the brink of the pour-off. With so much heavy rope hanging below adding friction to his rappel device, Sellers had to almost force the rope through as he crept down the wet, slippery cliff. More than 100 feet down, he could finally see the end of the first 300-foot section of rope dangling in the breeze far above the canyon bottom. With careful study he determined that while the first 300 feet wouldn't be enough, the second 300 feet would see him all the way down.

A trickle of very cold water was dribbling down the cliff, slowly soaking Sellers as he hung suspended in space. He was getting cold and continued his rappel, shouting his findings up to Brock. He dropped off an overhang and hung free of the cliff at the end of the first 300 feet of rope. Hanging free directly under the overhang caused the trickle of water to pour right down onto him, chilling him rapidly in the December weather.

With slow, difficult communication from way down the cliff, Brock prepared to lower Sellers the next 300 feet. Sellers hoped that Brock was doing everything right up above. His life was literally in Brock's hands. The switchover went smoothly, but some webbing had jammed in the braking system above, delaying Brock's ability to lower Sellers. Finally, after an interval that seemed interminable to Sellers, Brock freed the jam and lowered a shivering, thoroughly chilled Sellers.

Sellers quickly reached the bottom, unclipped from the rope, and yelled up at Brock to lower his pack. He was getting hypothermic and needed dry clothes. With the great distance between them, echoing canyon walls, and blowing wind, communication was difficult, but Brock soon understood and lowered Sellers' pack to a grateful recipient. He quickly started a small fire and changed clothes to warm up.

Sellers, who has spent an enormous amount of time in the outdoors in all conditions, later said, "I have never been so cold in my life."

It was getting late in the day and both climbers were exhausted. They decided to camp where they were for the night—Brock at the top, Sellers at the bottom. Talk was difficult, so they both soon settled in for the night, Sellers probably with thoughts of awe over his descent, Brock probably with dread over the next morning's descent.

The morning of December 16 started relatively warm and pleasant. Sellers got up early and scouted down canyon to find the place where the detour route they had used the previous year joined the main canyon. After some difficult scrambling, he found the spot where he hoped to be meeting Brock in a short time. He hiked and climbed back up canyon to his camp at the base of the huge pour-off.

Brock called down to Sellers soon after Sellers returned, saying that he wanted to rappel down the high pour-off rather than take the easier, but time-consuming detour route. Sellers was very concerned that Brock did not have the necessary equipment or expertise to do the descent without someone helping on top. He wanted Brock to come down by the detour route. By yelling in slow motion because of the echoes and wind noise, Brock described how he would do it. Sellers didn't think it would work and suggested an alternate method. Brock, however, wanted to use his. Sellers was unable to change Brock's mind. Sellers, unable to persuade Brock otherwise, told Brock to put on plenty of clothes because of the cold water. Brock put on some extra clothes and lowered his pack to Sellers.

After spending an hour setting up his rigging, Brock backed off the lip of the drop and began his descent with Sellers nervously watching from below. For the first 60 feet or so the descent seemed to go normally, then Brock appeared to slip on the wet cliff and lose control. His descent rapidly accelerated and he flew down the wet rope, slamming to a stop at the knot in the line. The rope he was descending is known as a static rope because it has very little stretch. Climbing ropes in which you expect to take a fall are designed to stretch substantially to lessen the impact when you hit the end of the rope after a fall. However, static ropes are easier and safer for rappelling. Although Brock said that he was fine, the sudden stop at the knot must have at least shaken him up if not done some injury.

Unless Brock had managed to regain control during his free-fall down the rope or Sellers had managed to put enough weight onto the bottom end of the rope quickly enough to add friction to Brock's rappel braking system to slow him down, it's possible that Brock would have plummeted all the way down the rope to the bottom and been seriously injured or even died without the knot to stop him. The knot connected the two ends of the 600-foot rope that they had cut in two in their descent of the canyon on the previous day. It's possible that the knot saved Brock's life. However, it quickly became apparent that the knot had created a serious problem.

Brock was hanging about 170 feet down the cliff so communication was improved, but Sellers was unable to see what the problem was. Brock called down to say that he was getting ready. After about ten minutes he reached below for the rope under him, but then flipped upside down and yelled that he was having trouble breathing. He managed to right himself and the breathing problems eased. The knot was jammed in his jury-rigged rappel braking system and he couldn't continue the descent.

Passing a knot while on rappel is a difficult, tricky maneuver that needs to be practiced many times in controlled conditions before attempting it on a serious rappel in the field. It requires the use of prusik knots or one of several types of mechanical rope ascending devices. Prusiks and the devices are designed to attach to the climbing rope and support a person without sliding down. They allow a climber to stay in place on a rope or, in pairs, to ascend the rope by releasing one ascender at a time, sliding it up the rope, and relocking it to the rope. Then the process is repeated with the other one. When done over and over, it allows ascent of a vertical rope. To pass a knot when rappelling, the devices are needed to allow the person to attach himself to the rope using the prusiks or ascending devices. When his weight is off of the rappelling equipment, he can detach it from the rope where it is stuck above the knot and reattach it to the rope below the knot. Then using a series of carefully practiced moves, he unweights each of the prusik knots or ascenders in turn so that they can be detached from the rope (it's impossible to remove them when the climber's weight is suspended by them) and transfers his weight back to the rappel device. He then continues his descent down the rope.

Unfortunately, Brock had no prusik knots or ascenders with him. Frigid water trickled relentlessly down onto him, chilling him and sapping his strength. Sellers grew increasingly concerned and quickly assembled two loops from which Brock could tie prusik knots and tied them to the end of the rope about 280 feet below Brock. However, Brock didn't have the strength to pull the heavy, wet rope up to him so that he could get the loops. He was chilled, his efforts to pass the knot through his equipment had exhausted him, and his hands were numb. In addition, he was only wearing a seat harness, so one hand was constantly occupied in holding himself upright on the rope. A chest harness would have made the process much easier by holding him upright, but he wasn't wearing one.

Sellers, desperate at this point, grabbed the 165-foot rope which was at the bottom of the drop and some climbing gear, and raced down the canyon to the bottom of the detour route. He hoped to get above Brock somehow to be able to drop down to him or somehow lower him. By pushing the limits of climbing safety he was able to get even with Brock, but could find no possible way to get above him. As it was, Sellers said later, "I got a little farther up than I should have." The detour had worked with a rope when rappelling down last year, but was impossible to climb without a safety belay and better equipment. Dispirited, he climbed back down the difficult route, jury-rigging rappels in two spots that he had somehow managed to climb in minutes in his adrenaline rush earlier.

He arrived back at the base of the pour-off at about noon and wracked his brain to come up with a way to help Brock. He could find no way to get above Brock. Even if he was somehow able to prusik all the way up the rope to underneath Brock with the cold water trickling down on him, he didn't see how he could help Brock from that position. He finally yelled up at Brock that he was going to race to the Basin to get a helicopter and help. Brock replied very simply, "Okay." Sellers changed to his hiking boots, strapped the rope to his shoulders, jammed some nuts in a pocket, guzzled as much water as he could drink, and trotted down the canyon.

Sellers knew that he had an ordeal ahead. He had to climb east out of Cattail Canyon through cliffs, thick vegetation, and loose scree. He had to cross at least one deep canyon before he could finally descend into the Basin. He had done a somewhat similar route before on his 1977 trip and it had taken 12 hours. He was with two other men then, all burdened by backpacks stuffed with camping gear, water, and food. This time he was traveling light, pushed along by fear and adrenaline. Maybe he could make it by 4:00 P.M., four hours away.

He ran when possible, he pulled himself up cliffs, and he fought sliding scree. His pants were torn my thorny brush and cacti as he scrambled about 1,200 feet to the top of a ridge above the canyon. He looked back and could see Brock just hanging there, helpless. Brock had a wife; he was going to have a baby. Panic nipped at Sellers' heels.

He raced pell-mell down into the next canyon, the bottom lying 700 feet below. Cuts opened on his hands, arms, and legs from hitting cacti and grabbing brush to control his steep descent. He puffed and panted. Thirst gnawed at him, but there was no water in the canyon bottom. He pushed his body onward and climbed back out of that canyon to the top of the next ridge to the east, thinking that it would be the rim of the Basin. It wasn't. It was the rim of another canyon, although not as deep as the last.

He plunged downward into the canyon, grateful to find a trickle of water in the bottom. He dunked his head in a pool to cool off and drank as much as possible. He wolfed down some of the cashews he'd stuffed in his pocket earlier, took another drink, and began another ascent to the next ridge to the east. Surely it had to be the Basin rim.

As he neared the top he thought that he heard Brock calling his name. He stopped and yelled back, but it was impossible to have heard Brock's voice. His fevered imagination was working overtime. When he summited the ridge, relief flooded him. The Basin was spread out below, the lodge and Basin ranger station visible more than 1,000 feet below. Much of the rim was cliff, so he carefully picked out a scree slope and did a rapid, controlled slide to the bottom. When he hit the tiny creek at the bottom, he drank heavily again even while worrying about the horse and foot traffic upstream and the possible contamination with microbes. But he had to have water.

He climbed a few hundred feet out of the creek at the bottom of the Basin. He soon hit the Laguna Meadow Trail. Even though the trail was almost flat there, Sellers had to push his exhausted body to cover the remaining half mile at even a fast walk. He had no idea what time it was.

He pushed on the ranger station door, but it was locked and closed. Through the window he could see a clock with a time showing of 1:50 P.M. He had crossed some of the roughest terrain in the entire park in less than two hours, an incredible feat. He went over to the store, tripped, and fell on the floor and asked for a helicopter and water. His clothes were torn to shreds and he was bleeding from multiple cuts and scrapes. The woman behind the counter was shocked, but got a ranger on the phone for him and brought him some food and water.

"The woman at the store thought I was nuts," Sellers said later.

Chisos District Ranger Bob Andrew quickly responded and took Sellers over to the ranger station to determine the exact location of his climbing partner and get more details.

Andrew rapidly organized a search and rescue operation. He was skeptical of Sellers' report of a 435-foot pour-off in Cattail Canyon, but he did know that it was extremely difficult country in which it was easy to get into trouble. Andrew called Ranger George Howarth and asked him to come up from Panther Junction as soon as possible. He arrived at about 2:30 P.M. Howarth was an expert climber and probably more familiar with the Cattail Canyon area than anyone else in the park. Sellers and Howarth tried to determine the exact location of Brock in Cattail Canyon and the place that Sellers had used to exit Cattail Canyon. The USGS topo maps of that area are incomplete and inaccurate. As best they could tell, they concluded that Brock was somewhere in the middle section of the canyon.

While Sellers and Howarth talked, Andrew called the Chisos remuda and organized wranglers and pack horses to carry climbing, camping, and rescue gear to as close to Brock as was possible. He called other park personnel to get rescue teams organized. Sellers tried to rest and eat while the rangers and their equipment were getting organized.

At the time, Ranger Vidal Davila and his wife were walking their dog at Panther Junction on his day off. "A ranger drove up to me quickly and asked me to help with a rescue," Davila said. "It was life or death the ranger said. I jumped in the truck, leaving my wife, and went straight to my house to get minimal gear. When I got to the ranger station, George Howarth was there with John Sellers all geared up to go. Sellers was all scratched up. At the time I didn't think it (the rescue) would take long. I was wrong. We headed out ten minutes later."

At around 3:30 P.M. the two teams headed out. Rangers Bob Andrew, Dee Renee Ericks, Susan Roe, and Steven Minter headed up the trail with the horses and wranglers to Laguna Meadow. Outfitter and experienced climber Mark Mills soon caught up to them on the trail. Andrew and Howarth thought that the best way to get heavy ropes and equipment down to Brock was by following Cattail Canyon down from above, similar to what Sellers and Brock had done the day before.

A smaller party made up of Howarth, Davila, and Sellers headed out to attempt a very fast trip straight up over the nearly sheer face of Ward Mountain, similar to what Sellers had done earlier that afternoon. However, they planned to drop into the bottom of Cattail Canyon upstream of the drop from which Brock was hanging, rather than below where Sellers had climbed from earlier. They went very light, with a rope and minimal climbing, survival, and first aid gear to speed their travel. The plan was for them to get to Brock first if possible, pull him up the cliff or lower him down if he hadn't already managed to do that himself, render first aid, and keep him alive until the larger party could arrive with more equipment by following the long route down the canyon from above.

The park dispatcher called the park's helicopter contractor in Odessa to see about getting a helicopter to aid in the search and rescue operation, but it was already too late in the day. The shortest day of the year was only a few days away and sunset was coming soon. By the time the helicopter arrived, along with extra fuel brought in by truck, it would be too dark to operate.

Meanwhile, George Howarth's team made steady progress up the rim of the Basin toward Cattail Canyon. The country they entered was remote and virtually unknown. At the hearing about 10 days after the operation, Howarth said about the rangers who were setting up the rescue plan, "Several of us were familiar with the lower sections of the canyon, and upper sections, but due to the extreme involvement of trying to get into that middle section, I had never been there, and I don't think anybody else in the park had been into that section before." It was truly unknown, wild territory as Sellers could attest. It was a blank spot on the map.

When Howarth, Sellers, and Davila made it to the top of Ward Mountain, only 15 to 20 minutes of daylight remained. Regardless, they carried on with great difficulty in the fading light, crossing probably the same two canyons that Sellers had crossed earlier that afternoon, but farther upstream. The two smaller canyons are side canyons that feed into Cattail Canyon downstream of the huge pour-off where Brock was hanging. Like the main canyon, much of their walls are sheer rock and difficult to traverse.

"Catclaw tore into our clothes and hands," Davila said later. "There was lots of loose rock. It was a really rough few miles. I'm glad I was young and in good shape."

By the time the party reached the rim above the main part of Cattail Canyon, it was pitch dark and they had a risky descent of as much as 1,000 feet in front of them to get to the canyon bottom. They could vaguely see a route down, but were afraid of hitting the top of a cliff in the darkness when they weren't roped in. Howarth finally decided to take the risk and descend into what seemed like a black abyss.

"With our headlamps we could only see about fifteen feet ahead," Howarth said. "Maybe it was good that we couldn't see what we were getting into. Things that you would do in daytime and not think much about got very different at night. It was a bit daunting. We were lucky we didn't get stopped by cliffs. I kept telling the other guys, 'don't do anything stupid, don't rush.'"

With great care they worked their way down a steep talus slope to the bottom, arriving sometime around 7:30 p.m. They had gotten lucky and had found one of the few spots where it was possible to descend into the canyon without ropes.

A radio conversation made right before the descent confirmed that the other larger party had reached the upper end of Cattail Canyon near Laguna Meadow. The wranglers had unloaded the gear and headed back down to the Basin. The two strongest members of that team, Mark Mills and Dee Renee Ericks, were starting down the canyon.

In the darkness, Sellers was unable to tell for sure whether they were above or below Brock although he felt strongly that they were in the right place above Brock. Nothing was recognizable in the dim, limited light of their headlamps.

"If we were too far above him, we couldn't make it because we would have to leave fixed ropes in place or otherwise we couldn't get out," George Howarth said later in the park hearing. "If we got below, there was no way we could go up a 400-foot pour-off."

Howarth's party slowly worked their way downstream in the inky darkness. A radio transmission indicated that Mills and Ericks had made it to and down the first pour-off up stream. Finally, as Howarth was beginning to have serious doubts, Sellers recognized a short drop that he and Brock had descended the day before. With care the three made it down the drop without using the rope. They continued downward, soon reaching a second drop, this time of about 100 feet. It required use of their only rope, so they had to leave it attached to be able to escape the canyon later. Davila stayed at the top of the drop. Howarth and Sellers continued downward. They down-climbed a 50-foot drop without using a rope and then reached yet another drop.

Sellers knew that this was the last drop above Brock and was desperate to get back to him. However, Howarth was very concerned at this point. "At that point I was deciding to terminate our movement because of our people being strung out and it was getting to the point where it was extremely dangerous for us to continue on," he said at the park hearing later. "After talking to Sellers, he felt that the area (where) he and I stopped was one pour-off above where he thought Brock was. He said he had climbed down this pour-off before and it was probably a 5.6 climb, with water on it, meaning that it is a fairly difficult climb, especially in the dark and without any protection. He felt that he could climb it and wanted to climb down to get to the point where he could be above Brock and since he had done it before, we discussed it and he wanted to do it so I said 'O.K. I'll stay at this point. If you want to, go ahead and climb down, we probably shouldn't go any farther, because somebody could get hurt,' but he wanted to do this and I didn't think I could stop him from going on."

Despite Howarth's grave concerns, Sellers safely made the difficult climb down in the dark, feeling blindly for hand and footholds that lay at the limits of his reach. He raced down the last few yards in the narrow slot of the canyon above the giant pour-off. The rope still hung taut from the anchoring tree to and over the lip of the massive cliff. He yelled frantically for Brock and thought he heard a reply. He yelled again and again, but there was nothing but silence once the echoes of his voice crashing back and forth on the canyon walls faded away. He carefully moved to the brink and tugged on the rope. He couldn't move it a bit, indicating that Brock was still hanging down below.

Sellers headed back to Howarth, climbing safely back up to Howarth without a rope. Climbing up is usually considerably easier and safer than down-climbing. Sellers relayed his findings to Howarth. Together they went back up the canyon to where Davila was waiting, using the rope fixed there to belay each other up to Davila. They built a small fire, ate some food, and rested while deciding on a course of action.

"We had to make some decisions...because we were extremely exhausted at that point and I was afraid somebody was going to get hurt," George Howarth said later. "To get safely to where Brock was, we would have to take down our safety line, which meant we were committed—we couldn't come out, and if the other team couldn't come get us and weather got bad, we were in just as bad shape as Brock was."

Much to Sellers chagrin, Howarth decided to wait until the support team coming down the canyon arrived with more gear to allow them to safely reach Brock. He just couldn't be sure that Sellers had actually heard Brock and didn't want to put his party at further risk without a more positive sign.

During the park hearing afterward Bob Andrew was quizzed about whether Sellers had actually heard Brock. Andrew responded "No, he wanted to hear it. What he is saying is, 'I wanted badly to hear something.'"

Sellers later wrote, "George's decision crushed me. The helpless frustration of sitting while Bryan hung just a few hundred yards distant was taking its toll (on me). George was reassuring and helped keep everything in perspective. Under normal circumstances I could think of no finer men to share an experience such as this in the wilderness. As it was, it was the nearest thing to hell I could imagine."

Meanwhile, far up the canyon Mark Mills and Dee Renee Ericks continued their descent down the first pour-off and along the narrow treacherous edges of many pools in the dark. When they reached the second pour-off, they had difficulty finding a good anchor point for a rope. They finally set up a multiple point anchoring system, but they weren't confident in it and had used up most of their gear setting it up. The descent would get them wet with water trickling over the drop, plus they knew that there were many more drops ahead for which they would not have the necessary equipment. At about 10:30 P.M., they discussed the problem with Howarth and Andrew over their radio and decided to retreat and rejoin the main party near Laguna Meadow for the night. When they got back to the bottom of the first drop, they could not find their earlier descent route in the dark, so they ended up spending a cold night there.

When Howarth got the word from Mills and Ericks that they could not make it down the canyon that night he changed the plan. "We were real concerned about firewood because we were getting wet in rappelling, and as soon as we stopped and sat there in the wind, we were all starting to get slightly hypothermic," he said later.

Sellers climbed back down the pour-offs to Brock. Brock had left about 100 feet of rope coiled at the top of the big drop for some reason. Sellers cut it free and brought it back up to the last pour-off which he had been climbing and descending without protection. Howarth, Davila, and Sellers used it to get down the pour-off and then proceeded to the lip of the big cliff from which Brock was hanging.

"Even George (Howarth) didn't believe that there was such a big drop until we actually got back in there," Sellers said years later.

They called down to Brock and pulled on the rope, but got no response.

They were cold and wet, so they gathered wood and built a fire just above the drop, both to warm and dry themselves and to allow them to see. Their lamps were getting dim after heavy use. After warming up a bit, they returned to the brink of the drop and attempted to lift Brock.

"We all pulled on the rope with as much as we could pull, three of us at once, and it never moved an inch," Howarth said later. Brock's weight, the heavy wet rope, and the extreme friction where the rope was pulled tight across the rock made lifting Brock impossible. More equipment and people would be necessary to raise Brock.

The team settled in for the night at about 2:30 A.M. With no camping gear, the group spent a miserable, sleepless night trying to stay warm and get comfortable on the hard, rocky ground. The temperature dropped to about freezing and a steady, cold breeze flowed down canyon all night. Several times they were forced to scrounge more wood from the limited supply in the narrow, flood-scoured canyon bottom.

"There wasn't much wood," Howarth said. "We found a log that was maybe 16 inches in diameter and ten feet long. Somehow we got it burning. That log saved us. It slowly burned down its length over the course of the night. We sat as close as we could. We'd be cooking on one side, freezing on the other. We couldn't sleep, but it kept us from getting hypothermia. My canteen had some ice in it the next morning."

"We sat all night in the canyon with the wind coming down," Davila said. "I only had a jacket and a long-sleeved shirt. It was a long, cold night."

At dawn Howarth turned the radio on and reestablished communication with the other team and headquarters. At about 8:15 A.M. the helicopter arrived at the park. Rangers Jim Bellamy and Tom Alex climbed aboard and flew to the scene to do a reconnaissance trip. Upon hearing the helicopter, Howarth's team threw leaves on their fire to create smoke to help guide the helicopter to them. Soon they saw the chopper hundreds of feet below, snaking it's way up the canyon toward them. The pilot, Gary Carter, expertly flew his craft up the narrow canyon, its rotors coming perilously close to the canyon walls.

Alex described the flight up the deep canyon to the rangers and Bryan Brock.

"This will sound cliché, but it was more awesome than I ever imagined," Alex said. "I was looking out at the rotors and the nearby canyon walls and thinking, 'this would not be a good time for wind problems.'"

The chopper crew hovered even with Brock about 170 feet down the cliff below Howarth's party. The news was bad. In the hearing later

Bellamy said "The body was hanging at an angle to the vertical of about 30 to 40 degrees, with its head back and its arms back. The arms were extended backwards from the body and it appeared lifeless."

Sellers heard the radio conversation between Bellamy and Howarth. "He (Bellamy) confirmed what we had feared for over 8 hours," Sellers later wrote. "It was the news I expected, but still my heart sank."

The chopper flew higher and hovered above Howarth's party while they worked out a plan to retrieve Brock's body. Howarth thought that it would be virtually impossible to carry Brock out overland, so they set up a plan to extract the body using a long line and the helicopter. Carter flew the chopper up to the landing point where the other team was waiting near Laguna Meadow. They loaded two packs of rescue gear, rope, and some food and shuttled it back to Howarth's group, lowering it by a 150-foot rope.

Howarth's party set up a pulley system to gain a six-to-one mechanical advantage. Despite the mechanical advantage, with great effort they were only able to pull the rope with Brock's body up about 15 to 18 feet in more than an hour. Even re-rigging the pulley system to give them more advantage didn't help. Howarth finally radioed in that he needed two more people to help. They sat down and waited.

The pilot flew in and located a marginal landing site high above them. He then flew off and picked up climber Mark Mills and Ranger John Morlock and flew them to the iffy landing site. Like Mills and Howarth, Morlock was an experienced climber.

The landing site was a jagged ridge top that was too narrow to really land the chopper. "It was a hot landing," Morlock said. "The pilot put one skid down while still under full power, and we hopped out onto the narrow ridge."

After Morlock and Mills climbed down to the top of the large pour-off, they began pulling again using the six-to-one pulley system. They also added rollers on the lip to help reduce the friction. After they pulled the rope up about 15 feet, they had to lock off the rope with ascender devices to keep it from slipping back down the cliff. They then had to reset the pulley system, essentially a block and tackle system. It was tedious, but it worked. After about 30 minutes of steady hauling and resetting the pulley system, the rope hung up and wouldn't budge.

Sellers went to the edge to see what the problem was.

He later wrote "I should have sent someone else. I climbed out to the edge, following the rope over the lip. There, just a few feet from me was Bryan. Bryan appeared to have been dead for some time...His eyes were open, his complexion ashen. His body was stiff, stone-cold, and completely water soaked. Even his hair was wet."

"Sellers was pretty emotional when Brock's body was pulled up into view," Davila said. "I wasn't surprised. It was his climbing buddy."

Sellers stumbled back from the lip, as Howarth tried to comfort him. He walked up the canyon a bit to regroup while the others waited. After a bit he rejoined the party. Brock's body was jammed under a large chockstone just below the lip. John Morlock, who hadn't done the hike yesterday or spent the cold night out was the strongest, so he rigged up another rope.

"I rappelled out over the chockstone at the top," Morlock said. "I had to pull Brock and all that rope and rigging away from the wall while they pulled from above. We had to do it three or four times. Made about a foot with each try." It was exhausting work. "They're pulling him up which tended to pull him into the cliff while I was trying to pull him out." With great effort Morlock and the four men above finally pulled Brock the rest of the way up the cliff. Morlock followed Brock's body up.

Although it seemed pointless, they checked for a pulse and found none. They cut the ropes off Brock, but left the harness and rappelling gear attached to study later. Howarth and Sellers examined Brock's rappelling system, but didn't really understand it. Howarth said later, "How it worked I couldn't explain. It did not look like a normal system for rappelling down a long distance."

The men prepared Brock's body to be air-lifted out. The helicopter moved into position above and lowered a 200-foot rope to the waiting men. Later, Howarth said, "That was a tricky situation. It wasn't just as easy as throwing a rope down because there were overhanging trees, rocks, and the rotor blades were floating in between the canyon walls. That was a difficult maneuver to make."

In the later hearing, Ranger Jim Bellamy, who was in the helicopter managing the lift, described the operation from above. Because the helicopter wasn't equipped with a quick-release long-line system, they rigged a system with the seat belt clasp that would allow them to immediately drop the load in an emergency. The pilot, Gary Carter, and the other men had to constantly watch the rotors because of the very close proximity to the canyon walls. A light wind was blowing, making keeping the craft stable even more difficult.

"That pilot was exceptional," Howarth said. "He was very good, but not reckless."

"They (Howarth's team) did hook up the long line and we lifted the victim up," Bellamy said at the hearing. "He did start to become entangled in some overhanging small trees, but passed right on through them without getting hung up at all. The helicopter lifted him from that position and carried him down canyon to the Oak Springs Road area where we met Ranger Susan Roe. The helicopter pilot landed the victim alongside the road and we put him in a body bag."

Bryan Brock was out of the canyon, although not in the way everyone wished.

Howarth, Sellers, and the others gathered up the gear and began the long climb up to the landing spot.

"It was a pretty exposed route to climb out of the canyon to the helicopter landing site," Morlock said.

The men arrived at about the same time as the chopper. It hot-landed again, hovering with just one skid barely touching the ground, while two of the men with some of the gear hastily piled aboard. It took another trip to get the rest of the men and gear down to the parking lot in the Basin. A small crowd awaited them. Family members of Brock had been notified and were on their way to Alpine where Brock's body was being taken.

After answering many questions of the rangers, Sellers finally went to a room that the park had reserved for him at the lodge. He showered and spent a little time by himself before going to a pay phone and telling his family the bad news. His family made arrangements to come to the park. Sellers ate dinner at the lodge and then called Mark Mosier, a friend who had been on the 1983 trip to Cattail Canyon. He asked if

Mosier could come to the park and help retrieve all the gear left at the bottom of the huge pour-off. Mosier agreed to come right away. Finally Sellers went to bed, spending a restless night with little sleep, thoughts of the last two days' events racing around in his head.

The next day Sellers made difficult calls to Bryan Brock's parents and wife. His father and friend Mark Mosier arrived at the park at around noon. Mosier, Sellers' wife's brother Del, and a fit man he met in the lodge restaurant that morning headed out that afternoon to retrieve the 100 pounds of gear left at the bottom of the falls. Although Sellers wanted to go, the park and his family wouldn't let him. It was a long, hard, treacherous slog in and out, but the three emerged the next morning, tired but with gear in hand. The physical part of the ordeal was over, but it would take a long time for the mental scars of everyone involved to heal.

The park held a hearing on the incident on December 27. The Board of Inquiry concluded that Bryan Brock's death was accidental and was due to either asphyxia or hypothermia. An autopsy was not performed, so it was impossible to determine the cause with certainty. "The fatality was a direct result of an inexperienced climber attempting a solo move without properly rigged equipment or protection," stated the report.

It also stated that "the rescue plan and team response was appropriate…The actions of both teams were professional and responsive. In fact, several members of the rescue party partly endangered their own lives in order to reach the victim."

In 2009 the 50-year-old Sellers is a pastor of a church and a mission director for an organization that helps people in Nicaragua. He has been going to Big Bend every year since 1977 and has been to many places that few if any other people have been.

In conversation, he comes back to his friend's decision to rappel down the big pour-off instead of going down the detour route as they had agreed the night before. One hard lesson that he took from the experience "is to stick with the plan that you agree on unless circumstances force a change. If Bryan had come around the detour around the pour-off, he'd be alive today."

PETER BASTIEN

On June 3, 2004, Ranger Aaron Scott noted a white Ford Taurus parked at the Mule Ears overlook at Big Bend National Park. He wasn't too concerned as the lot is a popular trailhead for hikes into the desert surrounding the craggy, twin volcanic peaks of Mule Ears. It's less popular in the heat of June, but still used occasionally. After he noted that the car was still there three days later on June 6, park rangers began to get concerned. Temperatures had reached 104 degrees in nearby Castolon in the intervening days.

The next day, June 7, Ranger Brian Sikes made a hasty search to the Mule Ears Spring area via horseback, but found no sign of any people, footprints, or other evidence. The Mule Ears Trail travels through broken desert country past Trap and Mule Ears springs, over a low divide just north of Mule Ears Peaks, and down into the massive, dry drainage of Smoky Creek. Sparse desert plants dot the tortured volcanic landscape. Rocky basalt peaks and ridges rise above narrow canyons and gullies that carve up the desert floor. Someone could be hidden within a few yards of the trail and not be seen.

On June 8, Ranger Laura Van Inwagen began investigating the car while Ranger Sikes retrieved the vehicle and took it to the impound yard at Panther Junction. He searched the car and found items that belonged to someone named Peter Bastien, including a billfold with credit cards, a cell phone, and a checkbook, but no driver's license. ATM slips and store receipts were dated as late as May 30. Even though a withdrawal of $1,300 had recently been recorded, no cash was found in the wallet or car. He turned over what he had found to Van Inwagen.

She found that the car was owned by Peter Bastien, a 37-year-old resident of Dallas who had not been seen in about a week. The 1996 Taurus had recently been purchased by him. Van Inwagen found a business card with Bastien's name on it and the Dallas company EM Solutions. She called the company and found that Bastien had not been employed there since January. After explaining the situation, the company gave her his emergency contact information, which had his family's names and phone numbers. She called and left messages with Bastien's parents and sister, Margaret. The sister returned Van Inwagen's call first. She told Van Inwagen that she had not heard from him since May 17. From Margaret, Van Inwagen learned that Bastien and his girlfriend, Melissa Hern, had been arrested for possession of cocaine when they were stopped by Dallas police officers on the night of February 10. Later, the parents called Van Inwagen back and told her that they had not talked to their son in several weeks, which was unusual. They didn't know where he was. She described the situation to them and they answered her questions for the park's Lost Person Questionnaire.

Through further investigation, Van Inwagen learned that Bastien's bank account had seen no activity since May 25.

He had a court date for the drug charge on June 7 for which he had failed to appear. Both his lawyer, Kevin Ross, and a bail bond company were looking for him. When interviewed by Van Inwagen, the lawyer said that Bastien had been indicted for drug possession and was usually good about returning phone calls, but hadn't done so in a few weeks.

Van Inwagen interviewed Bastien's girlfriend, Melissa Hern. She said that she had not heard from him in about nine days, and that he had lost his $60/hour job and had spent his life savings. According to Van Inwagen's report, Hern said that she had received a phone message "to the effect of 'I love you, I have to do this, feel free to use anything in the apartment, I need to do this, I'm not going to give you any clues.'"

That afternoon, a Border Patrol helicopter flew an aerial search of the area along the trail at Mule Ears, but found nothing. Rain and lightning from afternoon thunderstorms forced the ship to end its search at about 5:15 P.M. While the aerial search was underway, Chief Ranger Mark Spier organized personnel and equipment for a full-scale search to begin the next day.

At 5:30 A.M. on June 9, the searchers met for a quick briefing before heading out. By 7:00 A.M., Rangers and search personnel John Morlock, Mark Yuhas, Joe Sirotnak, and Scott Jacobs were on the ground hiking in on the Mule Ears Trail. Ranger Kathleen Hambly rode in on a horse and proceeded all the way down the Smoky Creek Trail to the River Road. Frank Aguirre drove the River Road looking for tracks. A Texas Department of Public Safety helicopter arrived in the park and began searching at about 9:00 A.M. The heat was horrendous. The temperature at Castolon reached 104 degrees that afternoon.

"It was hot as hell every day," Yuhas said. "Thank goodness for Mule Ears Spring. We'd go by there periodically and get some shade and splash water on ourselves."

Hambly reached the River Road by a little after noon and called it quits because of the heat. She had found nothing on her long ride. By early afternoon, the search largely ended for the day, although Morlock and Yuhas went back out to look at a spot where the DPS helicopter had seen vultures congregating. Hambly checked with the village of Santa Elena across the river from Castolon, but no one there had seen any Anglos for the past few days. The four ground searchers, Morlock, Yuhas, Sirotnak, and Jacobs were released until June 11 to recover from the heat. All had drunk at least two gallons of water each during the course of the day.

A dog team was brought to the park that day. Adrian Evans and her air-scent dog headed out that evening with Ranger Aaron Scott to attempt to find and follow a scent. They stayed out overnight and resumed their search early the next morning. Spier and Ranger Don Corrick set up the next day's search, calling in even more people.

On June 10, the ground teams met again at 5:30 A.M. for a briefing and then headed out. Evans and Scott reported finding a possible scent trail that led from Mule Ears Spring to the junction with the Smoky Creek Trail. The four ground teams of two people each covered four different geographic areas that seemed most likely to contain Bastien in the Mule Ears Spring area. The DPS helicopter returned and flew over some new terrain in addition to again flying some of the areas that it had covered the day before. The heat was oppressive once again, reaching 107 degrees that afternoon.

Ranger Mary Kay Manning remembers the heat of that day well. Like most of the searchers, she was able to do only one day at a time and had to have a recovery day before going out again.

"It was just hot," she said. "We started hiking at first light and had to quit by early afternoon."

She got hopeful at one point when she saw some vultures land and then saw a fly buzz by as she approached the birds' landing spot.

"But we found nothing," she said.

By noon the dog team had arrived back at the trailhead, and the DPS helicopter departed soon thereafter. The various ground search teams trickled in that afternoon, exhausted and dehydrated. The park began distributing missing person flyers. A bloodhound team arrived in the park and prepared for the next morning.

Because the heat was so hard on the SAR (search and rescue) teams and because bloodhounds can track better with higher humidity, the next day's search operation was moved much earlier in the morning.

"It was so hot that we started at 2:30 one morning," Yuhas said. "We were using headlamps to get us out into the right area, so when daylight hit we could start looking."

On June 11, the search teams assembled at 2:30 A.M. before heading for Mule Ears. After a quick briefing at 3:45 A.M., the teams headed out into the desert. The dog teams also started out in the darkness. A slight scent trail was found at about 7:00 A.M., but it led nowhere.

The temperature began to soar the moment the sun peeked over the horizon. Rangers Morlock and Yuhas returned for another round of misery, along with many others.

"The heat and conditions were definitely affecting the rescuers," Morlock said. "After one or two days, we were having to pull people out. We weren't as effective as we could have been. That level of heat will sure teach you your level of heat tolerance. It doesn't matter how tough you are, you have to be smart, take breaks, and listen to your body."

The helicopter returned again at about 10:00 A.M. The rough terrain and problems with the radio repeater tower on Emory Peak hampered field communications. A little earlier, at 9:15 A.M., the dogs had returned to the trailhead, done for the day because of the heat. Other factors were hurting the dogs' performance.

"The dogs were from East Texas and just weren't used to this kind of terrain," Manning said. "The dogs were used to going straight through, following the scent, right through cacti and sharp rocks, and dragging their handlers along with them. Their paws got torn up."

By 1:00 P.M., the searchers gave up for the day, finished off by the heat and relentless summer sun. Other than a few cottonwoods and the occasional ledge or north-facing cliff, shade was nonexistent. The next day's search was planned out.

At 3:00 A.M. the next day, June 12, the SAR teams gathered at the Mule Ears parking lot for a quick briefing before heading out to their assigned search areas. Much effort was spent on the dogs in hopes that they could find Bastien. At 5:45 A.M., one of the dog teams picked up a scent, but the dog teams failed because of the heat and rugged terrain.

Ranger Raymond Skiles was with one of the dog teams that day. "We did everything possible to mitigate the heat by starting well before dawn," Skiles said. "The dogs did okay when it was cooler before dawn. Late that morning one dog just cratered, probably suffering heat exhaustion. We had to call for a litter and rescue the dog. It went from a search for a human to a dog rescue. The dog weighed at least 100 pounds."

The other dog wasn't in much better shape even though it was just mid-morning. In an attempt to get the two dogs re-hydrated, Ranger

Dan Leavitt hiked out with IV bags, and drips were started for the two animals. The dog teams were at least three miles from the trailhead, so getting the dogs back proved to be quite an ordeal. A wheeled litter with four rangers started out from the trailhead toward the dog team. Rather than sit there waiting for them with the sun beating down, Skiles figured out a way to start moving the sickest dog toward safety.

"We rigged a litter with sotol stalks, shirts, and straps," Skiles said. "It didn't work well. It kept coming apart and was hard to carry."

Once they met the rangers coming in with the wheeled litter, the dog was transferred to it, and the group tag-teamed carrying it back to the parking lot. They got back at about 3:30 p.m., tired and depleted. The search wound down for that day, with the last searchers leaving the field at about 5:15 p.m. Despite some active scent trails, no trace of Bastien had been found that day. Meanwhile, Chief Ranger Mark Spier conducted a conference call with Peter Bastien's family—his father, mother, sister, and uncle—in an effort to learn something that might help the SAR teams find him.

At the debriefing afterwards, the park decided to try to shuttle the dogs in via helicopter to help limit their exposure to the heat and rough terrain. However, one of the helicopters that they were considering using was at its flight limit because of the extreme heat. The hot air didn't offer enough lift for the ship's rotors, similar to being at high elevation.

June 13 was a recovery day. The dogs and searchers needed a break, and because of mechanical problems and the heat, no helicopters were available. Guy Foley made and donated booties to protect the dogs battered paws. The SAR team members met at 8:00 that night at the Mule Ears parking lot to resume the search. One of the dogs was carried in by litter, while the other rested for work the next day. The dog was able to again follow a scent trail to the junction of the Mule Ears Trail and Smoky Creek, but lack of vegetation in the large dry wash prevented further progress. Peter Bastien's uncle, Ron Sherlock, arrived in the park that night where he was briefed on the search operation. The dog team searched through the night, but finally gave up and got back to the trailhead at about 5:45 the next morning, June 14.

Ron Sherlock met park pilot Nick Herring for an over-flight of the search area in the park plane at 7:00 A.M. While Herring and Sherlock were making their flight, the dog handlers met with Spier and the rest of the searchers. The group concluded that there just wasn't enough scent remaining for it to be worthwhile for the dogs to continue. After days of extensive ground and aerial searching, the probability of success was thought to be low. The rangers decided that the active phase of the search would be ended and that a lower level, extended search period would begin.

Nick Herring brought Sherlock to Panther Junction after the flight to meet with Mark Spier and other rangers. That afternoon, Sherlock was taken out to Mule Ears to see the search area from the ground and to discuss future search plans with him. The Dallas Police Department officially added Bastien to their missing persons list and arrangements were made to get Bastien's dental records in case remains were found.

"That search was the most taxing emotionally and physically of any that we've done here in recent years," Spier said. "It was a grind. We hope not to do that again anytime soon."

"We risked a lot of people and dogs and helicopters on that search," Laura Van Inwagen said.

By the time the massive operation wound down, the ground teams had searched about 5,600 acres, the helicopters about 11,000 acres, and the park plane about 33,000 acres. Despite the enormous effort made to find him, Bastien's whereabouts remained a mystery. Rangers wondered if he was even in the park. Over the following months, park rangers continued to follow up any new leads and did additional searches in the area when reports of any evidence appeared. It was all to no avail. Time went by and the search memories slowly faded.

"His parents called once a month on Thursday afternoons to ask me about progress," Van Inwagen said.

More than nine months later, on March 23, 2005, a bit of luck came into play. Two park visitors from Britain hiking in the Mule Ears area found a canvas backpack partly buried in a dry wash. They thought they would do their part in keeping the park clean and carried it back to the trailhead with them on their hike out, planning to dispose of it as trash. By chance, a park volunteer happened to be at the trailhead, so they gave the backpack to that person as found property. The volunteer recalled the massive search for Peter Bastien in the area the previous year, and called Ranger Kathleen Hambly. The ranger talked with the British couple. Because they couldn't locate the spot on the map where they had found the backpack, they graciously agreed to hike out there again with rangers the following morning. The next day, the visitors guided Van Inwagen and Ranger Whitney Hibbard to the spot.

"They had found the backpack below the confluence where a little dry feeder wash joined a bigger wash," Hambly said.

Van Inwagen and Hibbard hunted around the area, looking for additional items. They found a human skull about 200 yards upstream from the pack in the little feeder wash. The teeth were still in the jaws and a little decayed brain matter remained in the skull. Another ten yards beyond the skull, they found more bones concealed under a shaded overhang at a small pour-off in among some big boulders. The human bones were bleached and scattered, some still within clothing. Peter Bastien had been found at last.

"It was amazing we ever found his remains," Van Inwagen said. "We would never have found those remains if those British visitors hadn't brought in the pack."

"That's how a lot of SARs (search and rescues) eventually get solved," Spier added, "when something turns up years later."

Because the location of the remains was within the massive search area, John Morlock visited the location, curious how they had missed the body.

"I think that Yuhas and I came closest to his body," Morlock said. "I was hiking up a drainage while Yuhas was going up another one nearby. I came to a fork in the drainage and looked up one fork that ended soon in a little pour-off. I could see most of it, and it didn't amount to much. There were a bunch of boulders between me and the pour-off. It was hot as hell, and I had to meet Yuhas who was getting ahead of me, so I didn't go up the little drainage. Sure enough, that's where he was and I missed him. He was dead already, but it sure would have been nice to have had some closure sooner."

Van Inwagen and Hibbard radioed in their find and asked for assistance in documenting the scene and collecting evidence.

"I took horses out to help bring the bones and evidence back with park volunteer Samantha Schroeder," Hambly said.

The park rangers and the volunteer carefully documented the scene and collected the bones and other evidence. The park sent the remains to a forensic anthropologist from the University of North Texas to confirm the victim's identity and to try, if possible, to learn a cause of death. The dental records, when compared to the jaws and teeth of the victim, confirmed that the body was that of Peter Bastien. No trauma had occurred to the parts of the skeleton that were recovered. However, because not all of the skeleton was recovered, the bones were bleached and disarticulated, and little tissue remained, it was impossible to determine a cause of death. Was it heat stroke? Was it dehydration? Was it a drug overdose? Was it snake bite or some type of trauma that didn't show up on the recovered bones? It will probably never be possible to determine what caused his death.

Peter Bastien was a very smart, successful young man. He had a bachelor's degree in electronics and computer engineering and a master's degree in computer science. He had served in the United States Navy as a lieutenant commander in a nuclear submarine in the Gulf War and elsewhere. He had worked as a software engineer for MIT's Lincoln Laboratory and for EM Solutions, a company that offers microwave communications services for military and commercial customers.

Was Bastien at a low point in his life? He was unemployed, broke, and had been indicted on a drug charge, so that would not be an unrealistic assumption after achieving so much success earlier in his life. His message to his girlfriend "I love you, I have to do this, feel free to use anything in the apartment, I need to do this, I'm not going to give you any clues" raises questions. Was he just going on a solitary hike in the desert to clear his head and the desert got the best of him? Temperatures reached 111 degrees on June 1 and 2. As is documented elsewhere in this book, the desert has claimed other victims. Text messages indicate to Van Inwagen that he planned on returning to Dallas.

"He had sent text messages to his girlfriend like 'I have to face my monster. See you soon,'" Van Inwagen said.

Van Inwagen still speculates as to what happened.

"He was a really smart kid, he had an engineering degree, he had a top-secret clearance," she said. "He was from a solid East Coast family. In Dallas he somehow got swept into the drug and prostitute scene. The women in his life used up all his money up their noses and then disappeared after Bastien disappeared at Big Bend."

"I think he was going out there to go cold turkey and kick his cocaine habit and the desert heat just got him," Van Inwagen added. "I think he just shaded up under that pour-off, one of the few places out there with any shade. We have no idea why he chose Big Bend. The backpack had some drug paraphernalia in it. We didn't find any water bottles or any camping gear. The remaining brain matter still showed cocaine metabolites."

Van Inwagen thinks that Bastien was not in a good frame of mind to deal with the horrendous heat of the Big Bend desert in summer, nor was he well equipped. Whatever his intentions were, the desert may well have taken away his choice in the matter.

"It was tragic," Mark Spier said. "One year he was sitting on top of the world, the next he's circling the drain. He went (to Big Bend) to kill his dragons, but grossly underestimated what he was getting himself into."

Peter Bastien's remains were finally recovered, but no one will ever know exactly what transpired at Mule Ears in June 2004, under the burning desert sun.

RILEY KNIGHTSTEP

On January 5, 1987, a Voyageur/Outward Bound party was paddling its canoes down the Rio Grande below Castolon in Big Bend National Park. The group was beginning a trip through the least traveled section of the river in the park between Santa Elena and Mariscal canyons. The river slowly winds for miles through desert flats with cane and tamarisk lining its sandy banks. Because it doesn't pass through any spectacular canyons, most boaters don't float that stretch of river. Some call it a "no man's land."

The Outward Bound group expected adventure on the trip, but nothing on the order of what happened. At one point, the group paddled toward the bank to pull out of the river for a break. One canoe with two girls eddied out by the Texas bank of the river.

"The two girls bumped a body (floating in the river) and a hand rolled up out of the water," Ranger Kathleen Hambly said. "They were very upset. It was a real horror story."

The two counselors, Cheryl Nelson and Billy Perkins, attempted to calm the group of boaters. They stayed at the location for almost an hour, trying to decide what to do about the body. Finally, they paddled downstream to where the River Road came close to the Black Dike primitive campsite on the Rio Grande. They hoped to find someone at the campsite or driving the road who could report their discovery to a ranger. After arriving at the campsite and beaching their boats, Nelson and Perkins walked up to the River Road.

Coincidentally, Ranger Tom Alex was driving two researchers to their campsite destination at Black Dike. At about 4:30 P.M. he saw Nelson and Perkins on the road.

"The two counselors flagged me down and told me what they had found," Alex said.

They had discovered the body of a white man wearing blue pants, socks, and shoes. The body appeared slightly battered and skin was torn off in several places. Because they were concerned about disease, they did not touch the body and left it where they found it in the river.

While traversing the River Road prior to running into the two counselors, Alex had heard radio traffic about a possible drowning in Santa Elena Canyon upstream. He assumed that this could be the victim and relayed the information obtained from the Outward Bound instructors to park headquarters via radio. He remained with the canoeing group for another 45 minutes, getting as much information about the body and its location as possible before returning to headquarters at Panther Junction.

Rangers John Morlock and Kathleen Hambly took the park's jet boat down to the river, arriving at the Santa Elena Crossing at 5:35 P.M. They launched the boat and started down the river toward the area where the Outward Bound group had found the body, about three miles downstream of the crossing. They reached the appropriate area at about 6:00 P.M. as the sun was setting below the Sierra Ponce to the southwest. Along the way, Hambly made two foot patrols on beaches on the Texas side. At about 6:15 P.M. they encountered two Mexicans. When asked if they had seen the body, they replied that they had not, although they had heard from boaters that there might be a body in the river.

The rangers continued moving slowly downstream, mostly searching the Mexican side of the river with the intention of searching the Texas side on the way back upstream. Increasing darkness was quickly making the search more difficult. They had a spotlight and flashlights, but neither were anywhere near as good as sunlight. They arrived at the Black Dike campsite at almost 8:00 P.M. without finding the body. Had it sunk to the bottom? Had it drifted farther downstream? Had they just missed it in the darkness. They didn't know.

"We found them (the Outward Bound group) sitting around a campfire," Morlock said. "They were sitting around all depressed and freaked out. Most of them just wanted to go home."

"We tried to calm them down," Hambly said. "We tried to tell the girls that they had helped someone find their loved one."

"That was one adventure they won't ever forget," Hambly said years later.

At Black Dike the rangers talked at length to instructors Nelson and Perkins and got more detailed information on the location of the body, including a sketch map drawn by Perkins. After talking to the group for about an hour, the rangers began their search back upstream in the darkness.

"It was a little spooky out looking for a body in the dark," Hambly said. "We were using a spotlight that we kept on the boat."

The rangers slowly cruised back upstream, looking carefully as they went. When they reached the area that seemed to match the description given by the two counselors, they pulled the boat up to the shore on the Texas side.

"We got out of the boat and started walking up and down the bank where they had told us," Morlock said. "I went maybe ten or fifteen steps and found him right away."

The victim was submerged and not visible from their boat in the river. Their foot search with lights along the Texas bank succeeded at 8:50 P.M. In the dark they had somehow located the body about 2.9 river miles below Santa Elena Crossing and what turned out to be 18 miles below the scene of the accident that led to the drowning.

"I've never seen anyone float that far with the ten drowning victims that I've had to pull out over the course of my career," Morlock said.

The rangers took photos of the body both before and after removing it from the river. Morlock then did a cursory medical exam. The skin was red, possibly from sunburn and the stomach was bloated. The only significant injury that they observed was a depressed area on the upper right cheek that might have come from a blow of some sort. The victim no longer had a shirt, but still wore jeans, shoes, and socks. They found no identification in the pockets, only a set of keys. They placed the victim in a body bag and loaded in onto the boat. They returned to the Santa Elena Crossing where they were met by Rangers Garrett Moynihan and Jim Unruh, Nova Knightstep, and several other people. They moved the body from the boat to a truck at a little after 11:00 P.M.

Ranger Jim Unruh performed another cursory examination of the body, finding no obvious evidence of any cause of death other than drowning and/or some sort of trauma. Eighteen-year-old Nova Knightstep viewed the body and positively identified it as being her father, Riley Knightstep. Her family's river trip had come to a terrible end.

Two days before on January 3, 1987, Riley C. Knightstep, his 18-year-old daughter, Nova, and her 20-year-old boyfriend, Les Montgomery, had driven to the park from their homes in Odessa, Texas to do an overnight river trip through Santa Elena Canyon. The canyon's sheer limestone walls rise as much as 1,500 feet above the narrow river chasm, making the trip very dramatic. While not highly experienced with whitewater rafting, Riley Knightstep had floated through the canyon several times before. Nova Knightstep and Montgomery had not floated the river before and had little experience.

"My dad loved adventure," Nova wrote years later. "He loved everything outdoors. My dad loved being on the Rio Grande. He hunted, fished, camped, rafted, canoed, and skied. He owned his own business, a machine shop, and was always very busy, but he always took the time to take trips with friends and family."

Generally, the Rio Grande is a relatively placid river with whitewater only in a few places, such as the Rock Slide in the middle of Santa Elena Canyon. It lies in a deep, narrow part of the canyon where a huge rockfall creates a hazardous maze of boulders and fast water that requires careful scouting before attempting to float through it. In very high water even experts will sometimes portage around it. While most of the river may seem peaceful and unthreatening, there are still deep holes, strong currents, and underwater hazards hidden by the muddy water. The park recommends that visitors not swim in the river and that boaters wear a life jacket at all times when on the river. While the river at the time of their trip was nowhere near flood stage, it was running a little high, meaning faster, stronger currents, deeper water, and more risk. It was significantly higher than it had been on any of Riley Knightstep's earlier trips.

Knightstep's party arrived that morning at the Panther Junction visitor center to get a permit for their river trip. Because they had not rented their boating equipment yet, they were asked to obtain their permit in Lajitas when they rented their gear. They proceeded to the Lajitas Trading Post and were given their permit and equipment by employee Clay Webb.

Webb instructed them in the use of the equipment, explained river safety rules, and warned them of the high river levels. He also recommended that they wear life jackets at all times when in the boats. According to Webb, they arrived at the Trading Post well after noon, although Montgomery and Nova Knightstep later said that it was right before lunch time. Webb said that they put into the river later than planned. According to Webb, Riley Knightstep wanted to camp near the Rockslide, but he warned Knightstep that they wouldn't be able to get that far before dark. He told them that it would be best to camp at the entrance of the canyon. Sunset was only a little after 6:00 that time of year.

The boating party got their raft loaded with their food and camping gear and pushed off into the river sometime around noon.

"The river was really running," Montgomery said later. "We floated for maybe two to three hours to the canyon."

Nova Knightstep wrote later that because the relatively high water made the river so smooth, her father thought that life jackets were unnecessary until they got well into the canyon.

With the high water they made very good time, even though they didn't paddle much. Although Webb had recommended that they camp for the night at the entrance, they chose to enter the canyon and continue downstream because there was still daylight.

"We had just entered the canyon Santa Elena," Montgomery wrote afterwards in his witness statement, "when we came upon some white-water which had filled the raft with water. We all got out on a bank and emptied the raft. After this we came upon some whirling water (an eddy) that took the raft into a spinning action. We worked our way out of this (which was on the Mexico side) and were heading for a wall on the Texas side. R. C. (Knightstep) had told us to lean toward the wall or the raft would flip. We leaned to the wall and the next thing I know we are all in the water."

His daughter Nova remembered her father telling them to use their paddles to push themselves away from the wall. She recalls their trying to do that without success as the boat rode up the canyon wall and dumped them in the river.

"He (Riley Knightstep) was in the front of the raft and he almost hit his head on the wall when we hit," Montgomery said years later about the accident. "Instinctively, he ducked away from the wall. I think that shifted his weight enough to maybe cause the boat to flip."

None of the three were wearing life jackets. The river's current pulled all of them under water, but all knew how to swim and struggled back to the surface.

"I'd heard all my life how powerful water was," Montgomery said, "but I'd never experienced it until then. I went under and fought and fought, but couldn't surface. I think Nova was under me at one point. Finally when I relaxed I popped to the surface."

Montgomery was in front, floating on the Texas side of the river, Nova Knightstep was in the middle, and her father was trailing behind on the Mexico side. The raft and their equipment were floating along behind them. Montgomery managed to grab some rocks and pull himself out onto the Texas bank. As he climbed out, he saw Nova and her father moving downstream.

"I felt so helpless," he wrote in his statement, "there was nothing for me to do. Both appeared to be struggling somewhat. I thought I heard both gasping for air. When I finally got to my feet both had disappeared. All I could see was the raft which was about 250 yards downstream."

Many years later, Montgomery remembered his last glimpse of Riley Knightstep. "The last time I saw him he was floating on his back with his hands behind his head and a smile on his face," he said. "I thought everything was going to be fine."

Nova Knightstep and her father continued downstream out of sight of Montgomery. Her father was behind her and seemed to be doing fine.

"I kept digging my heels into the sand and rock trying to slow my descent down the river because I knew that my dad and the raft were still behind me," Nova Knightstep wrote years later. "The raft had passed my dad, but he didn't attempt to reach for it. He was floating on his back with his arms folded across his chest. The raft hit me directly in the back and I was able to grab hold of the ropes that were fastened to it. At this point my dad floated on past me with a huge grin on his face, he seemed to be enjoying the fact that this had added to the adventure. He ended up way ahead of me and I eventually lost sight of him, all the while I was trying to get on top of the raft, which was upside down. This proved to be impossible. I decided to just hang on and let the current take me wherever."

"The raft finally became hung up on a huge rock (the raft was on one side of the rock and the drinks that were tied to the raft on the other)," she wrote. "I was able to make my way to a small sand bar on the Mexico side. It was evening by this time; the sun was going down. I realized that I had made it out of the river about 30 feet from the Rock Slide. My dad had spoken of the Rock Slide on numerous occasions and had told me that it was the most dangerous portion in Santa Elena Canyon because of all the rocks in the river and the current was really swift in this area."

Neither Montgomery nor Nova Knightstep had any idea where Nova's father was, nor did they have any idea of each other's situation. Both were trapped on separate beaches, cut off by sheer canyon walls from the outside world and each other.

"The water was pretty cool," Montgomery said. "I took off my clothes and wrung them out to help them dry faster."

Nova was more to the point. "The weather was cool, but the water was very cold!" she wrote later.

It was late; no one else came through the canyon that day. Temperatures that night fell into the low to mid 30s. Neither stranded boater had much water or food, but they survived the night, shivering with the cold and getting little sleep.

"There was no shelter or foliage of any sort on this sandbar," Nova wrote years later, "just wet sand. I curled up and went to sleep. I was cold and exhausted and I knew that no one would be coming down the river behind me."

"I wasn't worried about Les too much since I'd seen him make it out of the river," Nova wrote later. "I really didn't worry about my dad because I knew that he was a strong swimmer and that he was accustomed to this sort of thing. I seriously thought we'd find him waiting for us at the ranger station and him joking with us about the whole thing."

"It was pretty darn cold," Ranger Hambly said. "I was impressed with the two young people's survival skills."

"I slept right by the water the first night," Montgomery said. "The river was noisy, like a busy street in Odessa. It was really dark, without many stars."

The river water, while cold, was probably quite a bit warmer than the air temperature. It may have warmed the air some right near the river, helping the two survive the night.

The next day, the air warmed to a high of 69 degrees, but little sun penetrated the deep canyon, especially in winter. Montgomery got some sun in the morning; Nova Knightstep got none. The day dragged by for the two boaters; no one else floated through. Montgomery did the best he could.

"There had been some rain recently that was caught in some bowls in the rock," he said, "so I drank that. I ate some prickly pear, using my car keys to clean off the spines. It tasted like what aloe vera smells like. Not too good."

As the day wore on, he paced up and down the small bank area that he was trapped on, cut off by the canyon walls. He considered getting back in the river and trying to swim to find the others or even out of the canyon. Wisely he decided not to try because he didn't know what lay ahead. He didn't know it, but the canyon stretched ahead of him for seven miles and passed through a difficult obstacle, the Rock Slide. It would be a difficult and risky undertaking even with a life jacket in much warmer weather.

As the day slipped by and no one floated through, Montgomery made an effort to make his second night more bearable.

"I found a cut-out spot in the rock and gathered some Bermuda grass to make a bed in it for the second night," he said. "I slept a little better the second night."

Unlike her boyfriend, Nova had no vegetation on her sandbar and no means of creating shelter. Because she never got any sun, her clothes never dried out.

"There was no shelter, no way to get warm," Nova wrote years later.

"When I awoke that morning I was hoping that the raft was still hung up on the rock," Nova wrote later. "I had planned to try and flip it over and float farther down the river. The raft was gone. The rope broke from the rock and the force of the current. There was no sunshine at this location. I had been in constant shade during the day. I could see the sunlight on the Rock Slide and I debated over and over again if I wanted to get back in the river and try to make it that 30 feet to the Rockslide so that I could dry out and maybe find something to eat. I decided that it was too risky. I yelled for Les and my dad the entire day, but never heard a response. I never saw a plane, raft, or canoe. By evening I was seeing things, I thought I saw people scaling the canyon walls and waving to me. When darkness came and there had been no rescue, I curled up again and went to sleep."

As painful as it was, Nova's decision not to try to swim for the Rock Slide was a wise one. The obstacle course of boulders and swift currents would be dangerous to enter without a boat or life jacket. As the sun sank on the second night, the temperature fell again, leading to a second cold, hungry, miserable night trapped in the deep, narrow canyon.

"I shivered the entire time I was on that sandbar," Nova wrote later. "I quickly lost the feeling in my feet. I kept my hands clasped together and between my legs every time I'd lie down. I had nothing to eat. I had thought about drinking water from the river where it was flowing over the rocks, but I really didn't want to put something cold inside my already freezing body. I did without, which is probably why I was hallucinating about people scaling the canyon walls."

At 8:30 the morning of January 5, Les Montgomery's parents phoned the park to inquire about their son's overdue rafting party. According to the parents, the trip was supposed to end the previous day, but the group had not checked in with them. The park dispatcher got vehicle information from the parents and offered to call back when he learned more.

The dispatcher checked the files for the Knightstep's rafting permit, but couldn't find it. He called the park maintenance personnel at Castolon and the Lajitas Trading Post and asked them to look for the two Knightstep vehicles. One vehicle was found at the Santa Elena Canyon boat take-out and the other was at Lajitas, indicating that the party had not returned from their trip. While locating the vehicles, he learned that Big Bend River Tours had a trip planned for that morning for Santa Elena Canyon.

Upon getting the information from the dispatch office, Ranger Jim Bellamy called Big Bend River Tours and talked to the guide. Because the commercial trip was imminent, it would be able to search the canyon before the park could put together a search and rescue team.

"On Monday I sat by the river," Montgomery said, "hoping someone would come by."

The morning wasn't much different for Nova Knightstep.

"The next morning was pretty much the same routine," Nova wrote years later. "I watched the river, yelled for Les and my dad. Eventually started seeing people scaling the canyon walls again. Still no sight of a plane, a raft, or a canoe. At some point I remember lying back down, facing the Mexican canyon wall, saying a few prayers, and basically giving up."

As it turned out, a commercial tour with its guide and two guests led by Outback Expeditions entered the canyon first that day, with the Big Bend River Tours trip following close behind. Larry Humphreys, the guide for Outback, and his party found a thoroughly miserable Les Montgomery on the bank a short distance into the canyon.

"Finally at about noon," Montgomery said, "I saw a raft group upstream that had stopped at a bar. I yelled at them and the outfitter came down to me."

The Outback Expeditions group loaded him onto their raft, gave him food and water, and continued downstream. About an hour later they found Nova Knightstep on the beach above the Rock Slide where boaters usually stop to scout the rapid.

"When we got down to the Rock Slide," Montgomery said, "I saw the raft caught on some rocks and then looked over and saw Nova lying motionless on the sand. I yelled and she popped up. I was greatly relieved."

"I was awakened by my name being called," Nova wrote year later. "I remember opening my eyes and then re-closing them because I thought I was just hearing things. This went on several times. I finally sat up and stared in disbelief that someone was actually there. I really thought I was just seeing things. I finally realized that Les was in one of the two rafts and was calling my name. The raft that Les was in worked its way to the sandbar where I was located and the other went to the Rock Slide area. I tried to stand up but my feet and legs were really cold and extremely shaky. The outfitter made me sit back down. Since I hadn't eaten anything he made me eat some peanut butter while he heated up some Gatorade for me. I couldn't eat peanut butter for years after this and I still cannot stand Gatorade!"

The Outback Expeditions and Big Bend River Tours groups then carried the two victims out of the canyon, retrieving the Knightstep's raft and some other gear that they found along the way. They searched carefully for Riley Knightstep as they went, but found no sign of him. They reached the canyon exit at about 3:45 P.M. where they used a radio to call for assistance and to explain what they had found. Ranger Jim Unruh left a class he was attending and drove down from Panther Junction to the boat take-out to interview the two young people.

"When we got out of the canyon I seriously expected to find my father waiting for us at the ranger station and saying something like 'What took you so long to get here, I've been here for hours!'" Nova wrote years later. "When I learned that he was still missing I just figured that he was farther down the river somewhere and was making his way back somehow. One of the rangers (Jim Unruh) took us back to his house so that we could clean up, wash our clothes, and eat something. We then went back to the ranger station to fill out accident reports and write out, in our words, what had happened."

"The people on the rafts and the ranger couldn't have been nicer," Montgomery said later. Montgomery's father and brother-in-law arrived at the Castolon ranger station later that day. That night, Rangers Morlock and Hambly found Riley Knightstep's body after getting the report from the Outward Bound group. The Rio Grande had carried him about 18 miles down river from where the raft flipped and dumped the three into the water.

"I was informed that my dad had been found and that he was deceased," Nova wrote years later. "I remember the rangers asking Les and his brother-in-law if they would mind identifying my father. I remember throwing a fit and telling them that I wanted to identify him. They did not believe that it was a good idea, but I insisted that I would not believe them unless I went and saw for myself. I was escorted by one of the rangers down to the river where they had brought him in. I remember that I walked barefoot, my shoes were still wet and I had no feeling in my feet, all the way to the vehicle where my dad's body was located. I identified him and walked back. The rangers really wanted me to go to the Alpine hospital to have my feet checked out, but I refused. We stayed the night and then traveled back to Odessa the next morning."

Because there was absolutely no evidence of foul play, Brewster County Justice of the Peace declared the cause of death to be asphyxia from drowning. Contributing causes may have been trauma to the head and prior medical conditions.

At the park's Board of Inquiry on January 8, Big Bend Superintendent Jim Carrico presided. The hearing was held to determine the cause of the fatality on the river, to analyze the search operation to determine if improvements could be made for future search and rescue operations, and to find if anything could be done by the park to prevent such tragedies from happening again.

They found that Clay Webb, the person who had issued the permit and rented the rafting party their equipment had properly instructed them on safety rules, told them about the high water levels, and had encouraged them to wear their life vests. Board member Marty Ott asked Webb if they acted like the idea of wearing a life jacket was silly or was something that they didn't want to do.

"No," Webb replied. "I've had groups like that before that say this will make a good cushion to sit on or something. No, they were real attentive and everything. Especially the two younger folks because I guess it was one of their first river trips."

As always in a unwitnessed death like this, the park makes sure that no foul play was involved. According to Webb there was absolutely no tension or friction between the members of the party when he got them set up with the permit and raft. Because Ranger Jim Unruh had interviewed both Nova Knightstep and Les Montgomery right after they were rescued from the canyon, he was questioned by the board as to whether he had any evidence that the death was anything other than an accidental drowning. Unruh had largely interviewed the two survivors separately.

"No. Not at all," Unruh said when asked if he thought there was any possibility of foul play. "There was virtually no conflicting testimony between the two, especially considering that they had gone through quite a harrowing experience, even without the death of Nova Knightstep's father. Additionally, based on my experience of having interviewed I suppose several dozen individuals over the last 13 years in the Park Service, it is my professional opinion that these people were speaking from the heart and that they were as sincere as could be."

The board then questioned Unruh about the boaters' actions on the river leading up to the accident. Unruh explained about the boat getting partly filled with water and then being emptied by the group. He then explained about their being caught in the eddy.

"I think it may have caught them off guard, confused them a little bit," Unruh said. "They weren't on the river where they wanted to be. So they made some moves to negotiate out of that eddy and to move river left. That is to say toward Texas. Now at this point, and for reasons I was not able to determine and for reasons they were not able to express, they laid their paddles down and elected to simply drift. Actually, not only were the paddles not in the water but the paddles were not even in hand. They put the paddles on the floor of the raft. The raft encountered another eddy on river left which would be closest to Texas. Sometime after that, the eddy must have taken them close to I guess what's known locally as a wall shot, where the river current moves swiftly against a vertical rock wall. In this case, this was against the Texas side. Riley Knightstep must have realized that there was some degree of hazard imminent because he said something to the group about leaning into the wall or high-siding."

Unruh then explained the accident. "The boat was thrown against the wall and then flipped over to the right. It's a phenomenon that's happened several times this year at that location according to Larry Humphreys. Once the boat flipped, instead of three rafters, there were three swimmers. None of them had life jackets on at any time during this episode that I described. So three people are in the water. The water must have thrashed them around a bit. Nova Knightstep said that she took water in and that she had swallowed water and taken water into the lungs which she later coughed up. Leslie Montgomery said that he was under water for what seemed like a very, very long time and thought he felt another person beneath him. How he knew, I don't know, but he seemed to think it was Nova Knightstep. After what seemed like an awfully long time to them, everyone surfaced. Nova and Leslie did see, I guess everyone pretty much saw each other according to Nova and Leslie. They also saw Riley Knightstep. They said everyone appeared to be struggling at that point. I think at this point, everyone was just taking care of their own welfare."

Eventually, Montgomery and Nova Knightstep managed to pull themselves out of the river, but Riley Knightstep disappeared at some point after the initial spill from the raft. The two survivors were stranded for almost two days, not even knowing if the others were alive.

The board determined that several factors were involved in the death.

"I think lack of skill and lack of experience was one of the two primary contributing factors," Unruh said. "I think the other contributing factor that is equally important in this incident was that they failed to recognize a hazard. They seemed to recognize that white water and standing waves and hydraulics were hazards and this was something to reckon with. But I don't think they recognized what we call the wall shot. Water flowing swiftly against and into the wall of the Canyon.

Those are the two things I think are most important. Perhaps right up there with those two contributing factors was the fact that they were not wearing their life jackets. Although I think that if they had recognized the hazard of the wall shot, I think they would have worn their personal flotation devices. I never got the feeling that the reason they were not wearing them was because they were trying to defy the regulations or felt they weren't needed. I have the impression from that that if the hazard had been recognized, they would have put them on."

There was some speculation that Riley Knightstep's medical conditions may have contributed. He had high blood pressure and a mild case of diabetes. Being dropped unexpectedly in cold water could possibly have resulted in a stroke, heart attack, or some other condition. The board also speculated about the head injury. If Knightstep was knocked unconscious it could have led to his drowning. Or the injury could have happened after he had drowned. An autopsy was not done, so it was impossible to make any determination.

"Does anyone want to offer any suggestions on what we might have done to prevent the accident or to keep an accident like this from occurring in the future?" Jim Carrico asked.

"I don't have any suggestions that I think would be valid in this case," Marty Ott said. " I think that we have to remember that we have not had a drowning on the river—a raft related drowning on the river—for over five years. I think that the measures that we took were proper. A permit was issued also. The equipment was good and adequate. Due to lack of experience and lack of judgment, knowledge of the river and hydraulics, the accident occurred. I cannot think of anything we could do to prevent such accidents from happening again."

Les Montgomery and Nova Knightstep married three years later, in 1990. They went on with their lives, going to college, getting engineering and teaching jobs, and having two children, but the memories haven't faded much.

Nova still wonders about the cause of her father's death. "My father was also a diabetic and had high blood pressure," she wrote years later. "The rangers assumed that he drowned. There was no autopsy performed. I have a hard time grasping the idea that he just drowned. I believe that there was more to it than this, especially since I had seen him grinning from ear to ear when he floated past me in the river."

"Whenever I hear friends of mine are going down there to run the river, I caution them," Montgomery said years later, "'Get a guide,' I tell them if they haven't gone before. Be careful."

Nova agreed. "If you are rafting, canoeing, or fishing on the river, please wear your life jackets!" she wrote. "Please make sure that someone outside of the park is aware of how long you intend on being on the water or in the area!"

"I have a belief that my father managed to get out of the water at some point," Nova wrote. "I have no solid proof, though. When my father's body was found, the only thing he was wearing was his jeans. I believe that he got out on that first night, then the next day took all of the extra stuff off of himself and got back in the water to find a way out."

"I sometimes wonder if he (Riley Knightstep) got out of the river okay and then got back in to look for us," Montgomery said. "Nobody will ever know."

Riley Knightstep had planned a fun trip down the Rio Grande through Santa Elena Canyon, one of the most spectacular canyons anywhere in the country. He loved the river. His daughter, Nova, and her boyfriend, Les Montgomery, had never been to the canyon before. Unfortunately, their first trip ended in tragedy. Nova lost a father, her mother lost her husband, and many others lost a friend. Les Montgomery finally returned to Big Bend National Park in 2007 on a motorcycle trip, but his wife, Nova, has never returned.

"In the past, I had said that I would never go back but I believe that I could go back to the Big Bend area, my dad loved it there," Nova wrote years later. "I just don't believe that I would want to go rafting again."

"People always tell me that they hate that he died in such a tragic way," Nova wrote. "I usually say, 'Why? He died doing something he loved. How many people can actually do that?'"

DOUGLAS PAPPAS

Douglas Pappas worked as an attorney for Mintz & Gold in Manhattan, New York City, and lived in the suburb of Hartsdale a short distance north of the city. He was 42 years old, healthy, about 5 feet 10 inches tall, and 220 pounds.

Pappas was a nationally known authority on the business and economics of baseball. He was considered an expert on everything from the value of baseball franchises to the labor costs of the players. He ardently opposed taxpayer subsidies used to build stadiums and other facilities for professional sports. He maintained a website with many of his articles about the sport posted there.

In May of 2004, spring was rolling into New York. Green was painting the trees, flowers were blooming, and the days were cool and pleasant. It was a different world from Big Bend National Park where the air was dry, the desert was brown, and temperatures were pushing well over 100 degrees.

On May 14, Pappas flew out of Kennedy Airport to begin a vacation out west. He rented a red Ford Thunderbird convertible from Hertz at McCarran International Airport in his destination city of Las Vegas at about 1:00 early the next morning after arriving. As he drove across the West he sent emails to friends and family relating his travels. He generally worked his way southeast. On May 15, he visited the Grand Canyon. The next day, he traveled onward through Flagstaff and Phoenix to Tucson. On May 17, he drove to Alpine, Texas, a little north of Big Bend National Park. In his last message sent from Alpine, he wrote that he would be spending the next two days at Big Bend.

He entered the park the next morning at about 9:00. He explored the park that day and spent the night at the Chisos Mountains Lodge in the Basin in the center of the park. His vacation was about to take a turn for the worse.

The next day, May 19, park visitor Rex Box of Houston made a report at about 4:15 P.M. at the Panther Junction visitor center that indicated that all might not be well with Pappas. He had had an experience earlier that day in the Grapevine Hills that concerned him.

The Grapevine Hills are a low range of igneous hills a few miles north of the Chisos Mountains. The low hills lie in the Chihuahuan Desert and get very hot in summer. Most hikers avoid them after about mid-April. The rocky hills are noted for their interesting rock formations, particularly a large balanced rock that creates an arch at the end of the one-mile Grapevine Hills Trail. The hike is relatively short and easy with an elevation gain of 240 feet, mostly toward the end of the trail. It follows a dry, sandy wash up the bottom of a canyon into the hills to the south of the parking lot.

At Panther Junction, Rex Box reported that he arrived at the Grapevine Hills Trailhead at about 11:00 A.M. that day. He noticed another vehicle in the parking lot, a red Ford Thunderbird convertible. Box headed up the trail toward the balanced rock. About 30 minutes into the hike he ran into another hiker returning from the balanced rock at the end of the trail. Box thought the hiker looked overheated and poorly prepared for even a short hike. He was wearing shorts, a polo-style shirt, and athletic shoes. He wasn't wearing a hat and didn't seem to be carrying any water. The hiker, later identified as Douglas Pappas, said to Box, "good thing you have a stick, it's a hard climb, but a great view."

Box continued his hike out to the arch. He stayed out at the arch for awhile and returned to his car at the trailhead at about 4:00 p.m. By then temperatures were probably around 100 degrees in the shade and the sun had been beating down mercilessly for hours. Box was surprised to see the red Thunderbird still sitting in the parking lot. The obvious conclusion was that it had to be the car of the man he had met earlier on the trail, but no one was in sight. He thought that the other hiker would have left long ago because he looked stressed by the heat. Not surprisingly at that time of year, he had seen no other cars or hikers since he had arrived at 11:00 a.m. Box promptly drove to Panther Junction to express his concerns. He gave a description of the hiker and vehicle to rangers at park headquarters, and they moved into action.

Ranger Kathleen Hambly promptly drove the dirt road out to the Grapevine Hills Trailhead and found the car. She called in the plate number and found that the vehicle was owned by Hertz and had been rented to Douglas Pappas. Calls were made to his work and home numbers in an attempt to learn Pappas' plans and whereabouts. By then it was late in the day on the East Coast and the rangers were unable to reach anyone, so they left messages.

Hambly blocked the parking lot with her vehicle to prevent visitors from disturbing tracks around the car. She found a fresh footprint by the driver's side door of the Thunderbird that she thought was probably Pappas'. She then began to hike south up the Grapevine Hills Trail from the parking lot, calling out his name, scanning the surrounding hills with binoculars, and watching for footprints on the trail. She periodically found tracks that matched the one that she had found by the car. The tracks went both northbound and southbound, which would match Box's report that he had met the hiker coming back north toward his car from the balanced rock at the end of the trail.

She hiked about a quarter mile up the trail before turning around. The tracks that she thought were Pappas' did not return to the trailhead, however. Rather than exiting the sandy wash to the left on the trail, the tracks continued down the wash on a route parallel to the trail. The trail quickly reaches the parking lot. The wash crosses the dirt road just east of the parking lot and continues north out into desert flats above Tornillo Creek.

Hambly set up a search and rescue command post at Grapevine Hills and requested the assistance of park rangers, a Border Patrol tracker, and a Border Patrol helicopter to expand the search. Seven park rangers and one Border Patrol agent quickly responded to her call. The Border Patrol tracker and two park rangers began to follow the tracks that continued down the wash into the desert north of the road and trailhead. A pair of rangers began a search on the east side of the Grapevine Hills Trail to its end while another did the same on the west side. Hambly and Ranger Steve McAllister covered the tracks in the wash bottom to protect them and then drove the Grapevine Hills Road using their lights, siren, and horn in hopes of attracting Pappas. They also talked to campers at primitive campsite Grapevine Hills 5, apprising them of the situation and asking them to call the rangers if they saw Pappas.

The team following the footprints north of the trailhead managed to follow them for about a mile before darkness made progress impossible. They noted the coordinates of the last track that they found with a GPS unit to hasten finding the starting point the next morning. The other rangers reached the end of the Grapevine Hills Trail without finding anything but footprints. The search ended for the night at about 11:00 P.M. with no success in finding Pappas.

After darkness fell, Ranger Michael Ryan parked on the prominent highway bridge over the large dry wash of Tornillo Creek a few miles to the northeast of the search area. He stayed out there for the night with his overhead lights flashing in hopes of attracting the lost hiker.

At 6:00 the morning of May 20, the search team met for a quick briefing before heading out to Grapevine Hills to continue the hunt. Ranger Kathleen Hambly again served as incident commander. By 7:00 A.M. the search teams moved into position. Two rangers headed out to the last footprint found the night before to continue following the tracks. Other teams acted to contain the boundaries of the search area. The Border Patrol helicopter flown by pilot Clay Tippet arrived at the park to pick up Ranger John Morlock to act as spotter and medic.

"We were ready to give first aid if he was still alive," Morlock said.

The helicopter team began aerial reconnaissance at about 8:40 A.M. Unless Pappas was tucked tightly under a ledge or some brush, he should be easy to spot from the air. The desert there has only sparse vegetation with cacti, creosote shrubs, hardy clumps of desert grasses, and other widely scattered bits of vegetation. Sure enough, the search was short-lived. At about 9:00 A.M., pilot Tippet in the chopper spotted somebody lying on the ground and landed nearby.

"In open desert country like that a person really stands out from the air. It's hard to hide," Morlock said. "The pilot did a quick half circle and immediately landed. It was so quick that I didn't even see the body until we'd landed."

The two rangers following Pappas' tracks had gotten close by now and they quickly joined Morlock and Tippet by the helicopter. The men hustled to Pappas to render aid. Unfortunately, they were too late. Morlock radioed in that the person was dead and that a driver's license found in his wallet identified him as Douglas Pappas. He also reported that the tread on the shoes matched the tracks that the ground searchers has been following.

Pappas was lying on a north-facing slope of a small east-west-running dry wash about 40 feet below the ridgeline. His tracks indicated that he had wandered about three or four miles in a zigzagging path across the desert to the northeast of the trailhead. He finally collapsed about a mile north-northeast of the east end of the Grapevine Hills Road. The area is open desert with very little shade.

Investigating ranger Laura Van Inwagen hiked to the site at about 10:30 A.M. Morlock turned over Pappas's wallet to her. She photographed the scene and examined the body. The skin color of Pappas' arms and face varied from deep red to purple, probably from extreme sunburn. His body was hot to the touch. The only apparent injuries were scrapes on his right elbow and right knee. She didn't find any unknown footprints in the surrounding area, nor any evidence of any type of crime. Van Inwagen found car keys, three rechargeable AA batteries, a broken camera battery cover, a Palm PDA, two pens, and a small spiral notebook that appeared to be a record of photos taken and events on his trip in Pappas' pockets. On the ground uphill from Pappas' body, she found an Olympus digital camera that was covered in dust and had some surface damage. Its batteries and battery cover were missing.

Once she finished her investigation, she cleared Pappas' body for removal. A mule was brought in by Ranger Marcos Paredes to carry the body to the Grapevine Hills Road. The body was taken by truck from there to Panther Junction where Van Inwagen met the Brewster County coroner at about 1:30 P.M. The coroner took possession of the body, and it was transported to a funeral home in Alpine. Pappas' rental car was driven to Panther Junction by one of the rangers. All of Pappas' possessions in the vehicle were removed and logged in as evidence or held as property to be sent to his next of kin. The car was later picked up by a towing company under the direction of Hertz.

The next day, May 21, Chief Ranger Mark Spier was able to locate Pappas' mother, Carolyn Pappas, in New York. The difficult task of notifying her of her son's death fell to him.

In succeeding days the park completed its investigation of the death of Douglas Pappas. Rangers Van Inwagen and Dispatcher Meghan Hicks attempted to read Pappas' handwriting in the small notebook found in his pocket. The writing was difficult to read, but the last three pages appeared to be a record of his hike at Grapevine Hills. The first entry said "9:40 Start trail to balanced rock." The next entry said "find it and head back." The next said "think I'll be back by 10?," followed by "11: 0 - no car, go path, mtn nearby." Much is very cryptic. "keep walking 11:20 checked SE and W of." The next only said "I've." The next was a little more clear "should be back at 11:45 no problem." After that the entries get less and less understandable, although desperation shows through. Several said "Call for help." Another said "rest in shade." The last entry simply said "12:40 - ."

Rex Box, the hiker who met Pappas sometime around 11:30 A.M. on the trail, reported that Pappas made comments that seemed coherent. Little did Box realize that his brief conversation with Pappas would be the last words spoken by Pappas to another human being. Box did notice that Pappas seemed overheated and ill-prepared. From where Box met Pappas, it was less than a mile on a smooth trail with a gentle downgrade to the trailhead. The heat must have been severely affecting Pappas, maybe even more than Box realized. Although Pappas' notes are cryptic, it would seem that he might not have been thinking clearly even as soon as when he met Box. His last notebook entry was little more than an hour after meeting Box on the trail. The speed with which Pappas seemed to have declined physically is frightening. By then he had only hiked between one and two miles.

The high temperatures on May 19, 2004, reached 96 degrees Fahrenheit at Panther Junction and 104 degrees Fahrenheit at Castolon in the shade. The Grapevine Hills area where Pappas died lies about midway between the two places in elevation. Temperatures there very likely reached 100 degrees Fahrenheit that afternoon. When he did his hike in the mid and late morning, the temperatures would not have been that high yet, but the sun would have been beating down mercilessly. For someone coming from cool spring weather in New York, the heat may have proved too much to bear. In addition, it's possible that Pappas was particularly sensitive to heat.

"How did he get dehydrated that fast?" Van Inwagen asked. "We wondered if he was already dehydrated when he started, or if he had some underlying physical condition that contributed. That was a classic case of someone who didn't go far and died really fast. It shows how fast something can happen."

"He was a little overweight which probably didn't help," Morlock said. "Maybe he was also out of shape. His rapid decline was the remarkable thing about this case."

In an attempt to learn more about what happened to Pappas, Van Inwagen put batteries into his camera and turned it on. Only three photos were on the card. The three photos were recorded with the date and time when they were taken. She corrected the times (recorded in Eastern Standard Time) to the local time zone (Central Standard Time). The times seemed to correlate fairly well with the report by hiker Rex Box. The locations of the photos was determined by several of the park staff and Van Inwagen. The first photo, taken at 10:31 A.M. (CT), showed the area along the upper end of the Grapevine Hills Trail. The second was taken at 10:37 A.M. (CT) at the balanced rock at the end of the trail. The third was taken at 12:09 P.M. in the area where his northernmost tracks were found about 1.5 miles from the trailhead.

From the photos, it appears that Pappas was seriously lost in the desert only about 40 minutes after meeting Rex Box on the trail. His thinking must not have been clear by the time he met Box or shortly thereafter. When Pappas continued following the trail down the wash after leaving Box, he missed where the trail climbs a short distance to the left and out of the wash to the nearby parking lot. It's not difficult to miss the spot, but within about 100 yards, the wash crosses the Grapevine Hills Road. For anyone thinking clearly, the road is impossible to miss. The trailhead parking lot is only 50 yards away to the left on the road. However, Pappas, his body most likely now under severe stress from the heat, walked right across it and out into the empty desert to the north. He may have been suffering severe heat exhaustion or worse by then. Possibly he was already sinking into heat stroke. Mental ability fails rapidly with heat stroke. Disorientation and hallucinations are common. It surely happened at some point. The autopsy result was clear; the cause of death was hyperthermia, or heat stroke.

"It was amazing that he somehow walked across the road and missed his car," Van Inwagen said.

"The fatal error was walking right past his car," Morlock said. "You can't quite see the cars from where the wash crosses the road, but it's only ten or twenty steps up the road to where you can see the nearby parking lot. It's a shame. He was sorely missed in the baseball community."

As always after a fatality, the park studies the case to try to prevent such incidents in the future. The park makes a strong effort to warn people of the desert heat when hiking and doing other outdoor activities. Pappas' death showed the wisdom of those efforts. Although Pappas was found by helicopter, the tracks that he left were very important. The ground searchers would have found him soon even without the helicopter because of the footprints. The park report emphasized the importance of not contaminating an area with searchers' footprints when tracks are present. "Protect and photograph tracks!" was the conclusion of that part of the report. The report also concluded that GPS units were very valuable in marking the location of evidence. In this case, it allowed searchers to quickly resume their search at the location of the last footprint that they had found the day before as darkness descended.

To make it less likely that hikers would miss the spot where the Grapevine Hills Trail leaves the wash, a directional sign was placed to mark the spot. Other hikers that miss the spot easily find their vehicle when they hit the road. Whether a sign would have helped Pappas will never be known. He apparently walked across the road without seeing it, so he might have missed a sign. Regardless, the Park Service even placed a second directional sign pointing the way to the parking lot where the wash crosses the road.

The desert at Big Bend is a harsh place at any time of year, but particularly after temperatures start to really climb in April. Even a short, easy hike like the Grapevine Hills Trail in the middle of the day can threaten unprepared hikers. Pappas succumbed to the heat with frightening speed.

JUSTIN BAIZE

On Saturday, February 9, 2002, Justin Baize of Houston parked his car at the dusty trailhead along the road to Boquillas Canyon in Big Bend National Park. He donned his backpack and started walking north into the rugged, empty desert country of the Dead Horse Mountains, an extension of the higher Sierra del Carmen of Mexico across the Rio Grande to the south. Initially, the trail he followed is the combined Marufo Vega, Strawhouse Canyon, and Ore Terminal trail. It follows a broad canyon upstream that slowly narrows at it approaches the point where the Ore Terminal Trail forks off to the left. At about 1.4 miles Baize took the Marufo Vega Trail that splits off to the right. It climbs steeply up out of Strawhouse Canyon right before the canyon really narrows. The trail then crosses an uneven plateau on top of the Dead Horse Mountains and works its way northeast toward the rim of Boquillas Canyon, the route by which the Rio Grande carves its way through the

Dead Horse Mountains. The trail undulates through rough desert country, climbing in and out of dry washes. Eventually it splits, with each branch dropping way down to the Rio Grande and then reconnecting with the other near the canyon bottom. In effect, the trail makes a lollipop shape with a single trail in and a big loop at the end. Except for the river at the bottom of the loop, there's no water whatsoever on the hike. In fact, the entire Dead Horse Mountain Range is notorious for its lack of water. Only hardy desert rats brave the Marufo Vega Trail and other routes in the Dead Horse Mountains. The trail sometimes gets faint and easy to lose, especially where it crosses dry washes. It was out on the loop section of the trail that Justin Baize got into trouble.

"I was just doing an overnight hike," Baize said.

It turned out to be much more than that. At least he was well prepared for the ordeal to come with camping gear, food, and most important of all, lots of water. When he got his backcountry permit, he also filled out the solo hiker permit, a wise move as it turned out. His problems started on the first day of his trek.

"I got off the trail on the loop section before it dropped down into the canyon," Baize said. "It was faint and I just lost it. I thought I was in the middle of the loop, but I was outside the loop. So I kept getting farther away from the trail instead of hitting the other side of the loop."

Baize kept hiking, assuming he would hit the other side of the loop soon. The loop is large, nearly two miles across at some points, so it wasn't an unrealistic assumption. However, he kept hiking and didn't hit it. Possibly he missed it; it's faint in some areas, particularly in the dry washes. After awhile he realized that he must be outside the loop somewhere, but he wasn't sure where. Although it's possible to see the towering Sierra del Carmen in Mexico from many areas of the plateau upon which the trail lies, it doesn't help a lost hiker locate himself on a map very precisely.

After hunting for the trail for quite some time, Baize also started looking for a way back to the trailhead. The country is rocky and covered with lechuguilla, cacti, catclaw, and other spiny desert plants. Hiking cross-country through those mountains wears quickly on a hiker, especially one carrying a heavy backpack. By the time night fell, he was still unsure of his location, so he set up camp in an open area where he could lay out his pad and sleeping bag. It wasn't cold and the wind was calm, so he didn't bother with his tent. Although he was a little concerned, he slept pretty well that night.

The next morning, Sunday, February 10, Baize packed up his gear and started hiking again. He was still fairly confident that he could either find the trail or his way back to the trailhead. He hiked for awhile, still looking for the route.

"On Sunday after I hiked for a bit, I realized that I should stay put so that rescuers could find me," Baize said. "I found a shelter cave to camp in for the night. I didn't have to bother with my tent. I knew that people would look for me the next day. I was still okay on water."

On his solo hiker permit, Baize was scheduled to hike out on Sunday after only one night on the trail. The park's dispatch office keeps track of those permits so that a search can be initiated for a missing hiker. The park usually starts looking for people who haven't checked back in after about 24 hours. If they started looking too early, they would have too many false alerts. Often, hikes take longer than people anticipate, so getting in a few hours late is not uncommon.

The next day, Monday, Baize decided to leave his camp in the shelter cave rather than move it. Except for the fact that he was lost, it was another nice day. He saw no sign of rescuers that day, but it was a bit early to expect much action from the park staff.

"On Monday, I walked around hoping to see my way back out the trail, but stayed in range of my camp," Baize said. "I was bored, so I moved around some. I found the river far below in Boquillas Canyon. I spent another night in the same shelter cave."

Meanwhile, the rangers at park headquarters were starting to move into action. At about 5:00 on Monday afternoon, the park dispatch office called Ranger David Van Inwagen at his home to notify him that a hiker was overdue. Baize's permit said that he would return from his backpack sometime Sunday afternoon or evening.

Van Inwagen began some preliminary work. He drove down to the trailhead and found Baize's vehicle, a red Isuzu pickup. He saw no sign of Baize or his camping equipment in the truck, so he left a note asking Baize to call him if he returned to his vehicle. He then drove back home and called Chief Ranger Todd Brindle to plan a course of action. He then started organizing a search operation to begin the next morning. He called other rangers and located vehicles and the necessary equipment. At a little after 9:00 p.m., he called Baize's parents and got the information he needed to complete a missing person questionnaire. The form covers everything from the person's appearance to his shoe size and mental state. After talking to the parents, he determined that the search rated a measured response. By the time he went to bed that night, the search was set up to begin the next morning.

Van Inwagen got up early on Tuesday, February 12, and drove back down to the Marufo Vega trailhead near Rio Grande Village. At about 6:30 a.m. he discovered that Baize had still not returned. The undisturbed truck with his note was still there. Van Inwagen got the search and rescue operation underway.

By 9:45 a.m., two teams of two people each were on the trail starting a quick search of the Marufo Vega Trail. At 10:00 a.m., a team with two mules headed out to search the upper part of the trail. At 11:35 a.m., a third party of two people left the trailhead to begin searching. Another team in a truck drove the Old Ore Road looking for Baize in case he had somehow wandered that far west. A Department of Public Safety helicopter arrived at the park at about noon and picked up Ranger John Morlock as an observer. The chopper flew to the Marufo Vega area and began searching in a grid pattern.

"It's a really big country," Morlock said. "Even though it's pretty bare, it's broken up, rough, and large. People just disappear out there. People seek shade and shelter and they're hard to find."

Meanwhile, Tuesday dawned on Baize at his shelter cave. He still had some water, but he was carefully watching the dwindling supply. He was a little discouraged after not having seen any rescuers the day before.

"I decided that no one was coming," Baize said, "so I started to hike again. I saw a helicopter twice. I tried to signal it to no avail by using a cooking pan as a reflector."

In a dry desert area like Marufo Vega where there are no trees, and other tall vegetation like brush is sparse, aerial searches are often very effective. Unless a person is under a ledge or boulder, or trying to hide in some manner, aerial searches often find the subject very quickly. However, despite the aerial search and many people on the ground, Baize was not found. Days are short in mid-February, and the sun sets at about 6:40. With darkness falling fast, the day's search concluded at 7:20 P.M.

Baize knew that the helicopter was probably searching for him, but was discouraged that they hadn't seen him. The helicopter had been too far away. He had not seen anyone on foot, even in the distance.

That evening the weather began to change as a cold front rolled in. There was no precipitation, but the wind began to howl and the temperature fell rapidly.

"That night all I found was an exposed spot in the open for a camp," Baize said. He had moved his camp during the day. "It was windy and colder. It was so bad that my sleeping pad blew away in the night when I rolled off it, but it was too cold to go after it. I didn't want to get out of my sleeping bag. I had a miserable night and didn't sleep a wink. I wished I hadn't left my shelter cave. The ground was too hard to pitch my tent."

"The winds were terrible," Van Inwagen said.

With the onset of much colder weather and the strong winds, the searchers' concerns grew. Well before dawn at 6:00 A.M. on Wednesday, February 13, people signed in for the continuing search. After a brief planning meeting at 6:20, the searchers headed out again to the Marufo Vega area. The plan was similar to the day before with even more people and mules on the ground, and helicopters in the air. In addition, dog teams joined the ground searchers, and a canoe trip through Boquillas Canyon on the river was organized. Baize's parents had arrived at the park the night before, so a ranger took them down to the area so that they could see some of the aerial operations.

"We must have had 60 searchers on the ground," Van Inwagen said later. "We were already doing everything we could, but Baize's family had some good political connections, so we received quite a bit of pressure to find him. We shuttled many people in by helicopter so that they wouldn't already be tired after the long hike into the search area."

Baize slept only a little toward the end of the night. In the morning, Baize crawled out of his sleeping bag and shivered in the chill air. He was dehydrated and low on water, but not completely desperate yet. He never found his sleeping pad. He broke camp and loaded up his backpack again. He was tempted to leave his pack, because he was tired of carrying it. However, he didn't want to lose it and thought he might need some of the gear again if he wasn't found that day. "Besides, some of the equipment was expensive," Baize said, laughing.

"I climbed a low mountain and could finally see a search party about a mile away," Baize said. "I tried to signal them by waving, yelling, banging my pan, and jumping up and down, but it didn't do any good. I also saw the helicopter flying."

"I scrambled down toward them," Baize said. "It was steep and I was tempted to ditch my pack again, but I didn't. I lost sight of them as I descended, but I kept walking their direction. I was just hiking along a dry wash when one of the search dogs came up on me. It was friendly. Then several rangers came up. They asked if I was Justin and I said, 'Yes I am.' Everyone was happy, especially me. They gave me Gatorade and a sandwich. I still had water with me, but not much."

"When we found him alive," Van Inwagen said, "we were ecstatic."

Ranger David Yim offered medical treatment to Baize, but he refused it. Baize was tired and dehydrated, but not in bad shape. He didn't turn down a ride out in the helicopter, however. The pilot flew him to Panther Junction where his parents were waiting.

The helicopter returned to duty with the Department of Public Safety. The mules, dogs, and rangers walked out and the search wound down.

Justin Baize spent four nights out in the wilderness when he planned to do only one. He got lost probably because he wasn't paying enough attention to the map and trail. To give him credit, though, the trail does sometimes get faint. Running out of water or the cold weather that blew in could have killed him, but he did some smart things that kept him alive. He filled out the solo hiker permit at the visitor center. He took adequate camping gear to protect him from the weather. Once he realized he was lost, he mostly stayed put, rather than risk moving farther away from the search area along the Marufo Vega Trail and using precious water to do so. He carried plenty of water, although if he'd found a way down to the river, he could have survived on that, even with its dubious quality. He had plenty of food, much of which he wisely didn't eat. Digesting food requires water use by the body, not a good thing when it's in short supply. He kept his gear with him, rather than leaving it somewhere. If he had been caught without his sleeping bag on the night when the cold weather moved in, he could easily have died of hypothermia. Not chasing the sleeping pad that blew away was another good decision that mostly happened by default. Although he was so cold that he didn't want to get out of his sleeping bag to pursue it, it would have been a disaster if he had chased after his pad and had not been able to find his sleeping bag again in the dark.

"He had a map with him," Van Inwagen said, "but he really didn't know how to use it well. Otherwise he did really well out there. He was smart enough to conserve his energy and water."

Since his rescue, Baize has returned to the park about five times to hike again, but he tends to stay on the more developed trails now. He hasn't done the Marufo Vega Trail again.

"I'll do it again one of these days," he said.

Asked what he would do differently if he did the Marufo Vega Trail again, Baize said, "I'd take a GPS with me in the future."

"I still hike alone most of the time," Baize said. "I usually can't find friends to go and I like the solitude."

CURTIS LEWIS

The weather forecast for Saturday, January 4, 1986, was for highs of 58 to 78 degrees Fahrenheit and lows of 20 to 38 degrees, depending on the location in the park, with sunny skies and variable winds of 5-10 MPH. The mountains generally have highs that are quite a bit lower than the desert because of the higher elevation. The lows, however, are sometimes colder down in the desert along the Rio Grande because cold air often sinks to low spots. The extended forecast predicted mostly sunny for Sunday and "partly cloudy Monday through Wednesday, with a chance of light showers on Tuesday."

When 21-year-old Curtis Perry Lewis showed up on January 4 at Big Bend National Park to get his camping permit for a backpacking trip, there was nothing in the forecast that even hinted at what was to come.

The forecast for that day was accurate. The temperature reached a high of 58 degrees at the Basin where Lewis picked up his backcountry permit. Down at the river the highs reached well into the 60s.

At a later park hearing, Ranger Charles Callagan was asked what the weather was like on that day.

"It was nice—very nice," Callagan responded. "It was sunny, warm, and clear."

That would change.

Curtis Lewis had never been to Big Bend before, but set up an ambitious six-night, seven-day backpack into some remote areas of the park. He planned to do the strenuous Outer Mountain Loop with a lengthy side trip down toward Elephant Tusk Peak. The hike entails climbing 1,600 feet up out of the Basin on the Pinnacles Trail into the Chisos Mountains high country. After traversing part of the high country, the route drops down about 3,000 feet into the desert via the Juniper Canyon Trail. From there the route takes the Dodson Trail across the high desert country of the rugged foothills of the Chisos Mountains below the South Rim. The Dodson Trail has lots of ups and downs as it crosses several canyons draining south from the mountains. It ends at Blue Creek very near the Ross Maxwell Scenic Drive on the west side of the mountains. From there, the Blue Creek Trail makes a grinding ascent back into the high country of the mountains. A long descent then leads from the high country down the Laguna Meadow Trail to the Basin. The Elephant Tusk Trail, his possible side trip, leads southwest from the middle of the Dodson Trail into very remote, rugged country. It's very lightly traveled.

Lewis was a very fit young man of average height and weight. He had just passed the Marine Corps flight physical and was a straight A physics student. He could jog for hours at a time. He planned to go into flight training with the military. According to his family, he was a very organized person.

Lewis had never been to the park before, but was determined to do a challenging, lengthy hike. However, he had very little experience. He'd done some hiking around Lubbock and had camped at Brazos Bend State Park. His gear was borrowed or had been given to him.

He initially wanted to do his hike in the Mule Ears area, but was talked out of it by park rangers at Panther Junction who were concerned about his lack of experience. The trails in that part of the park are faint and often difficult to follow, and the terrain is rough and unforgiving. However, the rangers managed to convince him to do the Outer Mountain Loop, which, while rugged and remote, has more easily followed trails.

Lewis first got his backcountry permit at the Basin Ranger Station from park volunteer Alan Van Valkenburg. He was delayed for several hours because he had to take his dog to Alpine, so went back to the ranger station and altered his permit with the assistance of Ranger Charles Callagan. Callagan reviewed Lewis' permit and saw that he had not been to the park before. He tried to talk Lewis into doing a couple of two or three-day backpacks instead of one long trip, but Lewis wanted to do a strenuous, one-week backpack. He had originally planned to camp the first night at the Southeast Rim, but by the time he was ready to start in mid-afternoon there wasn't time to get there. Sunset is only a little after 6:00 that time of year and the Southeast Rim is about seven hard miles away. Callagan did convince him to change his first night's campsite to a much closer site, Pinnacles 1. Callagan checked to make sure Lewis had enough water and knew the places where he could obtain more later on the hike.

Lewis headed up the trail at about 3:00 P.M. It was a pleasant day for a hike. As far as the park knows, Lewis spent his first night out at Pinnacles 1 as planned. The next morning, Sunday, January 5, dawned clear and chilly, with lows a little above freezing. It soon warmed up into the fifties even in the mountains. It was another beautiful sunny day, great for Lewis to continue his hike down into the desert via Juniper Canyon. He probably camped in Juniper Canyon on the second night as planned. On his second morning, Monday, January 6, temperatures were probably near freezing again, but the sun soon warmed up the dry desert air. Some parts of the park reached highs in the mid-70s that day. Lewis continued onward, reaching the end of the Juniper Canyon Trail and turning west onto the Dodson Trail. That night he set up camp along Fresno Creek about 50 yards north of the Dodson Trail, blissfully unaware of the changes brewing far to the north.

The Monday, January 6, forecast for the next day, January 7, said simply, "Partly cloudy and cooler, winds NE 10-20 MPH." The forecast never hinted at a storm bearing down on the park. The Tuesday morning forecast finally predicted some significant changes, but still greatly underestimated what was about to happen. It predicted, "Becoming cloudy and colder. 40% chance of rain changing to snow in the afternoon with accumulations of 1"-2" possible at higher elevations. Winds NE 15-25 MPH." For that night the forecast said, "40% chance of snow with an additional accumulation of 2"-3" possible at higher elevations. Much colder. Winds NE 10-20 MPH."

For Lewis, the day dawned like the rest on his trip. Lows on the Dodson Trail were probably somewhere between freezing and the low 40s. Nothing would have seemed different. There was no reason not to do his long hike down toward Elephant Tusk Peak.

In the park hearing after the storm, Ranger Charles Callagan was questioned about the weather.

"This is really worth stressing," he answered. "Up until the day of the storm and the day before the storm, the weather was nice. The weather forecast had no prediction at all of any rain, or any precipitation—even the extended forecast."

When Callagan was asked how often the rangers got weather updates, he replied "Every morning at 9:00 A.M. I don't find them overly reliable."

That turned out to be an understatement. Callagan wondered if "somebody (at the National Weather Service) was just sleeping."

He went on to describe the events of January 7. "And I would stress," he said, "that day of the storm, I was at the Basin, we had the weather forecast that morning, but it was sunny and warm in the Basin. The clouds were held back by the mountains and were also held back by the South Rim. Around noon, they broke through, and within an hour it was snowing and the temperature of 42 degrees had dropped 17 degrees within a couple of hours."

Lewis encountered a small group of hikers at the junction of the Elephant Tusk and Dodson trails at about 11:00 on the morning of January 7. His original plan was to hike down the Elephant Tusk Trail to spend the night somewhere on it and then return to the Dodson Trail the next day. However, most likely he decided that it would be easier just to leave his gear set up at his camp in Fresno Creek at the

Dodson Trail. He could do a long day hike down the Elephant Tusk Trail and not have to carry all his gear down and back. He planned to return to the Dodson Trail anyway for the night of January 8. In his chance meeting with the other hikers, he told them of his altered plans. If he followed the Elephant Tusk Trail all the way to its end on the Black Gap Road and back, he would be looking at a 16-mile round trip hike through rough country. With sunset hitting at about 6:00, it was a long haul, especially since he was just getting going at 11:00 A.M. However, he was in great shape so it wasn't impossible.

So off he went, down the Elephant Tusk Trail at 11:00 A.M. with minimal gear and little extra clothing. He had no reason to worry. The forecast when he got his permit predicted fair weather. The mornings had all started chilly, but quickly warmed up. The sun was shining; it looked like another beautiful day at Big Bend. The South Rim of the Chisos Mountains towered above him to the north, blocking his view in that direction. Sometime around 2:00 P.M. that all changed.

By the time Lewis saw the storm coming, it was almost upon him. It poured over the ramparts of the Chisos Mountains above, driven by a cold northeast wind. Initially, Lewis probably saw clouds rapidly thickening over the mountains, followed soon by increasing wind. Thin veils of moisture falling from darkening clouds probably starting obscuring his view of the South Rim. The chilly wind cut through his flannel shirt and jeans. Probably, he was smart enough to turn around and start back to camp. As the temperature plummeted, the first flakes started to fall. Within a short time, the snow cloaked the desert in white—beautiful, but potentially deadly. His thin cotton clothes quickly became soaked with moisture and offered no warmth at all as the temperature plunged into the 20s. The trail probably became hard to follow as snow hid it from view and the footing grew slick and treacherous. The heavy falling snow made orientation difficult. Fear and desperation probably crept in as Lewis hiked back to his camp, moving as fast as conditions allowed.

In the park hearing after the storm, Ranger Bob Andrew talked about the weather event.

"As near as we can tell, and the way that storm came in, he was down below the South Rim, he probably never even saw it coming," he said. "He could have been two or three hours down the Elephant Tusk Trail before it really hit him. The weather forecast, up until the day of the storm and for the day that he got his permit, had indicated fair weather. So, he had no reason to expect the storm."

The storm hit the entire park. Snow fell everywhere; even the low-elevation desert by the Rio Grande received some. However, the mountains and the high desert foothills where Lewis was hiking were hardest hit. Snow fell for hours at approximately one inch per hour. By 10:00 P.M., eight inches had fallen at Panther Junction and 12 inches in the Basin. By midnight, Panther Junction, which lies in the high desert at an elevation more than 1,000 feet lower than parts of the Dodson Trail, had twelve inches on the ground. The Dodson Trail probably received a similar amount of snow.

"I was concerned when that storm came in," Ranger George Howarth said. "It came from the north, it came fast and freakish. It was serious enough that we decided to do a welfare check on the hikers that we knew were out there."

He and other park rangers planned a ground search for the next day to check on hikers in the backcountry of the Chisos Mountains. It was meant to be solely a general welfare check. Rangers would walk the trails and check hikers and campsites to make sure people were warm and dry. However, by the next morning, Wednesday January 8, the continuing severity of the weather necessitated a change in plan. Hikers and campers would be evacuated from the backcountry. Rangers headed up into the Chisos high country and found everyone known to be up there from the backcountry permits. All were escorted down out of the mountains. Snow in the high country was close to an incredible two feet deep on the level.

Ranger Gordon Ellison went to the Blue Creek area to talk to hikers coming off the Dodson and Blue Creek trails. There he met the hikers who had encountered Lewis at 11:00 A.M. the day before at the Dodson/Elephant Tusk trail junction. From them he learned of Lewis' plans, and that Lewis was probably not properly equipped or clothed for the severe weather that descended on the park.

The weather did eventually clear out that day, leaving a heavy coat of snow on the mountains and foothills, but it was very cold and Lewis was still out there somewhere.

Ranger Callagan filled out a list of all the people who were out in the backcountry Wednesday night after the storm was over and underlined Curtis Lewis's name.

"I think Bob Andrew came in that morning, and I said, 'I'm concerned about this fellow. Let's check on him,'" Callagan said at the hearing a week after the storm. "I guess that if he had been going with someone else I wouldn't have felt so strongly, but going out alone (concerned me)."

By the night of January 8, all the known hikers had been accounted for except Curtis Lewis. A plane was found in McCamey, Texas to begin an aerial search the next day. Plans were made for a ground search of the Dodson Trail.

At 8:00 A.M. on Thursday, January 9, the plane arrived at Panther Junction to begin the search. Unfortunately, low overcast and ground fog over the search area prevented any flights that morning. Ranger Gordon Ellison received a call at Castolon from George Howarth at about 11:00 A.M. requesting that he hike the west end of the Dodson Trail to its intersection with the Smokey Creek Trail to see if there was any sign that someone had hiked into the Smokey Creek area. Ellison hiked into the area from the Blue Creek/Homer Wilson Ranch trailhead at about noon, carrying a backpacking stove, enough clothes to get him through the night if necessary, and a few extra clothes for Lewis if he found him. He walked east on the Dodson Trail to its junction with the Smoky Creek Trail without seeing any sign of anyone. There was still four to six inches of snow on parts of the western end of the trail. On north facing slopes near Fresno Creek that received little sun, he sometimes trudged through knee-deep drifts. Even though the snow had melted down quite a bit, it still obscured the trail at times. Generally, he could see a depression in the snow without vegetation where the trail was, but he did lose it once and had to backtrack to find it again.

"It didn't look like anyone had hiked up the Dodson Trail since the snow fell," Ellison said at the park hearing a week later. "At that point, since I was already up on the Dodson Trail, I decided that I would hike on over to see if I could locate Lewis's camp."

The weather improved slightly by afternoon, so the plane made its first flight into the search area at about 2:00 P.M. The pilot and spotter found a tent camp at Fresno Creek in the location described by the hikers who had encountered Lewis on January 7, but saw no sign of Lewis.

"There was an aircraft in the air and they had spotted the camp, and I hiked on over, reaching the campsite (at) about 4:00 or 4:30 P.M.," Ellison said at the hearing.

The tent was still standing, although it sagged, probably because of the weight of snow that had fallen on it.

"I announced very loudly, asked if anyone was inside, and proceeded to open the tent and see if Lewis was inside," Ellison said. "I looked for items in the tent, looking for anything that would indicate a direction of travel. I also looked to see what equipment he had in the tent so we might have a better idea of what he might have taken with him, or not had with him. I didn't find any signs—any footprints or tracks that would indicate to me the direction of travel. Apparently, there had been a good deal of snow there and it had melted. It was hard to read any tracks at all."

"The contents of the tent were very wet," Ellison said. "Some articles of clothing in the tent were very wet. The sleeping bag was very wet. From looking at the tent, I couldn't tell if he had come back to the tent and had gone somewhere else and tried to hike out, or if he had gotten caught out and not made it back to the tent at all."

Ellison also found Lewis' backpack in the tent, along with quite a bit of food and even a gallon-sized glass jar half full of water. The tent had a rain fly, but Ellison didn't think it was coated or treated with waterproofing very well. "It looked kind of flimsy," he said. It didn't have a ground cloth underneath the floor to protect it, so he thought that most of the moisture soaking everything in the tent had come up through the floor.

It was getting late, and the temperatures were falling into the 40s. After reporting what he had learned by radio, Ellison hiked out by continuing east to the Juniper Canyon trailhead. At 4:30 P.M., Rangers Gary Kiramidjian and Steve Winslow drove to the trailhead to hike to Lewis' campsite to spend the night so that they could begin an early search the next morning. Ellison met them on the trail as he was walking east and briefed them on his findings. He used their vehicle to return to park headquarters.

The next day, Friday, January 10, the search expanded hugely in scope as concerns grew. Lewis' tent had been found with most of his gear and clothing. It was likely that Lewis was lost out there somewhere with little to protect him from the harsh weather.

Border Patrol trackers arrived to begin searching from the point where Lewis was last seen by the group of hikers. Rangers Kiramidjian and Winslow started early, searching the Elephant Tusk Trail by walking south from its north end at its junction with the Dodson Trail. Two other small groups left Rio Grande Village at 6:30 A.M., long before sunrise, and drove to the south Elephant Tusk Trailhead on the Black Gap Road. One group began working its way north on the trail toward rangers Kiramidjian and Winslow. The other hiked north up Fresno Creek. The trail roughly parallels Fresno Creek for its entire length, and even lies within the drainage for a mile or two.

Two other rangers hiked the sections of the Outer Mountain Loop other than the Dodson Trail. One did the Pinnacles/Juniper Canyon trail combination that Lewis did on the first part of his hike; the other did the Laguna Meadow/Blue Creek trail combination. Neither found any sign of recent travel.

Rangers John Morlock and Jim Vukonich hiked in from the Dodson trailhead in Juniper Canyon to search the area between there and Lewis's camp at Fresno Creek. They also searched the upper part of the Fresno drainage above the camp and carefully inventoried Lewis's camp. A Texas Department of Public Safety (DPS) helicopter arrived at 12:30 P.M. to ferry the Border Patrol trackers to the junction of the Dodson and Elephant Tusk trails. With George Howarth aboard as a spotter, the pilot then began an aerial search of the area, along with the same fixed-wing aircraft from McCamey that had been used the day before. At about 6:00 P.M., as the sun was sinking below the western horizon, the search was called off for the day and the searchers returned to their bases. Another helicopter was brought in late that day to assist in the next day's search.

Curtis Lewis' father, Rufus Lewis, was located and notified of the search for his son. At the hearing, Chief Ranger Marty Ott told of his experiences with the parents.

"The father felt that he should come down," Ott said, "especially after he thought about it for about eight hours, and considered the implications, and stressed that they didn't want to be in the way, but would it be okay? At that point, we said, 'Certainly, come down, and we'll try to make you as comfortable as we can and answer your questions.'"

Curtis Lewis' father and step-mother arrived the next day after the search was well under way again. Ott spent much of the day with them, answering questions and asking questions of his own to learn more about their son.

"We even went so far as to go around the River Road—they got into the search at one point. On Black Gap Road we were looking at tracks. They saw exactly where the planes were flying, they knew where the people were searching, and most important, they could see what the situation was—the very complex nature of that country, and the difficulty for the searchers and other people."

Ott learned that Lewis was a very stable kid that did well in school. He was a bit of a loner who kept mostly to himself. His solo hiking trip to Big Bend was no surprise to his parents.

After Rufus Lewis had seen the rough country and had a feel for the seriousness of the problem, he called his son's mother and suggested that she come down. She started for Big Bend the next day.

The search on that day, Saturday, January 11, resumed full tilt. Two search teams with dogs and handlers were brought in in an attempt to find a scent trail. Ranger John Morlock guided one team of bloodhounds down Fresno Creek from Lewis' camp. The other team, led by Ranger Misha Kokotovic, picked up a scent trail and followed it down the Elephant Tusk Trail almost to Elephant Tusk Peak. Then the subject began to wander, but the dogs may have been tired and were missing the scent.

The operation was becoming increasingly complex. The two helicopters involved stayed busy shuttling personnel and dogs to various locations, plus continuing the aerial search. A fuel truck was brought in to minimize ground time for the choppers. An infrared vision scope was used by one of the choppers to try to pick up a heat signature, but it was only able to find a deer. Two planes also continued to search the subject area.

"There were only three (aircraft) operating at any one time, although there were four available," Ranger Jim Bellamy said at the park hearing a week later. "There was a high bird keeping track of the two low searchers. We didn't want to have any more in the air at any one time for safety considerations."

Using a horse, Ranger Kathleen Hambly searched the Mule Ears Spring and Lower Smokey Creek areas. Ranger Jim Unruh took three Border Patrol trackers to some tracks he had found the day before, but the footprints were later determined to have been left by another hiker. Ranger Paul Nordeen walked the Dodson Trail again, while Mark Yuhas drove the backcountry roads surrounding the search area by motorcycle.

All of the effort was in vain. By dark Lewis had still not been found. By now, some of the rangers wondered privately if Lewis would be found alive. It had been four days since the storm blew through and no trace of Lewis had been found, other than his camp.

"I think that everyone retained the hope that he was alive and was working on the search with that type of orientation," Ranger Bellamy said at the hearing. "But everyone, I think, was very cognizant of the fact that there was a strong possibility that he wouldn't be alive."

On Sunday, January 12, the search resumed with an even larger contingent of searchers. One group of dogs, handlers, and rangers was airlifted to the spot on the Elephant Tusk Trail where the dogs had seemed to find a scent the day before. The second dog team led by John Morlock was helicoptered to a location near the Elephant Tusk Trail and the Fresno drainage and began to work its way down Fresno Creek. A 16-member ground team led by Ranger Mike Fleming was carried into the upper Fresno drainage about 0.25 mile above Lewis' camp. The group split into five teams of three each. Each team began a thorough search of an assigned area, trying to cover every bit of ground. Each team consisted of a park ranger, and one volunteer each from Far Flung Adventures in Terlingua and the Civil Air Patrol. The country was steep, rugged, and covered with spiny desert plants and brush making a thorough search difficult.

Morlock's dog team of bloodhounds and handlers seemed to be following a scent four or five miles down the canyon.

"The scent trail petered out when the canyon opened out into the desert," Morlock said. "It was probably the spot where Lewis was when the storm hit. I expect he turned around and started racing back to camp at that point. If the dogs were right, Lewis probably made it five miles down canyon and almost back that day."

The sky above buzzed constantly from the helicopters doing their shuttles and planes searching in a grid pattern. Two planes flew at low elevations with a pilot and a Park Service spotter aboard. A third plane flew at much higher altitude to help the lower planes stay on their search grid, provide radio communications, and prevent collisions between aircraft.

At 2:21 P.M., the massive hunt achieved its objective, although the result was not what anyone wished. The ground team of three led by Ranger Steve Alvarez found Lewis under a rock ledge about twenty feet above the bottom of the Fresno Creek drainage where he was not visible to aerial searchers. He was a little less than a mile downstream from his campsite. Mike Fleming radioed in the bad news. Lewis was dead.

"There was very little shelter down in Fresno Canyon," Morlock said. "Maybe you could get out of the wind a little, but not out of the moisture. Lewis found the best spot there was, but it wasn't very good. I was at Panther Junction when the storm rolled in. It hit with ferocity, lots of wind, almost a whiteout. On the way down the canyon with the dogs, the lead dog circled around and around at the spot in the canyon near where the body lay. After hesitating for a bit, the main dog finally followed the trail down the canyon because it had the strongest scent. It had the strongest scent because Lewis had gone down the canyon and then back up, making that scent stronger."

Ranger and medic George Howarth was immediately flown in by helicopter to examine Lewis's body and investigate and photograph the scene.

"At the time I went out there," Howarth said at the hearing afterward, "we were all aware of the possibility that he (Lewis) might be in deep hypothermia."

To warm and revive a person with severe hypothermia requires great care. Even something as simple as gently moving a person can cause fibrillation of the heart. In the field it can be difficult to re-warm a victim safely.

However, as Howarth approached the body on foot he smelled the odor of decaying flesh. Also, he saw evidence of postmortem lividity in the body when he got a closer look. In postmortem lividity the red blood cells pool in the lower parts of the body, giving the skin a purplish red appearance in those areas. It usually starts about 20 minutes to three hours after death when the heart is no longer moving the blood through the body. Lewis was wearing only a t-shirt, blue jeans, and a long-sleeved flannel shirt.

"I was sure that Mr. Lewis was not alive, but I did follow the procedures, which the next step was to look for any thoracic movement, which there was none, and then place a stethoscope on his chest and got no heartbeat whatsoever," Howarth said at the hearing. "In touching the thoracic cavity, I couldn't say for sure, I'm not an expert in it, but it felt that the muscles were so tight or dense, it felt even more that the body may have been still frozen or partially frozen, but it could have been rigor mortis involved. It felt denser to me than I have ever felt a body that was in rigor mortis."

Once it was ascertained that Lewis was dead, his body was loaded in a helicopter and flown out. Following that, the search wound down and the airlift evacuation of the ground search teams began. By 5:30 P.M. all of the searchers had been brought back to Panther Junction. The personnel were debriefed and released.

Curtis Lewis' parents asked that an autopsy not be done after learning that their son was dead.

"I can request an autopsy," Chief Ranger Marty Ott said at the hearing later, "and I would request an autopsy if there were any suspicious circumstances. In any unattended death, an autopsy has to be considered, at least."

Ott consulted with Howarth, the search team bosses, and the coroner and decided that an autopsy wasn't necessary.

"There was absolutely nothing that was suspicious in any way concerning his ultimate death," Ott said.

Four days after Lewis' body was found, a board of inquiry was convened to discuss his death, to determine if there were ways to prevent such deaths in the future, to study how the search and rescue operation was conducted, and to determine if anything could be done in future incidents to improve such operations.

The board concluded that "All evidence and testimony indicate that the death of Curtis Perry Lewis was accidental with the probable cause being hypothermia. No autopsy was performed. The fatality was attributed to the inexperience of the hiker, a solo hiking situation, a camping expedition in unfamiliar terrain, and adverse weather conditions. Neither the camping equipment, nor the clothing used by Curtis Perry Lewis were adequate for the type of weather encountered."

In general the board felt that the search operation was conducted according to plan. While there were minor problems with radio communications in rough terrain, in transporting resources to the park and into such remote country, in locating outside resources such as helicopters, and in coordinating with other government agencies, overall, the board felt that the park conducted the operation effectively.

"The thing that everyone learned about this was that people need to carry some extra clothes," George Howarth said. "It might not be enough to make you comfortable, but it might get you through if something bad happens."

In a normal snowstorm that moved in more slowly and dropped far less snow, Curtis Perry Lewis might well have survived even with his level of inexperience. In a more normal storm he probably could have gotten back to his tent and worked to keep his other clothes and sleeping bag dry. He would have had a cold, miserable night, but he would have survived to hike out the next day. However, even in the dry, usually warm desert country of Big Bend National Park, severe winter weather occasionally happens. If Lewis had carried better clothing with him on his day hike, he probably would have survived even that severe storm. However, he got wet and so cold that even he, a young, very fit, intelligent young man, was felled by the storm less than a mile from his tent.

JON CRADIT
GEARY SCHINDEL

In May 2004, two seasoned cavers, Jon Cradit of San Marcos and Geary Schindel of San Antonio, decided to try to descend Cattail Canyon in the Chisos Mountains. They were used to long trips underground, sometimes several days long. They thought Cattail might make a fun canyoneering trip. No trails enter the canyon or even come close to anything but the canyon mouth and the extreme upper headwaters. Few have ever ventured into the canyon, not even most park rangers. Rumors of towering cliffs, multiple pour-offs, slick wet rock, and treacherous talus slopes hovered over the canyon. The two cavers knew little about what equipment would be necessary to traverse its length, nor did any of the rangers to whom they talked.

"It's the great unknown," Ranger Mary Kay Manning said.

Cradit and Schindel were experienced, having done plenty of technical rope work in caves over the years. They carried the right equipment and 300 feet of rope and went prepared to stay overnight should it become necessary. If anyone could get through the canyon successfully, it should be them. They would soon learn differently.

On May 31, 2004, Chisos Basin campground hosts Clara and George Willis reported to park dispatch that two hikers were overdue. Jon Cradit and Geary Schindel had left a note at their campsite which was found by the Willises. The note said that they would be hiking up to Laguna Meadow and then down through Cattail Canyon on May 30. Because the hike was a one-way hike, the note said that they would park a white Chevrolet Tahoe at the "Window parking lot." It added that they planned to finish their hike by dark, but were equipped to spend the night if necessary. The note asked for assistance if they had not returned to their campsite by 10:00 A.M. on May 31.

The hosts found the note and called the park dispatch office at about 10:30 A.M. The dispatcher proceeded to call Ranger Kathleen Hambly. She then called Ranger Manning, who knew the missing men.

"They were supposed to meet me for dinner that night," Manning told Hambly. "but I knew it was a really hard trip, so I wasn't too concerned when they didn't show up."

She told Hambly that the two men were prepared to spend the night in the canyon and that they were experienced climbers and cavers.

Cattail Canyon tumbles down through the heart of the most rugged and inaccessible part of the Chisos Mountains. Within a few miles the canyon drops about 2,500 feet in elevation, much of it happening at multiple pour-offs that range from a few feet in height to more than 400 feet. Because the middle and lower parts of the canyon are lined with towering cliffs of rotten rhyolite, shifting talus slopes, and thick brush, it is extremely difficult to climb around the many pour-offs.

To do a one-way trip through the canyon by rappelling down the pour-offs requires taking a rope of more than double the length of the biggest drop. Climbers place an anchor with webbing or other climbing equipment around a tree or boulder, or in a crack at the top of the drop and loop their rope through the anchor webbing. They tie the two rope ends together and make sure that it reaches the bottom of the drop. They then rappel down the cliff, untie the knot, and pull the rope down after them so that it can be used again at the next drop. Cattail Canyon is notorious for having a canyon bottom scoured clean of trees, boulders, or other good anchor points. Sometimes the anchor has to be set as much as 100 feet or more back from the lip of the drop where a decent anchor can be found. Hence, if climbers have a 400-foot drop to descend and have to go back 100 feet from the edge to anchor the rope, they need a rope at least 1,000 feet long. That length of rope is brutally difficult to carry even without other climbing gear, food, water, and camping equipment. Only one person has made it successfully all the way through the canyon using ropes, and that person's partner died in the attempt, chronicled elsewhere in this book.

"They (Cradit and Schindel) had talked to Michael Ryan and me," Manning said, "but we couldn't tell them exactly how much rope they would need."

"The only good advice that I could give them since I hadn't been there," Ranger Ryan said, "was to leave a note about when to expect them back."

Cradit and Schindel would agree with that. Neither Ryan nor Manning had been able to tell them how much rope would be needed for the descent. Out of the entire park staff at that time, possibly only three people, John Morlock, Raymond Skiles, and Mark Yuhas, had any idea how much rope would be necessary for the trip. Unfortunately, Cradit and Schindel did not know to talk to them. Very few park rangers had even been in anything but the easy upper headwaters of the canyon. Ryan and Manning knew that people had made it through the canyon before, but didn't realize that almost all of those people had done it by doing very difficult, dangerous, and hard-to-find climbs around the highest pour-offs.

Because the two men had not returned by that morning, Kathleen Hambly worried that they could be trapped in the canyon or injured. She quickly put a search operation into motion. At 11:15 A.M., Ranger Brian Sikes drove up to the Oak Springs trailhead from Castolon to see if the white Chevrolet Tahoe was there. Hambly rightly thought that

that was what the two climbers meant when they said "Window parking lot" in their note. The Oak Springs trailhead lies below the Window and is the most likely ending point for someone trying to hike one-way down Cattail Canyon.

As it happened, Ranger/pilot Nick Herring was already in the air in the park's Cessna 206 doing a patrol when Hambly radioed him. He flew to Cattail Canyon and began an aerial search of the canyon. Within about ten minutes Herring spotted a man waving a space blanket from the top of a major pour-off in the canyon. He circled the location but was only able to see one person. A few minutes later, Sikes reported to Hambly that the Chevrolet Tahoe was at the Oak Springs trailhead as expected.

"Although Nick saw the one guy," Ryan said, "we still didn't know if they were okay."

Hambly began the planning for a rescue. Rangers were called up to go into Cattail Canyon. An available Department of Public Safety helicopter was found and started flying to the park.

At 2:50 P.M. the DPS helicopter arrived at Panther Junction. The ship was refueled while the pilots were briefed on the situation. About an hour later, Nick Herring boarded and the helicopter flew to Cattail Canyon, only a few minutes away by air.

They quickly arrived on the scene, and now Herring spotted two people standing at the top of the same pour-off. There was nowhere to land anywhere close to the two men, so the chopper returned to the helipad at Panther Junction to pick up a radio that had been carefully prepared to drop to Cradit and Schindel. If the two men had a radio, rescuers would be able to learn their condition and coordinate a rescue with them.

"We wrapped it in a big ensolite pad with duct tape," Ryan said.

The helicopter returned to the canyon and successfully dropped the radio to the two men. They quickly unwrapped it and reported that they had no injuries of any sort, but that they were trapped.

"They were pinned between pour-offs," Ryan said, "and it must have taken a mental toll not knowing when they would be found."

"We thought it would be a very long day," Schindel said, "so we went light. We were used to long caving days."

Schindel had no idea just how long the day would turn out to be. The men had started hiking the day before at about 7:15 A.M. and reached Laguna Meadow in good time. They climbed up out of Laguna Meadow, and soon left the trail and began their descent into Upper Cattail Canyon. After about three miles of scrambling down the canyon, they encountered the first drop that required a rappel. They descended it with no problem. They continued down canyon and rappelled down several additional drops, for all of which they had enough rope to descend with a double-rope rappel. Each time they de-rigged and pulled the rope down behind them. Once the rope is pulled down, however, there is no way to climb back up the drop. Finally, at a point where the bottom of the canyon is nothing but a narrow slot within the bigger canyon, they hit the largest pour-off in Cattail Canyon. The pour-off is an incredible abyss where climber Bryan Brock had died years before. They tossed rocks down and listened to them hitting to try to estimate the height of the cliff. They guessed about 600 feet, far higher than the amount of rope that they had. In actuality, the drop is "only" about 430 feet by one person's estimate (480 feet by another's), but it was still far too high for their ropes. They had pulled the rope down behind them two pour-offs back. The canyon walls in between rose high and vertical. The men were trapped.

Because Cradit and Schindel had left the note at their campsite following the advice of Michael Ryan, they decided that waiting for help was their best option. They could have risked trying to free climb back up the drop from which they had pulled the rope. Because they didn't have any protection, however, they wisely decided not to try. All they needed was a rope to get out. If either of them got injured trying to make the climb, a simple rescue would turn into a nightmare.

"It wasn't a desperate situation," Schindel said about their thinking at the time. "People know where we are, somebody will come looking for us. We just hoped that nobody would get hurt coming for us."

They had an uncomfortable night out with minimal camping equipment.

"We took lights, space blankets, a water pump, and other items just in case," Cradit said.

Twisted humor made up for a little of the discomfort.

"The subject came around to Jeffrey Dahmer," Schindel said. "We sat there and discussed which body part you could eat for the most nutrition and be the least crippling. Our conclusion was that your buddy's body part was best."

Because the rocks were cold and hard, they tried to sleep on top of the ropes and a duffel bag pack.

"The wind blew down the canyon all night," Cradit said. "We tucked up under some boulders to get out of the wind and stay warm. Every time I'd move, the space blanket made a racket."

The next day one of them waved his space blanket at pilot Nick Herring when he flew by, while the other tried to get a smoky fire going, so Herring saw only one of them. They could read "NPS" on the plane's wings for National Park Service, so they continued to stay put, rather than risk the dangerous climb up the pour-off.

Once Hambly received word that the men were fine, she called Geary Schindel's wife, Susan, to alleviate her worries. His wife said that she would call Lisa Cradit, Jon's wife.

Fortunately, days are long that time of year, so the DPS helicopter carried Rangers Michael Ryan and Nick Herring to the closest possible landing spot high above the canyon bottom at about 6:30 P.M. Because there was no good, flat landing spot, the pilot did a "hot landing" on a rocky knife-edge ridge. Basically the pilot just hovers, barely touching down.

"It was a little exciting," Ryan said. "We had to do a one-skid landing and just jump out."

After a difficult descent around cliffs and down slickrock and talus, the two rangers reached the canyon bottom and followed it down to the two pour-offs above the stranded climbers. They rigged the ropes that they had brought and joined the two stranded men. Because the pour-off was too big even for the ropes of the combined group, they all climbed back up the smaller pour-offs where the rangers had left their ropes hanging. From there the four retraced the steep route the rangers had descended and climbed out of the canyon to the knife-edge ridge where the helicopter had dropped the rangers earlier.

"After little to eat for 24 hours," Schindel said, "that climb out of the canyon kicked my ass."

At the ridge top, the men ate some snacks that the rangers had brought and watched the sun set. As darkness closed in, they climbed 1,000 feet down a steep, treacherous, brushy ravine to the canyon bottom downstream from the huge pour-off and another sizeable pour-off.

"Nick told us as we were descending in the dark that here was where the park turned loose the bad bears and mountain lions that it traps elsewhere in the park," Cradit said.

By the time they finally scrambled to the bottom, it was completely dark and very hazardous for further travel down the boulder-strewn canyon bottom, so they bivouacked for the night. It was another hard night, with little sleep.

First thing the next morning, Cradit, Schindel, and the two rangers resumed their hike out of the canyon. At about the same time, Ranger John Morlock and search and rescue team member Mark Yuhas began hiking up into Cattail Canyon from below. The climb from below entails a steep, treacherous cross-country climb up a lengthy scree slope to a ridge to get around some unclimbable pour-offs in the mouth of the canyon. From the ridgetop, the route requires a hazardous descent back into the canyon. Morlock and Yuhas met the party at the top of the ridge and helped Cradit and Schindel carry their gear. Both men were about worn out by the ordeal. All four rescuers and the two climbers descended back down off the ridge and hiked back to their vehicles at the trailhead. The rescue ended successfully and the operation quickly wound down. Cradit and Schindel were very happy to be found, although their travails weren't over.

"To add insult to injury, Cradit said, "on the way home our truck broke down in Marathon. It had to be towed to the dealer in Fort Stockton for repairs."

Two days later Cradit and Schindel finally got home.

"They were very gracious," Ryan said about the two men. "They were good guys."

However, even good, experienced people can sometimes get in over their head, especially in places like Cattail Canyon. The two men were experienced in technical climbing. They let their wives know where they were going and when they expected to return. They left a note for the campground hosts. They tried, but were unable to get good information on Cattail Canyon because few rangers were familiar with it. They took enough gear with them to get through spending a night out with little difficulty. Once they realized they were trapped, they stayed put until rescuers came, rather than risking a fall on an unprotected climb. They made only one mistake —pulling their rope down behind them without knowing for sure what they would encounter farther down canyon.

"The moral in this case," Morlock said, "is don't pull your rope down behind you if you don't know what lies ahead."

"That rescue triggered a three-day SAR (search and rescue) training trip through the canyon," Manning said, "so that rangers would be familiar with that area."

In what has become possibly the most notorious SAR training exercise in park history, nine rangers spent three tortuous days getting through the canyon carrying 45-pound packs and a 500-foot rope. Rain fell several times, turning every one of the endless boulder hops in the rocky canyon bottom into a slick, ankle-risking maneuver. Everyone slipped and fell at least once, but amazingly no one was hurt. Even with a 500-foot length of rope, the men still had to climb around several pour-offs because it wasn't long enough. The rain turned the normally dry pour-offs into small waterfalls, sending water cascading down onto the rangers as they rappelled down the smaller pour-offs. Some parts of the canyon bottom form a narrow slot with no escape route, raising the men's fears of flooding with the rain falling. To top off the trip, they had to force their way through thickets of poison oak that flourish in the canyon. The rangers' conclusion after the trip? They hope they never have to rescue someone who has been injured in the canyon. As was demonstrated by the extremely difficult recovery of Bryan Brock's body from Cattail Canyon in 1984, the task would verge on the impossible.

DONALD TATE
BOSTON TATE

The incident that would become possibly the worst event in the history of Big Bend National Park started slowly and gradually built to a crescendo. It began, not exactly innocuously, but quietly with nothing to warn of the tragic events to come.

The park shares a lengthy border with Mexico. Since the mid-1800s, tensions have flared along the border over everything from smuggling to Pancho Villa's raids into the United States. Over time, such incidents simmer down to a low boil. In recent years, drug and weapon smuggling and illegal immigration, with their associated violence, are the primary problems affecting the border region. Because of the vast swaths of remote desert on both sides of the Rio Grande at Big Bend and the lack of nearby cities, the park escapes many of the problems suffered by other areas along the international border. However, it is not immune. Drug shipments do pass through the park headed north, and illegal immigrants periodically brave the miles of harsh desert to enter the United States.

On June 30, 1991, park rangers and Border Patrol agents began 24-hour surveillance of a white 1978 Chevrolet Caprice with Texas plates parked in the Black Dike area along the west end of the River Road. The car had been observed at the Del Rio, Texas port of entry three days earlier. Low-clearance sedans were not commonly seen on the River Road, a rough dirt road for which the park recommends a high-clearance, four-wheel-drive vehicle. The individual to whom the vehicle was registered could not be traced. The rangers and agents suspected that it was being used by Ramiro and Juan Gallegos to smuggle drugs into the U.S. The keys had been left in the ignition and there was perishable food inside.

At some point the vehicle was moved somehow without the rangers noticing. On July 4, rangers found that it had been moved about 0.4 mile downstream to a dry arroyo where it was concealed with brush and locked. The tracks leading to its hiding place were brushed away. The rangers continued the observation until the next day when surveillance was ended and the vehicle taken to the impound yard at park headquarters. Because no one returned to the car, rangers wondered if foul play was somehow involved.

Border activity calmed down for the next two weeks as the heat of summer marched on, at least until July 19. At about 9:30 that evening, San Vicente, Mexico residents Calisto Brito Morín, Franco Sánchez, and Tito Brito came to the home of Ranger Dave Evans at Rio Grande Village.

"We were having a little dinner party when these Mexican men came to the house," Evans said.

The men told Evans and Ranger Lisa Callaway that they had found a dead body in the Rio Grande near the San Vicente river crossing. With translation help from several other park employees, the three men related the story of what they had found. They and several other men had been riding horseback on the Mexican side of the river at about 5:00 P.M. when they saw some vultures circling near the edge of the river on the American side. Curious, one of the men, Juan Brito Morín, swam across the river on his horse to see what was attracting the birds. He found a body caught in some brush in the river at the mouth of an arroyo. He swam his horse back across the river to tell the other men of his discovery. The three men who were now at Evans' house then swam their horses across the river to the American side and rode to Franco Sánchez's truck parked at the San Vicente crossing. From there they drove to Evans' home at Rio Grande Village. The other men remained where the body was found to try to retrieve it. It had rained heavily, and they were worried that the river might rise and sweep the body away.

The dinner party was over. Evans reported the men's find to other park personnel and Ranger Patty Goodwin came to Evans' residence. Evans and Goodwin got in their vehicle and followed the three Mexicans in their truck out of Rio Grande Village at about 10:30 P.M. They all arrived at the San Vicente crossing at about 11:00 P.M. While the three Mexicans were getting Dave Evans, the remaining men had used a rowboat to pull the body from the river, wrapped it in plastic, and brought it to the San Vicente crossing where they waited until Evans and Goodwin arrived.

Evans asked the men to open the plastic so that he could examine the body. The only remaining piece of clothing on the body was a blue t-shirt, and there was no identification of any sort, not surprisingly. Although the body was partially decomposed and the hair from the head and eyebrows was gone, Evans was able to determine that it was a white male. Obvious injuries were broken front teeth and a leg. The men rewrapped the body, placed it in a body bag, and carried it to the park truck.

"The man's body was a real mess," Evans said. "The fish and turtles had worked on it. The smell was awful."

At 11:15 P.M. Evans told Callaway over his radio that they did have a body at the crossing and asked her to notify the county coroner, Chet Wilson. At 11:32 P.M., Callaway called by radio to tell Evans that Wilson had been called and that he had requested that Evans document as much as he could about the incident, including where the body was found and whether it appeared that foul play was involved.

Before Evans left the river for park headquarters at Panther Junction with the body, he asked Juan Brito, the "commandante" of the nearby Mexican village of San Vicente, if he and the other Mexican men could show Evans where the body had been found. They agreed to meet at the San Vicente crossing the next day at 2:00 P.M. Evans thanked the men for their assistance and drove up to Panther Junction with Goodwin and the body to meet the coroner, arriving at 12:34 A.M., July 20. Acting Chief Ranger Andy Ferguson was already there waiting for them. While they waited for the coroner to arrive, Evans called FBI Agent Mike Plichta in Midland, Texas to tell him about finding the body. If a man is murdered on federal land, the FBI usually leads the investigation.

At 1:15 A.M. Coroner Wilson arrived at Panther Junction accompanied by Brewster County Chief Deputy Sheriff Wayne Dial and Deputy Investigator Alfred Allee. Dial interviewed Evans about the body recovery while Wilson examined the body and pronounced the man dead.

"The coroner cracked open the body bag, took a quick look, said 'yep, he's dead,' and closed it up again," Evans said.

Goodwin and Evans headed for home in Rio Grande Village at 2:30 A.M. Evans would have a short night's sleep.

By 8:15 A.M. Evans was calling FBI Agent Plichta to update him in the case. Plichta told him that the case had been assigned to Agent Van MacDonald in El Paso. Evans proceeded to call MacDonald and relate the details of the case to him.

That afternoon, Evans loaded up his horse and drove to the San Vicente crossing and met the Mexican men at 2:30 P.M. Seven men met him, including Juan Brito Morín, the man who had found the body after seeing the vultures. They rode up river about a half mile on the American side. Because the terrain on that side became too rough for continued travel, they crossed over to the Mexican side and rode another two miles upstream. When they reached the spot on the Mexican side across from where the body was found, one of the Mexican men, Jose Brito, swam his horse across the river, rode up on a sandbar, and pointed out the arroyo where they had found the body. Evans took pictures of the location and the party rode back to the crossing. Evans thanked the men, loaded up his horse, and drove back to Rio Grande Village, arriving at about 5:00 P.M. Right after he arrived, he received a call from Agent MacDonald notifying him that the body would be autopsied at the Lubbock County Morgue.

For three days the park was quiet, but on July 23 events got far worse. That morning an ATL (Attempt to Locate) request was received by the park from April Trotter of Irving, Texas for a green Volkswagen van and its occupants.

"I called the park," Trotter said later, "and said my ex-husband might be at the park with our daughter and hasn't returned."

That afternoon, four park visitors, Doug Baxter, Sandy Baxter, Brad Baze, and Janna Cullins, drove to the old Basin visitor center and made a startling report to Ranger Rob Dean who was on duty there at the time.

"They walked in and asked me 'What do you know about that burnt-out van at Solis?'" Dean said.

By chance Dean had just driven by it the day before on patrol, but hadn't stopped to give it a look.

"Van fires weren't that uncommon at that time," Dean said later. "The river outfitters used old vans to transport people to the river. They sometimes would overheat and catch fire. People would usually come and get them sooner or later."

"Well," Dean told the visitors, "I just saw it yesterday and didn't pay much attention."

"There's a body in it," they told Dean.

"Are you crazy?" was Dean's first thought upon hearing the visitors' statement.

Unfortunately the visitors weren't at all crazy. They explained that they had found the body of a child in the burnt Volkswagen van that Dean had seen the day before at the remote Solis campsite on the River Road. The Baxter party then drove down to Panther Junction to describe their discovery in detail to Rangers David Vecera and Roger Moder, Chief Ranger Phil Koepp, Border Patrol Agent John Davies, and FBI Agent MacDonald who was already in the park investigating the man's body found several days earlier.

The Baxter group stated that when they first arrived at their campsite at Solis on July 20 that they had noticed the green, burned-out Volkswagen van about 50 to 100 yards from their campsite. Solis is a small area of relatively level floodplain between Mariscal Canyon and the smaller San Vicente Canyon. Before the park was created in the 1940s, it was farmed using river water to irrigate the dry desert land.

When the campers arrived at their site, they assumed that the vehicle was abandoned and that the park was aware of it. That first day several members of the party walked over and looked inside the van and saw what they thought was the burned body of a large dog.

"It was completely burned," Doug Baxter said, "and it was hard to tell what it was. 'It must be a dog,' one of my friends said, 'maybe a pit bull because of the large head.' I kept thinking in the back of my mind that something didn't look right. I went over that third morning (July 23) with a shovel and turned the body over. Then I could see the lower part of the jaw. I knew right then that it wasn't a dog. I went back over to my family and said, 'tell me that's not a child.' They came running over and my dad said, 'Oh my God! That's a child!'"

"There wasn't a whole lot left," Baxter added. "Her arms and legs were burned almost completely off. We just couldn't believe that the park didn't know about it. We got right in the truck and drove straight up to the Basin to report it."

The Baxter group also told the rangers and agents assembled at Panther Junction that a group of Mexican horsemen had visited their campsite before their discovery while they were in the area rounding up stray livestock. The Mexicans told them that they had seen a man and child in the area on the Saturday before the Baxter party had arrived at Solis. The Mexicans thought it was July 12, but July 13 would be the correct date if it was Saturday. They told the Baxter group that the man they saw was bathing in the river while the child played on shore.

Rangers Dave Evans and Martin Ziebell were the first rangers on the scene at Solis.

"I was down on the River Road when the park radioed me to go to Solis," Evans said later. "Finding that little girl was one of the most horrible experiences that I had in my Park Service career. Later when the FBI agent brought down photos of that girl when she was alive, it really brought it home."

Evans and Ziebell secured the scene. Soon Ranger Vecera and FBI Agent MacDonald drove down to the Solis campsite after the interview with the Baxter party, arriving at 8:10, a little before sunset. Soon afterward, more law enforcement personnel poured in, including Ranger Tom Alex.

The officers carefully inspected the scene while Alex took photos. Because darkness was descending, the officers decided to leave the scene and return in the morning to begin the investigation in earnest. Ranger Ziebell stayed overnight at Solis to protect the scene's integrity.

A license plate check showed that the van belonged to Donald Tate of Irving, Texas. No outstanding warrants of any sort were found for Tate, but the park had received an Attempt to Locate request earlier that day. Subsequent investigation found that he had come to the park with his five-year-old daughter, Boston Tate.

Evans relieved Ziebell first thing the next morning while a planning meeting got under way at Panther Junction. Attendees, which included law enforcement personnel from the Park Service, Border Patrol, FBI, and Sheriff's Department, established Chief Ranger Phil Koepp as the Incident Commander, Byron MacDonald as the Chief Investigator, and David Vecera as Assistant Investigator and Lead Park Service Investigator. Tom Alex was assigned as photographer and sketcher and Dave Evans as evidence collector, both under MacDonald.

A river patrol led by Ranger Marcos Paredes began at Rio Grande Village and worked its way upstream toward Solis to search for evidence or other bodies. They interviewed some Mexican nationals near Casa Piedra between Solis and the San Vicente crossing, but otherwise found little of value.

At a little after lunch time, Vecera and MacDonald arrived at Solis. Evans was on site, maintaining security since he had relieved Ziebell that morning. Border Patrol agents John Davies and Danny Burns were already there, walking the perimeter looking for evidence and footprints. They found only tracks and manure from Mexican horses and cattle that had trespassed into the park. They had only done a brief survey near the burned van to avoid disturbing the immediate scene.

The full scale investigation began. Deputies Alfred Allee and Steve Hunt and Justice of the Peace Ron Willard provided security while

MacDonald, Vecera, and Deputy State Fire Marshal Steve Judd identified evidence items for collection. Alex photographed the scene and
took measurements with the help of Vecera. Judd inspected the burned
vehicle and pointed out evidence items which were collected and inventoried by Evans and MacDonald.

At about 3:00 P.M., Dog Handler Eddie Howard and his air-scent
dog were flown in by a U. S. Customs Blackhawk helicopter to search
the area for additional bodies or evidence. The dog concentrated on the
thick areas of cane and brush on the river bank that were difficult for
the officers to search. Unfortunately, the dog did not react anywhere
except where the bagged body had been laid. Nothing of significance
was found by the dog. Working in the extreme afternoon heat in July
along the river took its toll on the men and dog.

Later that afternoon the burned van was loaded onto a flat-bed trailer
and hauled to the park's impound yard at Panther Junction. After it was
removed, the team conducted a careful grid search of a 400 x 1,100-foot
area centered on the spot where the van had been. At about 6:00 P.M.,
MacDonald and Vecera interviewed Sandy Baxter at their nearby campsite. They then interviewed Janna Cullins. The men from the Baxter
party were off fishing, so they postponed interviewing them for the time
being. The Customs helicopter began a search of the river corridor with
the pilot, copilot, and two observers. At about 7:20 P.M., the men met
with Assistant Chief Ranger Roger Moder. Because all evidence had
been collected and removed, the site was removed from protective security and the rangers and officers departed for Panther Junction. By the
end of the day, 35 people, primarily from the Park Service, had been
involved in the incident.

The next morning, July 25, a briefing was held at park headquarters.
Vecera was assigned to head a search of the Black Dike area. Rangers
thought that is was possible that the events with the car were related
somehow to the two deaths farther down river. At a little after noon,
Vecera used two dog teams to move in parallel to each other to search a
swath of land between the river and the River Road at Black Dike. The
dogs never showed a sign of smelling anything unusual and no evidence
was found. That evening, Vecera met with Koepp, Moder, MacDonald,
and Ranger Steve Swanke to discuss his findings. The group decided

that further searching of the Black Dike area would be unproductive.

The investigation continued on multiple other fronts. River patrols continued, one floating downstream from the Santa Elena put-in to Solis and the other coming upstream from Rio Grande Village to Solis. Although Ranger Lisa Callaway was not in the law enforcement division at Big Bend, she and Dave Evans drove the burn victim's body in a body bag to the Medical Examiner's office in Lubbock for an autopsy.

"Everyone was tied up in the investigation," Callaway said later, "so they asked if I could take her body to Lubbock. Because so many vehicles were involved in the investigation, the only vehicle available was a pick-up truck. They said that they would put her in the back, and I said that I was not taking her in the back. It's going to rain and I'm not getting her wet. She's been through enough. So they scrounged around and finally found a sedan. We put her in the back seat and I drove her to Lubbock."

State Fire Marshal Judd called MacDonald to advise that he believed that the van hadn't exploded, rather the fire was intense, but slow burning. He also believed that the fire started near the engine compartment, which is in the rear in those vans. He also thought that the engine may have been running when the fire started and that there was spraying of fuel from the fuel tank vent pipe onto the van's exterior caused by heat forcing the fuel up the pipe. He hadn't determined if the fire was intentional or not, but suggested that if it was intentional, it could have been made to look like an accident. Judd also thought that the child may have been on the bed that rests on top of the engine compartment because some bone was found there, and that as the fire burned the body may have fallen onto the location where most of the remains were found. Later, the theory of what caused the fire would change.

Agent MacDonald and Larry Villalva interviewed people in the San Vicente, Mexico area, particularly Noie Brito, because he reported seeing blue and white smoke coming from the direction of Solis. He had been near San Vicente on the American side of the Rio Grande at about 9:00 A.M. several days before the body was found in the river. He was unsure of the exact day, but it could have been as early as July 14.

MacDonald also talked to park volunteer Michael Anderson who had hiked from Mariscal to Talley to Solis on July 16. He had arrived at Solis at about 5:00 or 6:00 P.M. that day and had noticed the burned Volkswagon van. He saw no people in the area, but he did observe tennis shoes on the river bank, which he identified as the same ones that had been collected the day before by the evidence team. Anderson also saw meat wrappers and sandwich rinds on the river bank, but it didn't evoke much curiosity from him. He never looked inside the van. He camped that night near the junction of the short spur road into Solis and the River Road. The van's sliding door was banging in the wind, which sounded eerie.

On the same day, Chief Ranger Koepp heard from Medical Examiner Ralph Erdmann of the Lubbock County Morgue. By using dental records, Erdmann had confirmed that the body pulled from the river was that of the van's owner, Donald Tate. Erdmann ruled the death a homicide because of the trauma to the head and other injuries to the body. Overall the body was badly beaten, but a major blow to the head was probably the cause of death. He estimated that the time of death was six days prior to the body's discovery. Because the body was found on July 19, the probable date of death was July 13. However, a San Vicente resident, Noie Brito had observed smoke coming from the Solis area probably a day or two later. Erdmann still had not confirmed identification of the child found in the burned van, but had determined that it was a girl from examination of the pelvic area of the body. Although the child was not old enough for the bone structure of the pelvis to have changed enough to indicate the sex, Erdmann found what appeared to be the charred remnants of ovaries and a uterus.

By the end of the day, 55 personnel from multiple government agencies, state, local, and federal, were involved in the investigation.

On July 26, MacDonald, Villalva, and Vecera examined the evidence and interviewed villagers at Boquillas and San Vicente, Mexico. Ranger John Morlock began a river patrol down Boquillas Canyon from Rio Grande Village. After fruitless searching, the helicopter crew demobilized and returned to their base. Other groups began to wind down, reducing the number of people involved in the incident. By the next day, with no solid leads, Agent MacDonald departed for El Paso and the investigation was continued by the park staff as part of their normal duties.

On July 30, Dr. Erdmann called Chief Ranger Koepp again to tell him that the child's body had been positively identified as five-year-old Boston Michelle Tate, the daughter of Donald Tate.

Donald Tate's ex-wife and Boston Tate's mother, April Trotter, found out the terrible news. She had last spoken with Donald on July 11 when she had gone to pick up Boston from him.

"He wanted to take her camping one more time," Trotter said. "So he took her out there (to Big Bend)."

Trotter was going to pick Boston up from Donald on July 19. When they didn't appear, Trotter assumed that they would arrive over the weekend. However, when she had not heard from them by July 22, she called the Irving, Texas police. The next morning she called Big Bend National Park.

Rick Womack of the State Fire Marshal's office conducted significant parts of the investigation after the initial flurry of activity died down. On August 9 he met with pathologist Ralph Erdmann who had done the autopsies on the two Tate victims. Erdmann told Womack that Donald Tate had been badly beaten with severe trauma to the head, chest, and both legs. Cause of death was a severe blow to the right side of his head, a broken neck, and other injuries that led to shock and cardiorespiratory arrest. The girl died of carbon monoxide poisoning and her body was subsequently burned 100 percent. Little soft tissue remained; the body consisted largely of charred skeletal remains. Later Erdmann lost his medical license for legal reasons related to some of his autopsies, casting some doubt on his conclusions in the Tate autopsies. However, Womack attended the autopsies and doesn't doubt that Donald Tate was beaten to death.

"That river would not have caused all those broken bones," Womack said.

On August 13, 1991, Womack visited Panther Junction to further study the burned camper van. The initial examination indicated that the fire started in the engine compartment and thereby could possibly have been accidental in nature. However, that examination was done by a newer, less experienced investigator. Womack's more comprehensive study of the vehicle determined that the fire started in the sleeping/couch area of the van because it received more intense burning. The fire then spread to the engine compartment. Once the gasoline in the fuel lines ignited, the engine received its fire damage. Womack carefully examined the engine and electrical wiring, but was unable to find any sign of an engine or wiring problem. Because he was unable to find evidence of an accidental fire or any possible source of ignition at the fire's point of origin, Womack concluded that the fire was incendiary.

"It was an intentional incendiary act," Womack said.

The remains of the little girl were found face down in the rear of the vehicle where her body appeared to be lying on a couch that had been made into a bed. Both the sliding rear door and the passenger door of the van were open at the time of the fire. Everything flammable inside the van was consumed by the blaze. The van had been outfitted as a camper and contained wood cabinets, a sink, paneled walls, a carpeted floor, and a couch that converted into a bed. The van had a top that would raise for more headroom.

The fire was intense. Some of the aluminum window frames had melted by the couch and sink area. Aluminum melts at 1,218 degrees Fahrenheit. Even the glass, which melts at 1,400 to 1,600 degrees, had melted in this area.

A metal two-gallon gasoline can was found about 18 inches in front of the victim on top of fire debris. The container wasn't ruptured, indicating that its cap had been removed prior to the fire. Womack concluded that the fuel in the can was used to accelerate the fire.

Even the dry nature of the investigator's report can't hide the horror of what happened to five-year-old Boston Tate.

"Due to these facts it is my opinion that this fire was incendiary in nature and fuel from the metal container was used to accelerate this fire," Womack wrote. "It is also my opinion that the victim was possibly either unconscious or tied up at the time of the fire or she would have been able to get out of the vehicle after the fire started."

Womack went to Irving and visited the Police Department, where he teamed up with Detective Randel Johnson to interview witnesses. They first visited with Todd Minshall, a long-time friend of Donald Tate's. He had been staying with Donald, his mother, and his sister for some time. Minshall had gone camping with Tate and his family several times, including a trip to the Solis campsite in May 1990. He had last seen Donald and Boston at about 2:00 A.M. on July 11. Minshall hadn't known where the Tates were going, but said that it wasn't unusual for them to leave for a couple of days. He told the officers that Donald would have taken his fishing gear and fished in the river while there. He listed some of the specific items that Donald would have had with him, including fishing and camping gear, and a new children's compact disc player of Boston's. He also added that Donald always took his brass marijuana-smoking pipe.

The next day, August 20, Womack and Johnson met Todd Minshall again and Donald Tate's sister, Amy, at Donald and Amy's mother's house. Amy told them that Donald had been living with her and their mother since Donald had divorced April Trotter two years before. She helped them look through the storage room where Donald had kept his camping and fishing equipment to try to determine what gear he might have taken with him to Big Bend.

After talking to Amy Tate and Todd Minshall, the two officers met with the next-door neighbor, David Stobb. He told the men that he had seen Donald loading the camper van with some blankets the evening of July 11 and that Boston had had a red Sony CD player.

Later examination of the evidence inventory list from the crime scene showed that many of the items that Donald should have had with him and were not at his mother's house were missing, including camping and fishing gear, the CD player, many CDs, the brass pipe, a .44 handgun that he had purchased right before the trip, and other items. Womack believed that the items had been removed from the scene by persons unknown.

Over the succeeding months, the investigation tailed off with no new leads or information to follow. Occasional tips appeared which were followed up by park rangers, particularly Victor Carrasco who was transferred to Big Bend in 1992. A couple that lives in Fort Stockton, Texas, Enrique and Juanita López, called the park on September 6, 1992, to report the rumors that they had heard during a visit to the town of Piedritas, Coahuila, Mexico. Coahuila is the Mexican state that borders most of the park. They told Carrasco that a person from Piedritas named Kiko Villareal had killed the Tates at Talley (a primitive campsite and trailhead up river from the Solis) and moved the van to Solis where it was burned with the girl inside. They said that he was a big drug runner and now lived in Fort Stockton. They mentioned other people in Coahuila and Fort Stockton whom they alleged were involved in the drug trade, but nothing ever came of their allegations.

On October 14, 1992, Ranger Carrasco called bail bondsman José Hernández in Fort Stockton. He was related to Juanita López. He wanted to learn what Hernández and Enrique López had learned in Piedritas, Coahuila on their trip of the day before. In particular he wanted to know if they had heard anything about a Santos Vásquez, a man who might have been involved in a sniping case on the river near Solis in 1989. Hernández told Carrasco that the current rumor in Piedritas was that Vásquez had committed the Tate murders by himself. He had been in the area at the time of the murders and had apparently hidden himself in a mine afterward for several days. People in Piedritas considered Vásquez to be crazy. Rumors arose and died for some time after the Tates were killed, but no concrete evidence of a suspect ever developed.

In his report of October 16, 1992, Carrasco wrote "For the last few months, I have been trying to get information related to the Tate murders from the Mexican border communities. My feeling is that due to the code of silence practiced by all of these communities, no one has been able to talk even though they have or know of relevant information concerning the Tate murder case. I also feel that Hernández was able to relate this information because of his disassociation of Mexican community ties by living in Fort Stockton, and not visiting Mexico on a regular basis, by the nature of his work, and by the impact of a 5-year-old girl's murder."

"People were afraid," Carrasco said years later.

Investigators learned that Donald and Boston Tate arrived at their Solis campsite on July 12. What happened soon after that is still unclear years later. From evidence gathered from witnesses and the scene, they were brutally murdered within a day or two of arriving in the park. Some rangers speculate that the two may have interrupted or witnessed some sort of drug transaction, or that Donald may have been involved somehow in a deal.

Jim Northup replaced Phil Koepp as Chief Ranger when Koepp

changed positions while the investigation was still ongoing. Like the other investigators, he soon became frustrated by the lack of any evidence or progress.

"There was some conjecture that Donald Tate might have been involved in some sort of drug deal," Jim Northup said, "but we never found a bit of evidence that indicated that. It was truly tragic that we were never able to solve that case."

Tate's ex-wife, April Trotter, thinks that it isn't unlikely that Donald was involved in a drug deal that went wrong. "He was a drug user," she said. "He couldn't keep a job. He bought a .44 handgun right before going to the park and had pawned some of his stuff. He wasn't a person that bought guns. Plus, he was beaten so brutally. Maybe he thought that having Boston along would prevent the people he was dealing with from hurting him. Why would you take a five-year-old girl with you to the middle of nowhere in summer? If something happened to you, what was she going to do? So I wonder if he was trying to do some sort of drug deal."

"I don't think it was a random murder," Womack said. "I've never understood why he took his daughter. That's such a desolate area of the park. I think that it's the most desolate place I've ever been, especially knowing what happened there."

"I don't know if it just started as a robbery that escalated or as something else," Roger Moder said. "Maybe murder was planned right from the start. Two years earlier, someone on the Mexican side (of the river) shot at some boaters and even tried to hunt them down for a ways. The boaters managed to elude him."

Despite considerable effort, the investigation languished. The park posted flyers offering a reward to anyone who could offer concrete evidence or information that led to the arrest of the person or persons responsible for the crime. Even a psychic was consulted with no result.

"I'm not a big advocate of psychics," Womack said, "but I'm not proud. I'll take any help I can get."

"We just didn't get any evidence from the crime scene that really helped," Moder said.

"I've found that studying the forensics of a scene is satisfying," Ranger Tom Alex said. "I'm sad to see the death of somebody, but at least I'm helping to solve the case by finding evidence. This case was doubly bad because not only did this little girl die, but we just couldn't find much evidence to solve the case."

The strong possibility that the perpetrator or perpetrators were Mexican nationals did not help in successfully solving the case. Cooperation with Mexican law enforcement officers has always been problematic. In addition, corruption within Mexican police forces is endemic.

"We tried to get some help from the Mexican side, but didn't get much," Moder said. "There were suspicions that the son of a prominent person was involved, and that was why we weren't getting much information."

Womack is more blunt.

"We got zero cooperation from the Mexican authorities," Womack said.

Trotter pressed the park for several years to find the culprits. The frustration and anger at not being able to solve the crime was palpable. In a letter to FBI Agent Richard Schwein on July 21, 1993, Park Superintendent Robert Arnberger wrote, "This was an egregious crime, and despite the difficulties, it needs to be pursued with vigor. It is particularly important to us. Big Bend National Park was set aside as a public pleasuring ground. This incident, along with others, has tarnished the park's reputation. I want to do everything possible to correct this situation, and solving this case is key to that process."

"They (the FBI) just thought it was unsolvable," Womack said, "and didn't try as hard as they could have."

"Texas Ranger Joaquin Jackson came out to the park and offered his assistance," Koepp said, "but there were jurisdictional problems between agencies. I think it might have helped to have included him more. He had a great network of contacts on both sides of the river."

"A year later when I went down to the park," Trotter said, "no one would talk to me about the case. (Ranger) Patty Goodwin took me out to Solis the first year, but she didn't know much. Two years later (from the date of the incident), they finally opened up and told me more. I went down to San Vicente Crossing with Van McDonald and Victor Carrasco and talked with some of the San Vicente residents."

Years later, Trotter still thinks about her little daughter. She's married and has two other children, along with a good job. The memories are still strong, but she doesn't wallow in it today. Even a tiny amount of good has come of it. When Trotter tells people her story, they often realize that their problems aren't so bad after all.

"I still remember her," she said. "As the time goes by you tend to remember the good things more than the bad things. For the first five years I was totally engulfed in it. Finally, an FBI agent told me 'This case isn't ever going to be solved. You need to get on with your life.' I've had to let it go. You learn how to live with it. It was the hardest thing I've ever gone through. I wouldn't wish it on my worst enemy. My faith helped carry me through."

The killings were never solved, but Trotter thinks that justice has probably been served by now.

"The way those murderers killed Donald and Boston so brutally," Trotter said. "I assume that they have been killed themselves by now."

Trotter may well be right. People who live a life of violence often have a short life span.

"It's still an open case," Womack said.

He hasn't completely given up. He recently put out a trace again on the gun that Donald Tate bought right before the trip and was never found.

"Sometimes a gun will turn up again in another crime," Womack said. "People rarely get rid of guns. They put it away for awhile and then use it again or sell it."

Memories have not faded much for many of the people involved in the case.

"It's been years," Ranger Evans said, "but I still occasionally have dreams about that little girl."

"The Tate murders disturbed me more than any other incident I've been involved in because this innocent little girl had been murdered," Tom Alex said. "That burned van stayed at the Panther Junction impound yard for many years afterward. Whenever I'd drive by, that van was a constant reminder to me of the death of that little girl."

SUMMARY

Don't let this book discourage you from visiting Texas's biggest park. Although this book highlights rescues and deaths at the park, it covers a period of almost 30 years. In reality, serious incidents are quite rare considering the number of people who visit the park every year. You are probably at much higher risk of death or injury walking through a shopping center parking lot or driving through Austin on Interstate 35 than you are hiking at Big Bend National Park.

Proper preparation will eliminate most of the risk of a visit to the park. Talk to park rangers about activities suitable for your level of physical fitness and outdoor knowledge. Read park brochures and guidebooks. Check weather forecasts.

Even if you're comfortable with taking risks in the outdoors, think also of the park rangers and volunteers who may have to risk their lives finding and rescuing you. In some of these stories, the rangers really pushed the boundary on their own safety in rescuing people and recovering bodies. Court decisions have shown that rescue personnel are in no way obligated to risk their own lives in an effort to save someone else's. And why should they?

In addition, the mental stress to rescuers of having to recover bodies wears on the psyche. Two rangers, John Morlock and Marcos Paredes, have probably been involved in more deaths than anyone else in the park. Morlock, who has helped with ten drowning recoveries over the years, just gets glum and shakes his head when the subject comes up. Whenever Paredes sees a park landmark, it usually brings to mind a body recovery he had to do there at one time or another. It's not a memory he treasures.

Besides the risk of harm to rescuers, the monetary cost of a major rescue can easily run into the tens of thousands of dollars. Some of the incidents in this book required the involvement of as many as 50 or more people for multiple days, often all getting paid overtime. Helicopters and airplanes can cost as much as $2,000 per hour to keep airborne. Dog teams are usually transported in from distant locations. Park budgets have limits. Don't risk the park's financial health and the lives of its personnel by taking foolish risks.

Big Bend National Park is huge, over 800,000 acres of rugged desert and mountain. That's a vast amount of land to get lost in should you be careless. Helicopters have to be flown in from cities hundreds of miles away. The nearest hospital is about 100 miles away in Alpine, a city of only about 6,000 people. There are no large cities anywhere close to the park.

I've spent my life hiking, climbing, canoeing, and doing other outdoor activities. I've never had a significant injury. Mostly it's because I've been well prepared and reasonably careful. However, luck sometimes enters in. I've been caught above timberline in Colorado when thunderstorms have moved in early in the day and lightning has been popping all around. I once hiked the Mariscal Canyon Rim Trail in April in temperatures of 100 degrees. I carried three liters of water for the half-day hike and needed every bit of it. Writing this book has made me even more careful and a little less willing to push the limit. I make sure I carry the extra jacket, the cigarette lighter, the space blanket, the extra liter of water, the extra granola bar. I don't like the additional weight in my pack, but as these stories show, sometimes those little items make the difference between life and death.

ABOUT THE AUTHOR

Laurence Parent was born and raised in New Mexico. After receiving a petroleum engineering degree at the University of Texas at Austin in 1981, he practiced engineering for six years before becoming a full-time freelance photographer and writer specializing in landscape, travel, and nature subjects. Hundreds of his photos appear in calendars every year.

His article and photo credits include *National Geographic Traveler, Men's Journal, Outside, Backpacker, Sierra, Natural History, National Parks, Newsweek, Arizona Highways, Travel & Leisure,* and *The New York Times.* He contributes regularly to regional publications such as *Texas Highways, Texas Monthly, New Mexico Magazine,* and *Texas Parks & Wildlife.* Parent has done 38 books. His latest is a large format color book, *Big River, Rio Grande,* that was released in the fall of 2009. Another large format color book, *Portrait of Austin,* was released in October 2008. In 2007, the large format coffee-table book, *New Mexico Wild and Beautiful,* was published. Also in 2007, he had three other books published: *Austin Impressions, San Antonio Impressions,* and *Santa Fe Impressions.* Additional books and credits appear on his website, www.laurenceparent.com.